Prentice Hall

GRAMMAR HANDBOOK

Grade 6

Upper Saddle River, New Jersey
Boston, Massachusetts
Chandler, Arizona
Glenview, Illinois

Prentice Hall Grammar Handbook Consulting Author
We wish to thank Jeff Anderson who guided the pedagogical approach to grammar instruction utilized in this handbook.

Grateful acknowledgment is made to the following for copyrighted material:

Brandt & Hochman Literary Agents, Inc.
"Wilbur Wright and Orville Wright" by Stephen Vincent Benét, from *A Book of Americans* by Rosemary and Stephen Vincent Benét. Copyright © 1933 by Rosemary and Stephen Vincent Benét. Copyright © renewed 1961 by Rosemary Carr Benét.

Alfred A. Knopf Children's Books
"April Rain Song" from *The Collected Poems of Langston Hughes* by Langston Hughes, edited by Arnold Rampersad with David Roessel, Associate Editor, copyright © 1994 by The Estate of Langston Hughes.

Longman Publishing Group, A Division of Pearson Education, Inc.
"Writing in a Second Language" from *Writing: A Guide for College and Beyond (2nd Edition)* by Lester Faigley. Copyright © 2010 by Pearson Education, Inc.

Note: Every effort has been made to locate the copyright owner of material reproduced in this component. Omissions brought to our attention will be corrected in subsequent editions.

Credits

Cover
Photos provided by istockphoto.com

Illustrations
Robert Neubecker

Photographs
All interior photos provided by Shutterstock, Inc.

ISBN-13: 978-0-13-363839-4
ISBN-10:   0-13-363839-1
2 3 4 5 6 7 8 9 10 V064 13 12 11 10

GRAMMAR

CONTENTS

CONTENTS

USAGE

CONTENTS

CHAPTER 14 Capitalization   283

    Numbered tags like this **EL1** are used on instruction pages of the Grammar Handbook to indicate where to find a related tip in the English Learner's Resource.

CHAPTER 1

NOUNS *and* PRONOUNS

Well-chosen nouns can help your readers picture the people, places, things, and ideas in your writing.

WRITE GUY *Jeff Anderson, M.Ed.*

WHAT DO YOU NOTICE?

Search for the nouns as you zoom in on these sentences from the story "Stray" by Cynthia Rylant.

MENTOR TEXT

> The puppy stopped in the road, wagging its tail timidly, trembling with shyness and cold.
> Doris trudged through the yard, went up the shoveled drive and met the dog.

Now, ask yourself the following questions:

- Which nouns name people, which nouns name places, and which nouns name things in these sentences?
- How can you decide whether the word *shyness* is an abstract or a concrete noun?

Doris is a noun that names a person. The words *road, yard,* and *drive* are all nouns that name places. The words *puppy, tail,* and *dog* are all nouns that name things. *Shyness* is an abstract noun because you can't recognize it through your five senses. It is a noun that names an idea.

Grammar for Writers Nouns are a powerful tool writers use to tell what they have observed or what they are thinking. Choose the right noun to exactly describe people, places, things, and ideas in your writing.

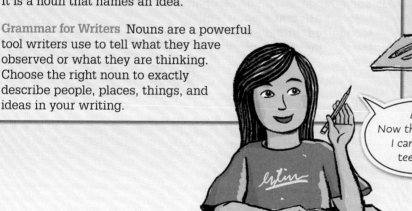

What's a noun that begins with the letter L?

Lunch! Now that's a noun I can sink my teeth into.

1

1.1 Nouns

Nouns are naming words. Words such as *friend, sky, dog, love, courage,* and *Seattle* are nouns.

RULE 1.1.1

A noun names something.

Most nouns fall into four main groups.

People, Places, Things, and Ideas

The nouns in the chart are grouped under four headings. You may know most of the nouns under the first three headings. You may not have realized that all the words in the fourth group are nouns.

PEOPLE	PLACES	THINGS	IDEAS
veterinarian	Lake Mead	bumblebee	strength
Dr. Robinson	classroom	collar	honesty
Americans	kennel	motorcycle	willingness
leader	Bunker Hill	notebook	obedience

See Practice 1.1A

Concrete and Abstract Nouns

Nouns may be classified as **concrete** or **abstract.** In the chart above, *People, Places,* and *Things* are concrete nouns. *Ideas* are abstract nouns.

RULE 1.1.2

A concrete noun names something that can be recognized through any of the five senses. An **abstract noun** names something that cannot be recognized through the senses.

CONCRETE NOUNS			
pencil	dog	tractor	river
ABSTRACT NOUNS			
courage	fun	honor	exploration

See Practice 1.1B

Collective Nouns

A few nouns name groups of people or things. A *pack*, for example, is "a group of dogs or other animals that travel together." These nouns are called **collective nouns.**

> A **collective noun** names a group of people or things.

See Practice 1.1C

COLLECTIVE NOUNS		
club	herd	army
troop	orchestra	committee
class	team	group

RULE 1.1.3

Count and Non-count Nouns

Nouns can be grouped as **count** or **non-count** nouns.

> **Count nouns** name things that can be counted. **Non-count nouns** name things that cannot be counted.

RULE 1.1.4

COUNT NOUNS	NON-COUNT NOUNS
orange	thunder
bench	rice
street	grass

Count nouns can take an article and can be plural.

EXAMPLE   an orange   the orange   three oranges

Non-count nouns do not take an indefinite article (*a* or *an*) and cannot be plural:

EXAMPLES   We heard thunder last night.
(*not* We heard a thunder last night.)

He needs clothing for the camping trip.
(*not* He needs clothings for the camping trip.)

See Practice 1.1D

PRACTICE 1.1A Finding Nouns

Read the sentences. Then, write the nouns in each sentence.

EXAMPLE   An ostrich is a type of bird.

ANSWER   *ostrich, type, bird*

1. Borneo is one of the largest islands in the world.

2. The zoo is a good place to learn about animals.

3. One of our neighbors has two dogs and a turtle.

4. Australia is sometimes called the land of parrots.

5. In winter, the sun sets earlier and days are shorter.

6. All planes have wings and a tail.

7. A bird may collect sticks, string, leaves, or rocks to build a nest.

8. Clouds are formed from droplets of water.

9. Each spring, bees pollinate the plants on many farms.

10. Many trees lose their leaves in the autumn.

PRACTICE 1.1B Identifying Concrete and Abstract Nouns

Read the sentences. Then, write the nouns in each sentence and label each one *concrete* or *abstract*.

EXAMPLE   The nurse used humor to cheer her patients.

ANSWER   *nurse* — concrete
humor — abstract
patients — concrete

11. The eager students wanted to learn about their futures.

12. His story was written on lined paper.

13. Actors must have active imaginations.

14. The carnival caused excitement throughout the school.

15. Some animals cannot live in a cold climate.

16. Many young people voted in the election.

17. Exercise is an important activity for both children and adults.

18. Engineers often find enjoyment in solving math problems.

19. Most people have a fear of public speaking.

20. Firefighters show amazing courage when they race into a burning building.

SPEAKING APPLICATION

In a small group, brainstorm a short list of abstract nouns (two or three more nouns than group members). Then, have each person choose one of the nouns and use it in a sentence.

WRITING APPLICATION

Write two sentences and include one concrete and one abstract noun in each sentence.

PRACTICE 1.1C **Finding Collective Nouns**

Read the pairs of nouns. Each pair includes one collective noun. Write the collective noun.

EXAMPLE   child, family

ANSWER   *family*

1. elephant, herd
2. student, class
3. employee, staff
4. team, player
5. coin, collection
6. Senate, Senator
7. panel, juror
8. soprano, choir
9. faculty, teacher
10. club, member

PRACTICE 1.1D **Identifying Count and Non-count Nouns**

Read the sentences. Then, list the count and non-count nouns. One sentence has only count nouns.

EXAMPLE   We crammed our luggage into the car.

ANSWER   *count noun — car*
non-count noun — luggage

11. We heard thunder before the storm began.
12. My little sister began to play hockey when she was ten years old.
13. All living things need oxygen.
14. There is too much furniture to fit into the room.
15. If you like to dance, you will love our neighborhood's block parties.
16. Has the mail come yet?
17. When they saw a skunk on the grass by the sidewalk, they waited to leave the house.
18. Traffic on the highway is always heavy on weekends.
19. Honesty is the best policy.
20. Everyone in the city lost electricity during the blackout.

SPEAKING APPLICATION

With a partner, take turns telling about a game you watched recently. Your partner should listen for and name two collective nouns, two count nouns, and two non-count nouns you used.

WRITING APPLICATION

Write three sentences and include one of the following in each: a collective noun, a count noun, and a non-count noun.

Recognizing Compound Nouns

Some nouns are made up of two or more words. *Classroom* is a **compound noun** made up of *class* and *room*.

RULE
1.1.5

> A **compound noun** is one noun made by joining two or more words.

Compound nouns are written in three different ways: as single words, as hyphenated words, and as two or more separate words.

COMPOUND NOUNS		
SINGLE WORDS	HYPHENATED WORDS	SEPARATE WORDS
crossbar	by-product	dinner jacket
firefighter	right-hander	pole vault
thunderstorm	middle-distance	pen pal
classroom	mother-in-law	chief justice

See Practice 1.1E

Using Common and Proper Nouns

All nouns can be divided into two large groups: **common nouns** and **proper nouns.**

EL2

RULE
1.1.6

> A **common noun** names any one of a class of people, places, things, or ideas. A **proper noun** names a specific person, place, thing, or idea.

Common nouns are not capitalized. Proper nouns are always capitalized.

COMMON NOUNS	PROPER NOUNS
inventor	Alexander Graham Bell
village	Tarrytown
story	"The Tell-Tale Heart"
organization	American Red Cross
idea	Germ Theory of Disease

See Practice 1.1F

PRACTICE 1.1E **Identifying Compound Nouns**

Read the sentences. Then, write the compound nouns, and draw a line between the words that make up each compound noun.

EXAMPLE   We have a doghouse in the yard.

ANSWER   *dog | house*

1. We built our campsite on the hilltop.
2. In high school we will study more science.
3. Wildflowers covered the countryside.
4. Always wear your seat belt when in a car.
5. Fireflies flickered in the moonlight.
6. Many children start day care at an early age.
7. Mr. Nguyen's brother-in-law is a firefighter.
8. Tomorrow we'll slide our homemade rowboat into the lake.
9. My grandfather used to play basketball.
10. All you need for this trip are a fishing pole and sunglasses.

PRACTICE 1.1F **Using Common and Proper Nouns**

Read the sentences. Then, rewrite them, replacing the underlined words with proper nouns.

EXAMPLE   My class took a trip to the city last month.

ANSWER   *My class took a trip to **Atlanta** last April.*

11. He pointed to an ocean on the classroom globe.
12. We saw a planet through the telescope.
13. Yesterday, I heard someone speaking a foreign language.
14. That store is my favorite store at the mall.
15. We went to the zoo.
16. When I started school, I met the teacher.
17. In class, we studied a country.
18. I would love to see a game at the sports stadium.
19. I walked slowly along the street, which is near my house.
20. I really enjoyed reading a book.

SPEAKING APPLICATION

With a partner, name as many things as you can related to your classroom and school that are compound nouns. Take turns saying how the parts create meaning. For example, *wastebasket* is a basket for waste.

WRITING APPLICATION

Write two or three sentences about places in and around your town. Use proper nouns to name places (streets, stores, parks, and so on) that you know or visit.

1.2 Pronouns

Pronouns are words that take the place of nouns. They are used rather than repeating a noun again and again. Pronouns make sentences clearer and more interesting.

> A **pronoun** is a word that takes the place of a noun or a group of words acting as a noun.

Imagine, for example, that you are writing about Aunt Jenny. If you were using only nouns, you might write the following sentence:

WITH NOUNS   Aunt Jenny was late because **Aunt Jenny** had waited for **Aunt Jenny's** computer technician.

WITH PRONOUNS   Aunt Jenny was late because **she** had waited for **her** computer technician.

Sometimes a pronoun takes the place of a noun in the same sentence.

EXAMPLES   My father opened **his** files first.
                pronoun

    Many people say exercise has helped **them**.
                                 pronoun

A pronoun can also take the place of a noun used in an earlier sentence.

EXAMPLES   My father opened his e-mail first. **He** couldn't
                           pronoun
    wait any longer.

    Students must take a science class. **They** can
                             pronoun
    choose biology or ecology.

A pronoun may take the place of an entire group of words.

EXAMPLE   Trying to make the team is hard work. **It** takes
                             pronoun
    hours of practice every day.

Antecedents of Pronouns

The word or group of words that a pronoun replaces or refers to is called an **antecedent.**

> An **antecedent** is the noun (or group of words acting as a noun) to which a pronoun refers.

1.2.2 RULE

EXAMPLES The **firefighters** described how **they** did **their**
antecedent   pronoun   pronoun
jobs.

Finally, the **rescue worker** reappeared. **She**
antecedent   pronoun
seemed to be unharmed.

How Kim was rescued is amazing. **It** is a story
antecedent   pronoun
that will be told often.

Although **he** was known as an expert software
pronoun
developer, **Darryl** enjoyed selling computers.
antecedent

See Practice 1.2A

Some kinds of pronouns do not have any antecedent.

EXAMPLES **Everyone** knows what the truth is.
indefinite pronoun

Who will represent the class at the town-wide
indefinite pronoun
school meeting?

The indefinite pronouns *everyone* and *who* do not have a specific antecedent because their meaning is clear without one.

See Practice 1.2B

PRACTICE 1.2A Recognizing Pronouns and Antecedents

Read the sentences. Then, write each pronoun and its antecedent.

EXAMPLE Many people are interested in dogs and their care.

ANSWER *their, dogs*

1. The children wanted to play, so they grabbed the ball.
2. Dad said he would be working in the basement.
3. Lianna thought she would like to try out for the school play.
4. That car is known for its reliability.
5. Most people can remember their phone numbers.
6. The teacher asked if Joseph had seen her ruler.
7. The squirrel looked as if it couldn't find any acorns.
8. The mayor knew that his job included balancing the budget.
9. My mother said the car on television is just like hers.
10. The students understood that they needed to finish the assignment.

PRACTICE 1.2B Supplying Pronouns for Antecedents

Read the sentences. Then, write each sentence, filling in the blank with the appropriate pronoun. Correctly identify and underline the antecedent of the pronoun you supply.

EXAMPLE Did Michael bring _____ camera?

ANSWER Did <u>Michael</u> bring *his* camera?

11. I like reading books. _____ always give me new ideas.
12. If I left the cupboard open, could you close _____ for me?
13. Farmer Johnson discovered that _____ liked organic farming.
14. Ahmed and Sepida went to _____ rooms to do homework.
15. Rosa wanted everyone to see _____ paintings.
16. Washington, D.C., is famous for _____ great monuments.
17. My mom is a great cook. I wonder how _____ learned to cook.
18. I returned the dress because _____ didn't fit.
19. By early autumn, the tree had lost all _____ leaves.
20. Billy ran because he was afraid the bus would leave without _____.

SPEAKING APPLICATION

With a partner, take turns telling about people you know. Your partner should listen for three pronouns and correctly identify the antecedents.

WRITING APPLICATION

Write two pairs of short sentences, using a noun in the first sentence of the pair and an appropriate pronoun in the second. Do not use the same pronoun twice.

Recognizing Personal Pronouns

The pronouns used most often are **personal pronouns**.

> **Personal pronouns** refer to (1) the person speaking or writing, (2) the person listening or reading, or (3) the topic (person, place, thing, or idea) being discussed or written about.

1.2.3 RULE

The first-person pronouns *I, me, my, mine, we, us, our,* and *ours* refer to the person or persons speaking or writing.

EXAMPLES **I** like the new design.

Please give **us** an example.

The second-person pronouns *you, your,* and *yours* refer to the person or persons spoken or written to.

EXAMPLES **You** will see the photo.

Your friend is at the door.

The third-person pronouns *he, him, his, she, her, hers, it, its, they, them, their,* and *theirs* refer to the person, place, thing, or idea being spoken or written about.

EXAMPLES **He** wants to listen to the radio show.

They wrote letters to the editor.

Some personal pronouns show possession. Although they can function as adjectives, they are still identified as personal pronouns because they take the place of possessive nouns.

EXAMPLES **Mary's** town paper comes out weekly.
possessive noun

Her town paper comes out weekly.
possessive pronoun

The chart on the next page presents the personal pronouns.

PERSONAL PRONOUNS		
	SINGULAR	PLURAL
First person	I, me, my, mine	we, us, our, ours
Second person	you, your, yours	you, your, yours
Third person	he, him, his, she, her, hers, it, its	they, them, their, theirs

See Practice 1.2C

Reflexive and Intensive Pronouns

The ending -*self* or -*selves* can be added to some pronouns to form **reflexive** or **intensive pronouns.** These two types of pronouns look the same, but they function differently within a sentence.

REFLEXIVE AND INTENSIVE PRONOUNS		
	SINGULAR	PLURAL
First person	myself	ourselves
Second person	yourself	yourselves
Third person	himself, herself, itself	themselves

RULE 1.2.4

> **A reflexive pronoun** directs the action of the verb toward its subject. Reflexive pronouns point back to a noun or pronoun earlier in the sentence.

A reflexive pronoun is essential to the meaning of a sentence.

REFLEXIVE   **Joy** helped **herself** to some turkey.
        noun   reflexive pronoun

           They poured **themselves** some milk.
        pronoun   reflexive pronoun

See Practice 1.2D

RULE 1.2.5

> **An intensive pronoun** simply adds emphasis to a noun or pronoun in the same sentence.

An intensive pronoun is not essential to the meaning of the sentence.

INTENSIVE   The mayor **herself** attended the carnival.

PRACTICE 1.2C ▷ Recognizing Personal Pronouns

Read the sentences. Then, write the personal pronouns in each sentence.

EXAMPLE   We took a trip to San Antonio, Texas, last summer.

ANSWER   *We*

1. I like having dinner with my family.
2. The neighbors say that ours is the nicest garden.
3. Is that T-shirt yours or mine?
4. Mom and Dad trusted us, and we didn't disappoint them.
5. Luis asked his mother to remind him to return the library books.
6. We forgot to bring food, but Carla and Shaun gave us some of theirs.
7. You can put your books over there.
8. Dad and Tim handed the usher their entrance tickets.
9. Do you want me to come along too?
10. My parents said they were going to a movie.

PRACTICE 1.2D ▷ Supplying Reflexive and Intensive Pronouns

Read the sentences. Write the reflexive or intensive pronoun that completes each sentence.

EXAMPLE   I painted that painting _____.

ANSWER   *myself*

11. We cooked this meal _____.
12. The coach _____ was amazed at the team's playing.
13. Those students painted the room _____.
14. Adam called the dentist _____.
15. Kim said she could do it by _____.
16. Allow _____ enough time for research.
17. The map _____ wasn't that detailed.
18. Help _____ to the free samples.
19. The trip _____ took one week.
20. The drivers congratulated _____.

SPEAKING APPLICATION

In a small group, have one person say a personal pronoun and the next person use it in a sentence. Additional pronouns may be used, as long as the one given is used.

WRITING APPLICATION

Write three sentences, each one using a reflexive or intensive pronoun to relate something done by friends or family members.

Practice   13

Demonstrative Pronouns

Demonstrative pronouns point to people, places, and things, much as you point to them with your finger.

A **demonstrative pronoun** points to a specific person, place, or thing.

There are two singular and two plural demonstrative pronouns.

DEMONSTRATIVE PRONOUNS			
SINGULAR		PLURAL	
this	that	these	those

This and *these* point to what is near the speaker or writer. *That* and *those* point to what is more distant.

NEAR

This is the desk where I sit.

These are my favorite books.

FAR

Is **that** the cafeteria down the hall?

Those sandwiches look good.

See Practice 1.2E

Using Relative Pronouns

Relative pronouns are connecting words.

A **relative pronoun** begins a subordinate clause and connects it to another idea in the same sentence.

There are five relative pronouns.

RELATIVE PRONOUNS				
that	which	who	whom	whose

The chart on the next page gives examples of relative pronouns connecting subordinate clauses to independent clauses. (See Chapter 7 to find out more about relative pronouns and clauses.)

INDEPENDENT CLAUSES	SUBORDINATE CLAUSES
Here is the book	that Betsy lost.
Dino bought our old house,	which needs many repairs.
She is a singer	who has an unusual range.
Is this the man	whom you saw earlier?
She is the one	whose house has a fire alarm.
This is the show	that he describes in the newspaper.
Tippy found her ball	that was under the chair.

See Practice 1.2F

Interrogative Pronouns

To interrogate means "to ask questions."

> An **interrogative pronoun** is used to begin a question.

All five interrogative pronouns begin with *w*.

INTERROGATIVE PRONOUNS				
what	which	who	whom	whose

Most interrogative pronouns do not have antecedents.

EXAMPLES   **What** did the doctor say?

          Which is the best treatment?

          Who wants to go with me?

          From **whom** will you receive the best advice?

See Practice 1.2G   **Whose** painting was chosen for the art show?

Indefinite Pronouns

RULE 1.2.9

An **indefinite pronoun** refers to a person, place, thing, or idea that is not specifically named.

EXAMPLES   **Everything** is ready for the field trip.

Everyone wants to see the medical center.

Anyone can learn to play tennis.

Something fell out of the cabinet when I opened it.

An indefinite pronoun can function either as an adjective or as the subject of a sentence.

ADJECTIVE   **Both** students want to be nurses.

SUBJECT   **Both** want to be nurses.

A few indefinite pronouns can be either singular or plural, depending on their use in the sentence.

INDEFINITE PRONOUNS			
SINGULAR		PLURAL	SINGULAR OR PLURAL
another	much	both	all
anybody	neither	few	any
anyone	nobody	many	more
anything	no one	others	most
each	nothing	several	none
either	one		some
everybody	other		
everyone	somebody		
everything	someone		
little	something		

See Practice 1.2H

PRACTICE 1.2E > **Identifying Demonstrative Pronouns**

Read the sentences. Then, write the demonstrative pronoun and the noun to which it refers.

EXAMPLE   This is an old camera.
ANSWER   *This, camera*

1. These are the new basketball uniforms.
2. This is a copy of the letter.
3. Do you know if those are the photographs that were chosen for the yearbook?
4. This is my favorite meal of the week.
5. That was a loud noise we heard during the play.
6. These are the blankets for the children in the hospital.
7. This is an amazing biography.
8. That was the house where my mom lived when she was my age.
9. Yes, these are my boots.
10. I think those are the two songs from the musical that Mrs. Brennan likes the most.

PRACTICE 1.2F > **Supplying Relative Pronouns**

Read the sentences. Then, write the correct relative pronoun for each sentence.

EXAMPLE   Rick Carson, _____ the players like, is leaving soon.
ANSWER   *whom*

11. The plumber, _____ has worked for twenty years, is scheduled for the job.
12. Players _____ like Stephanie want to join her team.
13. The team _____ they want to join hasn't won many games.
14. I met a writer _____ students adore.
15. The message, _____ Marcus is sending, will surprise everyone.
16. The driver, _____ car has a flat tire, is looking for a ride.
17. The only person _____ can solve the problem is gone.
18. Vanessa, _____ office is huge, is holding the meeting there.
19. The other horse _____ will race today is a palomino.
20. My grandmother, _____ we call every week, is coming to visit this summer.

SPEAKING APPLICATION

With a partner, take turns telling about a recent event you attended. Your partner should listen for and name two demonstrative and two relative pronouns you used.

WRITING APPLICATION

Write five sentences, including one of the following relative pronouns in each: *that, which, who, whom,* and *whose.*

PRACTICE 1.2G > **Identifying Interrogative Pronouns**

Read the sentences. Then, write the interrogative pronoun in each sentence.

EXAMPLE   Who invented the telephone?

ANSWER   *Who*

1. What was your sister's assignment?
2. Who will play soccer after school today?
3. Which building is your dad's office?
4. Who called the fire station?
5. What were the reasons given?
6. Whose book was left on the desk?
7. What are the answers to these questions?
8. With whom are you going to the library?
9. Which is the most interesting radio show?
10. What will happen next?

PRACTICE 1.2H > **Supplying Indefinite Pronouns**

Read the sentences. Then, write an appropriate indefinite pronoun (e.g., *all, both, nothing, anything*) for each sentence.

EXAMPLE   Would _____ close the door, please?

ANSWER   *someone*

11. Did _____ new happen while I was gone?
12. _____ must have moved the plants.
13. I'm sure _____ will be there tonight.
14. _____ of the copies of the book I need are missing!
15. There's _____ we can do about the squeak in that wheel.
16. Can _____ join this club?
17. I think there's _____ funny going on here.
18. If the one you want is gone, then pick _____.
19. Briana and Chai are here, but where are the _____?
20. _____ girls want to play shortstop, but only one of the two girls knows how to play the position.

SPEAKING APPLICATION

With a partner, take turns acting like a newspaper reporter conducting an interview. Ask at least four questions that use interrogative pronouns. Your partner should answer each of the questions, using one of the indefinite pronouns (e.g., *all, both, nothing, anything*) in each answer.

WRITING APPLICATION

Write a short paragraph about a story you have read that you think others should read. Use at least four indefinite pronouns (e.g., *all, both, nothing, anything*).

VERBS

When you write, choose verbs that show exactly what someone or something is doing.

WRITE GUY *Jeff Anderson, M.Ed.*

WHAT DO YOU NOTICE?

Chase down some verbs as you zoom in on these sentences from the story "The Tail" by Joyce Hansen.

MENTOR TEXT

> I saw a big brown and gray monstrous thing with tentacles reaching toward the sky, jutting out of the curve in the path. I screamed and almost ran.

Now, ask yourself the following questions:

- Who performs the action of the verb *saw* in the first sentence, and what receives the action?
- Do the verbs *reaching, jutting, screamed,* and *ran* have receivers for their actions?

The narrator *I* is the one who *saw*, and a *thing with tentacles* is what was seen. The *thing with tentacles* receives the action. *Saw* is a transitive verb because the receiver of the action is named. The verbs *reaching, jutting, screamed,* and *ran* do not have receivers of their action, so they are all intransitive verbs.

Grammar for Writers Think of verbs as the muscles that make your sentences move. When you use verbs that describe action, your writing is lively and interesting.

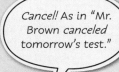

Name an action verb that you hope or expect to hear today.

Cancel! As in "Mr. Brown *canceled* tomorrow's test."

2.1 Action Verbs

Verbs such as *walk, sailed, played, migrate, raced, crossed, learn,* and *arrive* all show some kind of action.

RULE 2.1.1

An action verb tells what action someone or something is performing.

EL5

EXAMPLES   Father **carries** the ladder.

The ship **chugged** into the harbor.

I **believe** it will snow.

Sandor **remembered** to bring his puzzle.

The verb *carries* explains what Father did with the ladder. The verb *chugged* tells what the ship did. The verb *believe* explains my action about the weather. The verb *remembered* explains Sandor's action with the puzzle.

Some actions, such as *carries* or *chugged,* can be seen. Some actions, such as *believe* or *remembered,* cannot be seen.

See Practice 2.1A

Using Transitive Verbs

RULE 2.1.2

An action verb is transitive if the receiver of the action is named in the sentence. The receiver of the action is called the object of the verb.

EXAMPLES   Pete **opened** the **window** with great difficulty.
                    verb   object

The truck suddenly **hit** the **trashcan**.
                              verb   object

In the first example, *opened* is transitive because the object of the verb—*window*—names what Pete opened. In the second example, *hit* is transitive because the object of the verb—*trashcan*—tells what the truck hit.

EL5

Using Intransitive Verbs

> An action verb is **intransitive** if there is no receiver of the action named in the sentence. An intransitive verb does not have an object.

2.1.3 RULE

EXAMPLES

The race **began**.

The bus driver **raced** through the traffic light.

Seventh grade students **gathered** in the gym.

The clock alarm **rang** at eight o'clock.

Some action verbs can be transitive or intransitive. You need to determine if the verb has an object or not.

TRANSITIVE VERB   Kyra **painted** the **front door**.

INTRANSITIVE VERB   The artist **painted** in his studio.

TRANSITIVE VERB   The captain **sailed** the **ship**.

INTRANSITIVE VERB   The ship **sailed** out to sea.

TRANSITIVE VERB   The teacher **rang** the **bell**.

See Practice 2.1B   INTRANSITIVE VERB   The bell **rang** for class to begin.

PRACTICE 2.1A ▷ Finding Action Verbs

Read the sentences. Then, write each action verb.

EXAMPLE   I see a cocoon on that tree branch.

ANSWER   *see*

1. For breakfast, my mom usually eats cereal.
2. I saw an interesting show about Australia.
3. Traffic slows dramatically during rush hour.
4. The potter creates bowls out of clay.
5. Sometimes I forget my password for the computer.
6. Our flowers bloomed this weekend.
7. She said it would be a good movie.
8. My parents encourage my interest in music.
9. The new books arrived last week.
10. I walked the dog after dinner last night.

PRACTICE 2.1B ▷ Identifying Transitive and Intransitive Verbs

Read the sentences. Write each verb and label it *transitive* or *intransitive*.

EXAMPLE   Lisa rode her bike down the hill.

ANSWER   *rode* — transitive

11. The post office stands near the corner of Main Street and Hill Street.
12. The sun shone throughout the day.
13. A heavy blanket covered the bed.
14. The marathon runners came from many cities.
15. My brother threw his clothes into the washing machine.
16. I created small toys to take to the children.
17. Redwood trees grow amazingly tall.
18. Most animals protect their young.
19. The big balloon rose into the air.
20. We found the perfect place for a picnic.

SPEAKING APPLICATION

With a partner, take turns telling about something you enjoy doing on the weekend. Your partner should listen for and name three action verbs.

WRITING APPLICATION

Write two pairs of short sentences. In each pair, write one sentence using a transitive verb and one using an intransitive, in any order. For example, "I planted a flower. The flower grew."

2.2 Linking Verbs

Some widely used verbs do not show action. They are called **linking verbs.**

A **linking verb** is a verb that connects a subject with a word that describes or identifies it.

EXAMPLES

IDENTIFIES
Sheridan **was** a Union **general**.
subject / linking verb / predicate nominative

IDENTIFIES
The **winners** **were** Tony and I.
subject / linking verb / predicate nominative

DESCRIBES
We **felt** extremely **tired** after all our running.
subject / linking verb / predicate adjective

EL6

Recognizing Forms of *Be*

In English, the most common linking verb is *be.* This verb has many forms.

FORMS OF *BE*		
am	can be	has been
are	could be	have been
is	may be	had been
was	might be	could have been
were	must be	may have been
am being	shall be	might have been
are being	should be	must have been
is being	will be	shall have been
was being	would be	should have been
were being		will have been
		would have been

Using Other Linking Verbs

Several other verbs also function as linking verbs. They connect the parts of a sentence in the same way as the forms of *be*. In the sentence below, *calm* describes *chief*.

EXAMPLE   The **chief remained calm** during the battle.
          subject   linking verb   predicate
                                    adjective

OTHER LINKING VERBS		
appear	look	sound
become	remain	stay
feel	seem	taste
grow	smell	turn

Action Verb or Linking Verb?

Some verbs can be used either as linking verbs or action verbs.

LINKING   The water **looked** polluted.
           (*Looked* links *water* and *polluted.*)

ACTION   The inspectors **looked** at the water.
           (The inspectors performed an action.)

LINKING   The people **grew** unhappy.
           (*Grew* links *people* and *unhappy.*)

ACTION   The people **grew** poor crops.
           (The people performed an action.)

To test whether a verb is a linking verb or an action verb, replace the verb with *is, am,* or *are.* If the sentence still makes sense, then the verb is a linking verb.

EXAMPLE   The people **are** unhappy.
                        linking verb

See Practice 2.2A
See Practice 2.2B

PRACTICE 2.2A > **Identifying Action Verbs and Linking Verbs**

Read the sentences. Write the verb in each sentence, and label it either *action* or *linking*. One sentence has two verbs.

EXAMPLE   The coach called to the skaters.

ANSWER   *called* — action

1. The driver was unhappy with his car.
2. Sheila waved to the neighbors.
3. The players heard the coach's voice.
4. I don't feel very well.
5. The job you did looks really professional.
6. The two boys raced to the corner.
7. The sun shone on the new snow.
8. This story is about a lost rabbit.
9. We all helped Mom with the dishes.
10. They were happy with their grades.

PRACTICE 2.2B > **Using *Be* and Other Linking Verbs**

Read the pairs of words below. For each pair of words, write a sentence that uses a linking verb to connect them.

EXAMPLE   Patrick   busy

ANSWER   *Patrick looked busy as he prepared for the party.*

11. homework   easy
12. Sondra   puzzled
13. door   locked
14. Felipe   surprised
15. food   good
16. sweater   warm
17. idea   interesting
18. day   cloudy
19. puppy   happy
20. Alicia   careful

SPEAKING APPLICATION

With a partner, take turns telling about something you read about or saw on television. Your partner should listen for and name two linking verbs and two action verbs you used.

WRITING APPLICATION

Choose three different linking verbs, other than *be* verbs. Write three sentences, each one using a different linking verb.

Practice   25

2.3 Helping Verbs

Sometimes, a verb in a sentence is just one word. Often, however, a verb will be made up of several words. This type of verb is called a **verb phrase.**

> **Helping verbs** are added before another verb to make a **verb phrase.**

Notice how these helping verbs change the meaning of the verb *run.*

EXAMPLES   run   **might have** run

had run   **should have** run

will have run   **will be** running

Recognizing Helping Verbs

Forms of *Be* Forms of *be* are often used as helping verbs.

SOME FORMS OF *BE* USED AS HELPING VERBS	
HELPING VERBS	MAIN VERBS
am	growing
has been	warned
was being	told
will be	reminded
will have been	waiting
is	opening
was being	trained
should be	written
had been	sent
might have been	played

See Practice 2.3A

Other Helping Verbs Many different verb phrases can be formed using one or more of these helping verbs. The chart below shows just a few.

HELPING VERBS	MAIN VERBS	VERB PHRASES
do	remember	do remember
has	written	has written
would	hope	would hope
shall	see	shall see
can	believe	can believe
could	finish	could finish
may	attempt	may attempt
must have	thought	must have thought
should have	grown	should have grown
might	win	might win
will	jump	will jump
have	planned	have planned
does	want	does want

Sometimes the words in a verb phrase are separated by other words, such as *not* or *certainly*. The parts of the verb phrase in certain types of questions may also be separated.

WORDS SEPARATED

She **could** certainly **have come** earlier.

This **has** not **happened** before.

Marie **has** certainly not **contacted** us.

He **had** carefully **kept** all the records.

Did you ever **expect** to see an elephant?

When **will** we **open** our presents?

Can they really **build** their own home?

They **must** not **have taken** the bus.

Would you ever **want** to go skiing?

See Practice 2.3B

PRACTICE 2.3A > **Identifying Helping and Main Verbs**

Read the sentences. Write *main verb* if the underlined verb is a main verb. Write *helping verb* if it is a helping verb.

EXAMPLE   For weeks now, the weather <u>has</u> been cold and windy.

ANSWER   *helping verb*

1. The school construction <u>was</u> finished in August.

2. They must <u>have</u> believed they were doing the right thing.

3. The children had been <u>told</u> not to go there.

4. You <u>should</u> have seen their faces.

5. If I hadn't called the fire department, the house might have <u>burned</u> down.

6. I have <u>been</u> studying for three hours.

7. By the time we get home, the flowers may have <u>bloomed</u>.

8. The new sewing machine <u>does</u> work.

9. If you had missed the bus, you would have <u>been</u> late.

10. It's spring, and the birds <u>are</u> returning.

PRACTICE 2.3B > **Using Verb Phrases**

Read the verb phrases. Use each verb phrase in an original sentence.

EXAMPLE   were going

ANSWER   We *were going* to the movies.

11. had been dancing

12. must have known

13. might have finished

14. could stay

15. will study

16. have learned

17. did go

18. should rain

19. was growing

20. do wonder

SPEAKING APPLICATION

With a partner, discuss something you've learned in history class. Use helping verbs when you talk. Your partner should listen for and name two examples of helping verbs, along with the main verbs they help.

WRITING APPLICATION

Write three sentences about how things might have been different. You may use any main verbs and any additional helping verbs, but you should choose three of the following: *would, should, could, might,* or *may.*

CHAPTER 3

ADJECTIVES *and* ADVERBS

Make your writing more vivid by using adjectives to describe people, places, and things.

WRITE GUY *Jeff Anderson, M.Ed.*

WHAT DO YOU NOTICE?

Look for adjectives as you zoom in on these sentences from Russell Baker's autobiographical essay "Hard as Nails."

MENTOR TEXT

> Deems was short and plump and had curly brown hair. He owned a car and a light gray suit and always wore a necktie and a white shirt.

Now, ask yourself the following questions:

- In the first sentence, which adjectives modify the proper noun *Deems*, and which two adjectives in a row modify the noun *hair*?
- Which adjective in the second sentence modifies the noun *suit*?

The author describes Deems using the adjectives *short* and *plump* and uses the adjectives *curly* and *brown* to describe Deems's hair. The adjective *gray* modifies the noun *suit*. The word *light* is an adverb, rather than an adjective, because it modifies *gray*.

Grammar for Writers An artist crafts a picture with paint, but a writer uses words to create a picture in the reader's mind. Use a variety of adjectives to help bring your writing to life.

Which two adjectives best describe your book bag?

I only need one: heavy!

3.1 Adjectives

Adjectives are words that make language come alive by adding description or information.

Adjectives help make nouns more specific. For example, *car* is a general word, but a *red two-door car* is more specific. Adjectives such as *red* and *two-door* make nouns and pronouns clearer and more vivid.

An adjective is a word that describes a noun or pronoun.

Adjectives are often called *modifiers*, because they modify, or change, the meaning of a noun or pronoun. You can use more than one adjective to modify a noun or pronoun. Notice how *game* is modified by each set of adjectives below.

EXAMPLES   **old-fashioned** game

                new **video** game

                children's **board** game

                first **baseball** game

Adjectives answer several questions about nouns and pronouns. They tell *What kind? Which one? How many?* or *How much?* Numeral adjectives, such as *eleven*, tell exactly how many. In the chart below, notice how adjectives answer these questions.

WHAT KIND?	WHICH ONE?	HOW MANY?	HOW MUCH?
brick house	that judge	one daffodil	no time
white paper	each answer	several roses	enough raisins
serious argument	those sisters	both brothers	many hobbies
colorful shirts	this student	four books	some teams

Adjective Position An adjective usually comes before the noun it modifies, as do all the adjectives in the chart on the previous page. Sometimes, however, adjectives come after the nouns they modify.

EXAMPLES

┌─────── MODIFIES ───────┐
The legal system, **serious** and **complex**,
        noun   adjective   adjective
is sometimes hard to understand.

┌─────── MODIFIES ───────┐
The room, **narrow** and **dark**, frightened us.
  noun   adjective   adjective

┌─────── MODIFIES ───────┐
Graphics, **large** and **colorful**, covered the screen.
  noun   adjective   adjective

Adjectives that modify pronouns usually come after linking verbs. Sometimes, however, adjectives may come before the pronoun.

AFTER

┌─────── MODIFIES ───────┐
They were **quiet** and **thoughtful**.
pronoun   adjective   adjective

┌─────── MODIFIES ───────┐
They are **happy** and **talkative**.
pronoun   adjective   adjective

┌─── MODIFIES ───┐
She is **talented**.
pronoun   adjective

BEFORE

┌─────── MODIFIES ───────┐
Tall and **elegant**, **she** walked into the room.
adjective   adjective   pronoun

┌─────── MODIFIES ───────┐
Quiet and **sullen**, **he** sat in a corner.
adjective   adjective pronoun

┌─────── MODIFIES ───────┐
Intelligent and **active**, **they** won the tournament.
adjective   adjective pronoun

See Practice 3.1A
See Practice 3.1B

Adjectives 31

PRACTICE 3.1A ▷ Identifying Adjectives

Read the sentences. Then, write each adjective and list which question it answers. (*What kind? Which one? How many? How much?*)

EXAMPLE   Many people enjoy classical music.

ANSWER   *Many* — How much?
classical — What kind?

1. Australia is home to several unusual animals.
2. The parrot is a clever, friendly bird.
3. That music class was divided into four groups.
4. Some bright colors attract bees.
5. Nitrogen is an important chemical for all plants.
6. Some young people enjoy sports.
7. Eight advanced students went to the science museum.
8. In winter, bright days often bring cold weather.
9. Those little kittens went to five owners.
10. I think red paint will show up best on the gray wall.

PRACTICE 3.1B ▷ Identifying Adjectives and Words They Modify

Read the sentences. Then, write the adjectives and the words they modify.

EXAMPLE   Outside the dark house, the sky was blue and cloudless.

ANSWER   *dark, house*
blue, sky
cloudless, sky

11. The ground was covered with the sharp, fragrant needles from the tall pines.
12. It took a long time to build a huge, modern store.
13. The old dirt road was rocky and bumpy.
14. If one person leads, a thousand other people may follow.
15. A hollow tree makes a good place for some birds to nest.
16. The right attitude can make a big difference in many competitions.
17. The water, cool and inviting, tempted us to stop for a short swim.
18. The long blue skirt looks best with the red and white shirt.
19. Most people want a safe, reliable car.
20. Five heavy sweaters will not fit in a little cardboard box.

SPEAKING APPLICATION

With a partner, take turns describing a park near your home or school. Use adjectives to make your description more specific. Your partner should listen for and name three adjectives you used and what they modified.

WRITING APPLICATION

Write three sentences describing what you might see in a store you like. Use adjectives to help readers "see" what you are describing.

EL4

Articles

Three frequently used adjectives are the words *a*, *an*, and *the*. They are called **articles**. Articles can be **definite** or **indefinite**. Both types indicate that a noun will soon follow.

> *The* is a **definite article.** It points to a specific person, place, thing, or idea. *A* and *an* are **indefinite articles.** They point to any member of a group of similar people, places, things, or ideas.

3.1.2 RULE

DEFINITE   Mr. Ryan is **the** man to call. (a specific person)

Go into **the** gym. (a specific place)

I want to play **the** game. (a specific thing)

INDEFINITE   I want to see **a** game. (any game)

Please take **an** apple. (any apple)

You should see **a** teacher for help. (any teacher)

A is used before consonant sounds. *An* is used before vowel sounds. You choose between *a* and *an* based on sound. Some letters are tricky. The letter *h*, a consonant, may sound like either a consonant or a vowel. The letters *o* and *u* are vowels, but they may sometimes sound like consonants.

USING *A* AND *AN*	
A WITH CONSONANT SOUNDS	*AN* WITH VOWEL SOUNDS
a blue hat	an endangered water bird
a happy time (*h* sound)	an honest person (no *h* sound)
a one-way street (*w* sound)	an old map (*o* sound)
a unicorn (*y* sound)	an uncle (*u* sound)
a taxi	an opportunity
a pineapple	an angry look
a university (*y* sound)	an eraser

See Practice 3.1C

PRACTICE 3.1C ▸ **Identifying Definite and Indefinite Articles**

Read the sentences. Then, write the articles, and label them *definite* or *indefinite*.

EXAMPLE   A pair of cardinals built their nest in the tree outside my bedroom window.

ANSWER   *A* — indefinite
the — definite

1. During an average summer day in Antarctica, the temperature is around 20 degrees.

2. The children drew pictures of a waterfall they had seen in an encyclopedia.

3. Javier took a look through the telescope and saw one of the moon's craters.

4. An elephant is quite a sight in the jungles of Southeast Asia.

5. The first time I saw a shooting star, I didn't know what to think.

6. When visiting a new city for the first time, it is important to have a good map.

7. At the zoo, I hoped to see a lion or tiger, but I also wanted to visit the monkey house.

8. It is important when studying a subject like history to remember that the stories are about real people.

9. An unforgettable scene in the movie is when the hero saves a whole town from disaster.

10. After the storm, the clouds parted, and there was a beautiful rainbow.

SPEAKING APPLICATION

With a partner, discuss why picking the correct article—definite or indefinite—is important. Take turns creating examples that show how meaning changes with different articles: "A teacher talked to me" and "The teacher talked to me."

WRITING APPLICATION

Write three sentences, leaving blank spaces where there should be articles. Exchange papers with a partner and fill in the missing articles in each other's papers. Discuss whether the articles chosen were the ones the writer intended.

Using Proper Adjectives

A **proper adjective** begins with a capital letter. There are two types of proper adjectives.

> A **proper adjective** is (1) a proper noun used as an adjective or (2) an adjective formed from a proper noun.

3.1.3 RULE

A proper noun used as an adjective does *not* change its form. It is merely placed in front of another noun.

PROPER NOUNS	USED AS PROPER ADJECTIVES
Truman	the Truman Library (*Which* library?)
Florida	Florida wetlands (*Which* wetlands?)
December	December weather (*What kind* of weather?)

When an adjective is formed from a proper noun, the proper noun will change its form. Notice that endings such as *-n, -ian,* or *-ese* have been added to the proper nouns in the chart below or the spelling has been changed.

PROPER NOUNS	PROPER ADJECTIVES FORMED FROM PROPER NOUNS
America	American history (*Which kind* of history?)
Japan	Japanese cities (*Which* cities?)
Norway	Norwegian legends (*Which* legends?)
Inca	Incan empire (*Which* empire?)
Florida	Floridian sunset (*Which* sunset?)

See Practice 3.1D

Using Nouns as Adjectives

Nouns can sometimes be used as adjectives. A noun used as an adjective usually comes directly before another noun and answers the question *What kind?* or *Which one?*

NOUNS	USED AS ADJECTIVES
shoe	a shoe salesperson (*What kind* of salesperson?)
waterfowl	the waterfowl refuge (*Which* refuge?)
court	a court date (*What kind* of date?)
morning	a morning appointment (*What kind* of appointment?)

Using Compound Adjectives

Adjectives, like nouns, can be compound.

3.1.4

> A **compound adjective** is made up of more than one word.

Most **compound adjectives** are written as hyphenated words. Some are written as combined words, as in "a *runaway* horse." If you are unsure about how to write a compound adjective, look up the word in a dictionary.

HYPHENATED	COMBINED
a well-known actress	a featherweight boxer
a full-time job	a freshwater lake
snow-covered mountains	a sideways glance
one-sided opinions	heartbreaking news
so-called experts	a nearsighted witness

See Practice 3.1E

PRACTICE 3.1D **Using Proper Adjectives**

Read each group of words. Then, rewrite the words to include a proper adjective before the underlined noun.

EXAMPLE   a <u>shop</u> in Morocco

ANSWER   *a Moroccan shop*

1. a <u>visitor</u> from Russia
2. <u>birds</u> from South America
3. an <u>invention</u> from Australia
4. <u>food</u> from Mexico
5. <u>salmon</u> from Alaska
6. the <u>flag</u> of Britain
7. a <u>castle</u> built by a German
8. <u>pepper</u> from Brazil
9. the <u>artwork</u> of China
10. <u>pyramids</u> in Egypt

PRACTICE 3.1E **Recognizing Nouns Used as Adjectives**

Read the sentences. Write the noun, proper noun, or compound noun used as an adjective. Then, write the noun that the adjective modifies.

EXAMPLE   He enjoyed watching the trains in the railroad yard.

ANSWER   *railroad, yard*

11. December weather is usually cold.
12. The laptop computer might work.
13. We built a stone fireplace.
14. The Lincoln exhibit leaves soon.
15. It looked like a scene from a Dickens novel.
16. I need a guide to Chicago restaurants.
17. Both sides signed the cease-fire treaty.
18. Would you like to visit a South Pacific island?
19. The steel blade gleamed in the dim light.
20. The story came from a newspaper reporter.

SPEAKING APPLICATION

With a partner, take turns describing places around the world that interest you, being sure to use proper adjectives or proper nouns as adjectives. Your partner should listen for and name three or more of the adjectives.

WRITING APPLICATION

Write three sentences and include three of the following: a noun used as an adjective, a compound noun used as an adjective, a proper noun used as an adjective, or a proper adjective.

Using Pronouns as Adjectives

Pronouns, like nouns, can sometimes be used as adjectives.

> **A pronoun becomes an adjective if it modifies a noun.**

RULE 3.1.5

EXAMPLES   We see the ducklings on **this** side of the pond.

Which ducks are the males?

In the first example, the demonstrative pronoun *this* modifies *side,* and in the second example, the interrogative pronoun *which* modifies *ducks.*

Using Possessive Nouns and Pronouns as Adjectives

The following personal pronouns are often **possessive adjectives:** *my, your, her, his, its, our,* and *their.* They are adjectives because they come before nouns and answer the question *Which one?* They are pronouns because they have antecedents.

EXAMPLES

REFERS TO — MODIFIES
The **ducks** flapped **their** wings.
antecedent   pronoun

REFERS TO — MODIFIES
The **club** wants to increase **its** membership.
antecedent   pronoun

In the first example, *their* is an adjective because it modifies *wings.* At the same time, it is a pronoun because it refers to the antecedent *ducks.*

In the second example, *its* is an adjective because it modifies *membership.* The word *its* is also a pronoun because it refers to the antecedent *club.*

Note About Possessive Nouns Possessive nouns function as adjectives when they modify a noun.

EXAMPLES   The pond is on **Mrs. Smith's** property.

The **duck's** feathers are colorful.

See Practice 3.1F

38   Adjectives and Adverbs

Using Demonstrative Adjectives

This, that, these, and *those*—the four demonstrative pronouns—can also be **demonstrative adjectives.**

PRONOUN   We saw **that** .

ADJECTIVE   **That** lake is home to many geese.

PRONOUN   What are **these** ?

ADJECTIVE   **These** gulls are searching for food.

Using Interrogative Adjectives

Which, what, and *whose*—three of the interrogative pronouns—can be **interrogative adjectives.**

PRONOUN   **Which** do you think he will choose?

ADJECTIVE   **Which** parrot do you think he will buy?

PRONOUN   **Whose** can that be?

ADJECTIVE   **Whose** macaw can that be?

Using Indefinite Adjectives

A number of indefinite pronouns—*both, few, many, each, most,* and *all,* among others—can also be used as **indefinite adjectives.**

PRONOUN   I bought one of **each** .

ADJECTIVE   **Each** judge writes an opinion.

PRONOUN   I don't want **any** .

See Practice 3.1G   ADJECTIVE   I don't want **any** help.

PRACTICE 3.1F ▷ Recognizing Possessive Nouns and Pronouns Used as Adjectives

Read the sentences. Then, write the possessive noun or pronoun used as an adjective in each sentence.

EXAMPLE   Dad almost forgot his wallet this morning.

ANSWER   *his*

1. I walked by Mr. Levin's house.

2. Mom let me wear her bracelet.

3. The Sanchez children are going to visit their grandmother.

4. Mrs. Kamora's brownies are the best.

5. Why don't you bring your dog with you?

6. When we studied about Jamestown, I enjoyed John Smith's story.

7. Mr. Madorsky let me use his lawn mower.

8. Mrs. Cleary asked the three of us to talk about our vacations.

9. Freddie Johnson's home run tied the game.

10. Did you want me to show you my photographs?

PRACTICE 3.1G ▷ Identifying Demonstrative, Interrogative, and Indefinite Adjectives

Read the sentences. Then, write the adjective in each sentence and label it *demonstrative*, *interrogative*, or *indefinite*.

EXAMPLE   These shoes don't fit me anymore.

ANSWER   *These* — demonstrative

11. Which color do you think looks best on me?

12. Does this dress make me look too young?

13. That bowl will hold the fruit we bought.

14. I have only a few dollars, but I think it's enough.

15. What vegetable should I serve with fish?

16. Most doctors encourage people to eat right.

17. Call and find out if both boys are coming for dinner.

18. I wonder if those shirts will fit Johnny.

19. Whose books are those on the table?

20. Do you have many adventure movies in your collection?

SPEAKING APPLICATION

With a partner, take turns talking about something you or someone you know collects. Your partner should listen for and name two possessive pronouns.

WRITING APPLICATION

Write three or four sentences about your neighborhood. Write about people's houses, pets, and anything else that would give you an opportunity to use possessive nouns and possessive pronouns as adjectives.

3.2 Adverbs

Adverbs can modify three different parts of speech. They make the meaning of verbs, adjectives, or other adverbs more precise.

> An **adverb** modifies a verb, an adjective, or another adverb.

3.2.1 RULE

Although adverbs may modify adjectives and other adverbs, they generally modify verbs.

Using Adverbs That Modify Verbs

Adverbs that modify verbs will answer one of these four questions: *Where? When? In what way? To what extent?* These adverbs are also known as *adverbs of place, adverbs of time, adverbs of manner,* and *adverbs of degree.*

ADVERBS THAT MODIFY VERBS			
WHERE?	**WHEN?**	**IN WHAT WAY?**	**TO WHAT EXTENT?**
push upward	will leave soon	works carefully	hardly ate
fell there	comes daily	speaks well	really surprised
stay nearby	swims often	chews noisily	almost cried
go outside	exhibits yearly	acted willingly	partly finished
is here	report later	walk quietly	nearly won
jump away	come tomorrow	smiled happily	fully agree
drove down	went yesterday	moved gracefully	totally oppose

Negative adverbs, such as *not, never,* and *nowhere,* also modify verbs.

EXAMPLES   Helen **never** **arrived** at the party.
                       adverb   verb

I **could** **not** **answer** the question.
  verb   adverb   verb

The trail in the forest **led** **nowhere**.
                        verb   adverb

See Practice 3.2A

Using Adverbs That Modify Adjectives

An adverb modifying an adjective answers only one question:
To what extent?

> When adverbs modify adjectives or adverbs, they answer the
> question *To what extent?*

ADVERBS THAT MODIFY ADJECTIVES	
very upset	extremely tall
definitely wrong	not hungry

EXAMPLE   Forests can be **very beautiful**.

The adverb *very* modifies the adjective *beautiful*.

EXAMPLE   The building is **extremely tall**.

The adverb *extremely* modifies the adjective *tall*.

Adverbs Modifying Other Adverbs

When adverbs modify other adverbs, they again answer the
question *To what extent?*

ADVERBS MODIFYING ADVERBS	
traveled less slowly	move very cautiously
lost too easily	lived almost happily

EXAMPLE   The raccoon and beaver are **hardly ever** seen in
dry areas of the forest.

The adverb *hardly* modifies the adverb *ever*.

EXAMPLE   When running, I get tired **too quickly**.

The adverb *too* modifies the adverb *quickly*.

See Practice 3.2B

PRACTICE 3.2A > **Identifying How Adverbs Modify Verbs**

Read the sentences. Write the adverb in each sentence and list what question it answers. (*When? Where? In what way? To what extent?*)

EXAMPLE   Put the table there.

ANSWER   *there* — Where?

1. I hope this friendship never ends.
2. Carnations will grow well in this garden.
3. Rhonda seemed extremely excited at the fair.
4. Yesterday, I saw a bird fly out of the library.
5. Carlos seems very upset.
6. Jeffrey did his chores carelessly.
7. Mrs. Shapiro can take us home later.
8. You should put your boots outside.
9. Celia works on her science fair project happily.
10. Bring the flowers here.

PRACTICE 3.2B > **Recognizing Adverbs and Words They Modify**

Read the sentences. Write the word that each underlined adverb modifies. Then, write whether that word is a *verb*, an *adjective*, or an *adverb*.

EXAMPLE   In 1950, <u>very</u> few people had televisions.

ANSWER   *few* — adjective

11. By mid-afternoon, we had <u>successfully</u> completed our snow fort.
12. We washed the dishes <u>very</u> carefully.
13. The two scientists were <u>extremely</u> precise when recording their discoveries.
14. In the early days of airplane travel, flying was <u>quite</u> dangerous.
15. Some stuntmen have been injured <u>rather</u> seriously while making movies.
16. When we finally saw a gas station, the car's gas tank was <u>nearly</u> empty.
17. My grandmother returned <u>safely</u> from her first ride in a boat.
18. This book on rare animals is <u>definitely</u> interesting.
19. Did you know you can fly <u>nonstop</u> from Chicago to Beijing?
20. My sister <u>hardly</u> ever forgets to feed the dog.

SPEAKING APPLICATION

With a partner, take turns talking about activities you do regularly. Your partner should listen for three adverbs you use and say which question each adverb answers.

WRITING APPLICATION

Write three sentences about someone you admire—from your life or from history. Modify at least one verb, one adjective, and one adverb with an adverb.

Finding Adverbs in Sentences

Adverbs can be found in different places in sentences. The chart below shows examples of possible locations for adverbs. Arrows point to the words that the adverbs modify.

LOCATION OF ADVERBS IN SENTENCES	
LOCATION	EXAMPLE
At the beginning of a sentence	Silently, she approached the ocean.
At the end of a sentence	She approached the ocean silently.
Before a verb	She silently approached the ocean.
After a verb	She tiptoed silently into the ocean.
Between parts of a verb phrase	She had silently entered the ocean.
Before an adjective	Her father was always quiet.
Before another adverb	Her father spoke rather quietly.

Conjunctive adverbs **Conjunctive adverbs** are adverbs that join independent clauses. (See Chapter 5 for more about conjunctive adverbs.)

EXAMPLES She injured her leg; **therefore** , she couldn't play in

conjunctive adverb

the game.

Ben predicted his score in the game; **however** ,

conjunctive adverb

his prediction was not accurate.

See Practice 3.2C

Adverb or Adjective?

Some words can function as adverbs or as adjectives, depending on their use in a sentence.

> If a noun or pronoun is modified by a word, that modifying word is an **adjective.** If a verb, adjective, or adverb is modified by a word, that modifying word is an **adverb.**

3.2.3 RULE

An adjective will modify a noun or pronoun and will answer one of the questions *What kind? Which one? How many?* or *How much?*

An adverb will modify a verb, an adjective, or another adverb and will answer one of the questions *Where? When? In what way?* or *To what extent?*

ADVERB MODIFYING VERB	Lumberjacks **work** **hard** . verb adverb
	When the wolves reached the clearing, they **turned** **right** . verb adverb
ADJECTIVE MODIFYING NOUN	Lumberjacks accomplish **hard** **tasks** . adjective noun
	The **right** side of the road is a good **spot** adjective noun to view the wolves safely.

While most words ending in *-ly* are adverbs, some are not. Several adjectives also end in *-ly*. These adjectives are formed by adding *-ly* to nouns.

ADJECTIVES WITH -LY ENDINGS	a **kingly** feast
	a **friendly** person
EXAMPLES	At the restaurant, we enjoyed a **kingly** feast
	I like Andrew; he is such a **friendly** person.

See Practice 3.2D

PRACTICE 3.2C > **Locating Adverbs**

Read the sentences. Then, write each adverb and the word or words it modifies.

EXAMPLE   The chair was amazingly old and had almost broken when it was moved.

ANSWER   *amazingly, old*
almost, had broken

1. The hiker slowly climbed the very steep trail.

2. Suddenly, we came to a garden where flowers had been carefully planted.

3. Spring always seems nicer after a really harsh winter.

4. Our team easily defeated our rivals.

5. The mountains looked especially beautiful on that wonderfully sunny day.

6. Eventually, the boys learned that the plans they had quickly made would not work.

7. My mom gently placed the kitten directly behind my sister.

8. Noisily, the chickens rushed toward the recently filled feed bin.

9. The marathon runners crossed the finish line wearily.

10. We often return to the place where we had luckily found a good campsite.

PRACTICE 3.2D > **Recognizing Adverbs and Adjectives**

Read the sentences. Then, write whether each underlined word is an *adjective* or an *adverb*.

EXAMPLE   He answered <u>wisely</u>.

ANSWER   *adverb*

11. The fever is gone, and the doctor says Billy is <u>well</u>.

12. She loves ballet, and she dances <u>well</u>.

13. He worked <u>hard</u> at the math problems.

14. The farmer broke up the <u>hard</u> dirt.

15. Anna and Chen were there by 4:00, but Sasha arrived <u>later</u>.

16. They decided to take a <u>later</u> bus.

17. There's an <u>outside</u> chance we'll make it to the playoffs.

18. If you want to play ball, you need to play <u>outside</u>.

19. He held the book <u>close</u> to the light.

20. That was a <u>close</u> race!

SPEAKING APPLICATION

With a partner, take turns telling about an interesting book you recently read. Your partner should listen for and name three adverbs you used.

WRITING APPLICATION

Write two pairs of sentences, using the same word in each sentence of a pair—once as an adverb and once as an adjective.

PREPOSITIONS

Use prepositions in your writing to make connections between words and ideas clearer.

WRITE GUY *Jeff Anderson, M.Ed.*

WHAT DO YOU NOTICE?

Look for prepositions as you zoom in on these lines from the play *The Phantom Tollbooth* by Susan Nanus, based on the book by Norton Juster.

MENTOR TEXT

In this box are the letters of the alphabet. With them you can form all the words you will ever need to help you overcome the obstacles that may stand in your path.

Now, ask yourself the following questions:

- Which preposition shows the relationship between the letters and the box, and which preposition connects the word *letters* to the phrase *the alphabet?*
- Which preposition connects *stand* to *your path?*

The preposition *in* shows the location of the letters; they are inside the box. The preposition *of* connects *letters* and *the alphabet*. The preposition *in* connects *stand* and *your path* to show where someone might stand.

Grammar for Writers Making clear connections between words and ideas is an essential part of a writer's task. Think of prepositions as strings you use to tie together different parts of your writing.

Yesterday, my sister told me to balance a book in my head.

Wait a minute. She meant on your head!

4.1 Prepositions

Prepositions function as connectors, relating one word to another within a sentence.

They allow a speaker or writer to express the link between separate items. **Prepositions** can convey information about location, time, or direction or provide details.

RULE 4.1.1

A **preposition** relates the noun or pronoun following it to another word in the sentence.

EXAMPLES

RELATES ─── RELATES ───

The duck floated **on** the surface **of** the pond.
　　　　　　preposition　　　noun　preposition　　noun

RELATES ───

The dog ran **across** the yard and
　　　　　preposition　　　noun

RELATES ───

hid **between** the bushes.
　preposition　　　noun

In the first example, the duck floated where? (on the surface) It was the surface of what? (the pond) In the second example, the dog ran where? (across the yard) The dog hid where? (between the bushes)

FIFTY COMMON PREPOSITIONS				
about	behind	during	off	to
above	below	except	on	toward
across	beneath	for	onto	under
after	beside	from	opposite	underneath
against	besides	in	out	until
along	between	inside	outside	up
among	beyond	into	over	upon
around	but	like	past	with
at	by	near	since	within
before	down	of	through	without

See Practice 4.1A

Compound Prepositions Prepositions consisting of more than one word are called **compound prepositions.** Some of them are listed in the chart below:

COMPOUND PREPOSITIONS		
according to	by means of	instead of
ahead of	in addition to	in view of
apart from	in back of	next to
aside from	in front of	on account of
as of	in place of	on top of
because of	in spite of	out of

Because prepositions have different meanings, using a particular preposition will affect the way other words in a sentence relate to one another. In the first sentence, for example, notice how each preposition changes the relationship between *parade* and *City Hall.*

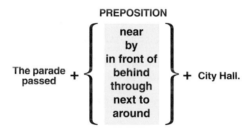

In this sentence, the preposition changes the relationship between *girls* and *gym.*

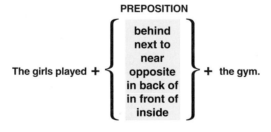

See Practice 4.1B

Read the sentences. Write the preposition in each sentence. Then, write the function of the preposition (to convey *location*, *time*, or *direction*, or to provide *details*).

EXAMPLE   Just tie a string around the middle.

ANSWER   *around* — location

1. Some people live on islands.
2. The ball got stuck underneath the car.
3. We heard a large crash in the next room.
4. Put the wood beside the fireplace.
5. Finally, the boat disappeared beyond the horizon.
6. Have you thought of a topic?
7. We were excited to find that it had snowed during the night.
8. There are mountains, valleys, and volcanoes under the sea.
9. We left before sunrise to go fishing.
10. There was a high fence between the two yards.

Read the sentences. Then, write the compound preposition in each sentence.

EXAMPLE   They worked hard and finished ahead of schedule.

ANSWER   *ahead of*

11. I'll have a salad instead of the soup.
12. Because of the storm, we have to go home.
13. Put the small picture in front of the larger one.
14. Some really fabulous food comes out of my mom's kitchen.
15. In addition to herbs, we planted several vegetables.
16. Don't get too far ahead of your sister.
17. The fire extinguisher is next to the fire alarm.
18. In back of the school, there's a large playing field.
19. The coach communicated by means of hand signals.
20. The game was canceled on account of rain.

SPEAKING APPLICATION

With a partner, take turns discussing a ball game, using prepositions to describe where players are in relation to the ball, other players, or positions on the field. Your partner should listen for and name four prepositions.

WRITING APPLICATION

Choose three prepositions and three compound prepositions from the sentences in Practice 4.1A and Practice 4.1B. Write six sentences of your own, using a different preposition or compound preposition in each to convey location, time, or direction, or to provide details.

Prepositions Used in Sentences

A preposition is never used by itself in a sentence. Instead, it appears as part of a phrase containing one or more other words.

> A **preposition** in a sentence always introduces a **prepositional phrase.**

RULE
4.1.2

Prepositional Phrases

A **prepositional phrase** is a group of words that begins with a preposition and ends with a noun or pronoun. The noun or pronoun following the preposition is the **object of the preposition.**

Some prepositional phrases contain just two words—the preposition and its object. Others are longer because they contain modifiers.

EXAMPLES

in water
preposition object

from the solar **system**
preposition object

in place of the old, broken **antenna**
preposition object

inside the large, modern **stadium**
preposition object

with us
preposition object

See Practice 4.1C
See Practice 4.1D

according to the new **coach**
preposition object

Prepositional phrases convey information about location, time, or direction or provide details. (See Chapter 11 to learn about prepositional phrases and their influence on subject–verb agreement.)

Preposition or Adverb?

Some words can be used either as prepositions or as adverbs. The following chart lists some examples. When the word is used as a preposition, it begins a prepositional phrase and is followed by the object of the preposition. If the word has no object, it is probably being used as an adverb.

PREPOSITION OR ADVERB		
above	inside	outside
after	nearby	past
around	opposite	underneath
before	out	within

PREPOSITION   The broken panel was **outside** the spacecraft.

ADVERB   The astronauts slowly stepped **outside** .

PREPOSITION   He appeared **before** the court.

ADVERB   I had not realized that **before** .

PREPOSITION   The ball flew **past** third base.

ADVERB   The umpire ran **past** quickly.

PREPOSITION   They sat **inside** the dugout.

ADVERB   Please come **inside** soon.

PREPOSITION   The umpire stands **behind** the catcher.

ADVERB   Harry stayed **behind** .

PREPOSITION   The team lined up **nearby** the water fountain.

ADVERB   Please play **nearby** .

See Practice 4.1E
See Practice 4.1F

PRACTICE 4.1C **Recognizing Prepositional Phrases**

Read the sentences. Write the prepositional phrase in each sentence, and underline the object of the preposition. Then, write the function of the prepositional phrase (to convey *location, time,* or *direction,* or to provide *details*).

EXAMPLE   I read it in the Sunday newspaper.

ANSWER   *in the Sunday <u>newspaper</u> —
location*

1. During recess, we played soccer.
2. He parked the car in front of their house.
3. The teacher hung the calendar near the clock.
4. He saved his money to buy a new pair of shoes.
5. A submarine can travel beneath the water's surface.
6. Maria will be going in place of Jolene.
7. The baker turned the flour into bread.
8. Wildflowers had bloomed along the path.
9. He pushed hard against the door but found it wouldn't open.
10. The nature photographer hiked through the old forest.

PRACTICE 4.1D **Distinguishing Prepositions and Prepositional Phrases**

Read the sentences. Write the prepositional phrases. Then, underline the preposition in each phrase.

EXAMPLE   Just leave the package inside the screen door.

ANSWER   *<u>inside</u> the screen door*

11. He wondered if he could climb over the fence.
12. Across from the store, there's a mailbox.
13. School was canceled today because of the snow.
14. The students gathered outside the classroom.
15. In the closet, you'll find extra blankets.
16. He put a flag on top of the fort.
17. We drove toward the next town.
18. Underneath the porch, the rabbit felt safe.
19. Dad helped me look for my lost homework
20. Is there anything interesting on television?

SPEAKING APPLICATION

With a partner, take turns describing your location. Use at least two prepositional phrases to convey location. Your partner should name the prepositional phrases and the prepositions.

WRITING APPLICATION

Write three sentences about your neighborhood. Use at least one prepositional phrase in each sentence to convey location, time, or direction, or to provide details. Circle the prepositions and underline the objects of the prepositions.

PRACTICE 4.1E > **Distinguishing Prepositions and Adverbs**

Read the sentences. Label each underlined word *preposition* or *adverb*.

EXAMPLE   My excitement grew as the day of the party drew <u>near</u>.

ANSWER   *adverb*

1. Leticia was afraid she would be left <u>behind</u>.
2. Is the library <u>behind</u> the school?
3. I left my wet boots <u>by</u> the door.
4. We watched the horses race <u>by</u>.
5. They built a bridge <u>over</u> the stream.
6. If you have time, why don't you come <u>over</u>?
7. He wondered if he'd ever learn what was <u>inside</u> the box.
8. To really appreciate the house, you have to go <u>inside</u>.
9. Stefan asked if he could come <u>along</u>.
10. Be careful that you cut <u>along</u> the dotted line.

PRACTICE 4.1F > **Supplying Prepositions and Prepositional Phrases**

Read the sentences. Then, expand each sentence by adding a prepositional phrase that begins with a preposition of your choice, or use one of these prepositions: *in, for, on, of, by, from, with, into, between, through,* or *about.*

EXAMPLE   We watched the dogs play.

ANSWER   *We watched the dogs play in the yard.*

11. There were many clouds.
12. I received a package.
13. May I bring my cat?
14. What did you find out?
15. She found her paper.
16. We saw a groundhog digging.
17. Gabriella put the book down.
18. Jeremy bought a watch.
19. I thought I would look.
20. There is a movie I want to see.

SPEAKING APPLICATION

With a partner, take turns saying a sentence. Use the sentences in Practice 4.1F as models. Have your partner repeat the sentence, adding a prepositional phrase.

WRITING APPLICATION

Use the sentences in Practice 4.1E as models, and write two pairs of sentences. Each pair should have one sentence with a preposition and one sentence in which the same word is used as an adverb.

CHAPTER 5

CONJUNCTIONS *and* INTERJECTIONS

Use conjunctions to connect and highlight important ideas in your writing; add interjections to help create emotion.

WRITE GUY *Jeff Anderson, M.Ed.*

WHAT DO YOU NOTICE?

Watch for conjunctions as you zoom in on these sentences from the book *The Pigman & Me* by Paul Zindel.

MENTOR TEXT

Life does that to us a lot. Just when we think something awful's going to happen one way, it throws you a curve and the something awful happens another way.

Now, ask yourself the following questions:

- Which idea does the subordinating conjunction *when* introduce?
- Which groups of words does the coordinating conjunction *and* link in the second sentence?

The subordinating conjunction *when* introduces the dependent idea *we think something awful's going to happen one way*. The main idea is *it throws you a curve and the something awful happens another way*. The coordinating conjunction *and* links *it throws you a curve* with *the something awful happens another way*.

Grammar for Writers You can add variety to your writing by placing subordinating conjunctions, such as *if*, in different locations in a sentence. *If it snows, they will cancel school. They will cancel school if it snows.*

I think I'll have a conjunction for lunch.

Okay. Are you having the soup and sandwich with a salad or vegetable?

5.1 Conjunctions

Conjunctions are like links in a chain: They help you join words and ideas.

RULE
5.1.1

A **conjunction** connects words or groups of words.

Conjunctions fall into three groups: **Coordinating conjunctions, correlative conjunctions,** and **subordinating conjunctions**.

Coordinating Conjunctions

RULE
5.1.2

Coordinating conjunctions connect words of the same kind, such as two or more nouns or verbs. They can also connect larger groups of words, such as prepositional phrases or even complete sentences.

COORDINATING CONJUNCTIONS						
and	but	for	nor	or	so	yet

In the following examples, notice the coordinating conjunctions that connect the highlighted words.

Connecting Nouns	My cousin and his wife left today for a trip to Washington, D.C.
Connecting Verbs	They printed directions but forgot to bring them.
Connecting Prepositional Phrases	Put the luggage onto the doorstep or into the garage.
Connecting Two Sentences	The flowers were blooming, yet it was still cold outside.

See Practice 5.1A

Correlative Conjunctions

Correlative conjunctions are *pairs* of words that connect similar kinds of words or groups of words.

CORRELATIVE CONJUNCTIONS		
both . . . and	neither . . . nor	whether . . . or
either . . . or	not only . . . but also	

Notice the correlative conjunctions in the following examples.

Connecting Nouns	Either the van or the bus will pick us up.
Connecting Pronouns	Neither he nor she is to be blamed.
Connecting Verbs	Every morning, she both runs and swims .
Connecting Prepositional Phrases	She'll come—whether by train or by plane , I can't say.
Connecting Two Clauses	Not only do they sing , but also they dance .

See Practice 5.1B

Subordinating Conjunctions

Subordinating conjunctions connect two ideas by making one idea dependent on the other.

5.1.3 RULE

FREQUENTLY USED SUBORDINATING CONJUNCTIONS				
after	as soon as	if	though	whenever
although	as though	in order that	till	where
as	because	since	unless	wherever
as if	before	so that	until	while
as long as	even though	than	when	

The Dependent Idea The subordinating conjunction always introduces the dependent idea. The subordinating conjunction connects the dependent idea to the main idea.

EXAMPLES   I did the planning **after** **he made the date** .

When **he phoned today** , he was unable to reach the doctor.

The examples show that the main idea can come at the beginning or at the end of the sentence. Look at the difference in punctuation. When the dependent idea comes first, it must be separated from the main idea with a comma. If the dependent idea comes second, no comma is necessary.

See Practice 5.1C

Conjunctive Adverbs

Conjunctive adverbs are used as conjunctions to connect complete ideas. They are often used as transitions, connecting different ideas by showing comparisons, contrasts, or results.

CONJUNCTIVE ADVERBS	
accordingly	indeed
again	instead
also	moreover
besides	nevertheless
consequently	otherwise
finally	then
furthermore	therefore
however	thus

Notice the punctuation that is used before and after the conjunctive adverbs in the following examples. (See Chapter 13 for more about punctuation with conjunctive adverbs.)

EXAMPLES   The film was great; **nevertheless** , I prefer the play.

The musical starts at 8:00 P.M.; we should, **therefore** , leave soon.

See Practice 5.1D

PRACTICE 5.1A > Supplying Coordinating Conjunctions

Read the sentences. Then, write each sentence, replacing the blank with a coordinating conjunction that makes sense in the sentence.

EXAMPLE   Was Mr. Kim born in Korea _____ the United States?

ANSWER   Was Mr. Kim born in Korea *or* the United States?

1. We weren't on time for the first show, _____ we went to the second show.

2. I like mustard _____ relish on my hot dog.

3. Tho necklace was expensive _____ seemed worth every penny.

4. We could not score a goal, _____ could we stop our opponents from scoring.

5. You may choose a sandwich _____ a burrito.

6. Marcel wanted to see his friends, _____ he went to their house.

7. The skater showed great skill _____ obvious confidence.

8. Put the key on a chain, _____ you might lose it.

9. Serena doesn't like algebra, _____ she does like geometry.

10. Flowers need water _____ sunlight in order to grow.

PRACTICE 5.1B > Writing Sentences With Correlative Conjunctions

Write ten sentences, using each of the correlative conjunctions below.

EXAMPLE   both . . . and

ANSWER   *Both* my sister *and* my brother went camping last weekend.

   Both her mom *and* her dad attended the school conference.

11. both . . . and

12. neither . . . nor

13. not only . . . but also

14. either . . . or

15. whether . . . or

16. both . . . and

17. neither . . . nor

18. not only . . . but also

19. either . . . or

20. whether . . . or

SPEAKING APPLICATION

With a partner, take turns talking about what you do when you have free time. Your partner should listen for and name three coordinating conjunctions.

WRITING APPLICATION

Write a short paragraph about someone you admire. Use two or more coordinating conjunctions and at least one correlative conjunction in your paragraph.

PRACTICE 5.1C > **Identifying Subordinating Conjunctions**

Read the sentences. Then, write the subordinating conjunction (e.g., *while, because, although, if*) in each sentence.

EXAMPLE   You can go to the park after you finish your chores.

ANSWER   *after*

1. Before a plane takes off, there is a safety check.

2. I wanted to see the movie because my friends all liked it.

3. As soon as I finish this math problem, I'll help you with your homework.

4. Unless we get a little more wind, we won't be able to fly our kites today.

5. I can make the sauce while you boil the pasta.

6. My sister makes friends wherever she goes.

7. If you do that, the teacher will be upset.

8. We worked hard on the snow fort although we knew it would soon melt.

9. Put those books on the lower shelves so that younger children can reach them.

10. Whenever you need me, just call.

PRACTICE 5.1D > **Identifying Conjunctive Adverbs**

Read the sentences. Then, write the conjunctive adverb (e.g., *consequently, furthermore, indeed*) in each sentence.

EXAMPLE   I studied for days before the test; thus, I was prepared.

ANSWER   *thus*

11. Cary scored the winning touchdown; thereafter, he was treated with respect.

12. Hannah wanted to go outside; however, she had to do her homework.

13. I don't want to go to the water park; besides, you just went last week.

14. We need to find a shortcut; otherwise, we'll never get there on time.

15. Maria is good at math; indeed, she volunteered to help us.

16. Manufacturers add safety features to cars; nevertheless, one must drive carefully.

17. I thought we had insect repellent; however, it's too late now to go back for it.

18. Something dug up our vegetable garden; therefore, we have no carrots or tomatoes.

19. Hoshi was very honest; consequently, he was put in charge of the money.

20. The class worked all day on the project; furthermore, some stayed late to finish.

SPEAKING APPLICATION

With a partner, take turns talking about a story you read. Use two subordinating conjunctions and two conjunctive adverbs. Your partner should listen for and name the subordinating conjunctions and conjunctive adverbs.

WRITING APPLICATION

Write two sentences using subordinating conjunctions and two sentences using conjunctive adverbs. You can use the sentences in Practice 5.1C and 5.1D as models. Be careful to punctuate your sentences correctly.

5.2 Interjections

The **interjection** is the part of speech that is used the least. Its only use is to express feelings or emotions.

> An **interjection** expresses feeling or emotion and functions independently from the rest of a sentence.

5.2.1 RULE

An interjection has no grammatical relationship to any other word in a sentence. It is, therefore, set off from the rest of the sentence with a comma or an exclamation mark.

Interjections can express different feelings or emotions.

JOY	**Wow!** I can't believe you won the race.
SURPRISE	**Oh**, I didn't expect to hear from you.
PAIN	**Ouch!** That hurts.
IMPATIENCE	**Hey!** How long do they expect me to wait?
HESITATION	I, **uh**, think we should leave now.

Interjections are used more in speech than in writing. They are informal, rather than formal, expressions. When you do see them in writing, they are often included in dialogue. The following chart lists words often used as interjections.

See Practice 5.2A
See Practice 5.2B

INTERJECTIONS			
ah	gosh	nonsense	ugh
aha	great	oh	uh
alas	heavens	oops	um
boy	hey	ouch	well
darn	huh	psst	what
eureka	hurray	shh	whew
fine	my	terrible	wonderful
golly	never	terrific	wow

PRACTICE 5.2A ▷ Identifying Interjections

Read the sentences. Write the interjection in each sentence. Then, write what emotion the interjection conveys.

EXAMPLE   Hey! Get out of there now!

ANSWER   *Hey* — anger

1. Ugh! That medicine tastes awful.
2. Oh! That's not what was supposed to happen.
3. Wonderful! You got straight A's!
4. Aha, that's where you hid it.
5. Nonsense! You should not believe everything you read in the newspapers.
6. Alas, he never returned from that last voyage.
7. Whew! I didn't think we were going to make it.
8. Darn! Why didn't I remember there was a test today?
9. Ah, these boots help my feet stay warm.
10. I, uh, don't want to go to that restaurant.

PRACTICE 5.2B ▷ Supplying Interjections

Read the sentences. Rewrite each sentence, using an appropriate interjection in place of the feeling shown in parentheses. Use a comma or an exclamation mark after each interjection.

EXAMPLE   (joy) Our football team won the championship.

ANSWER   *Hurray!* Our football team won the championship.

11. (impatience) I can't believe you were late again.
12. (pain) Be careful taking off the bandage.
13. (relief) I thought that test would never end.
14. (surprise) I didn't expect to see you here.
15. (anger) Get those dogs away from our picnic.
16. (pleasure) The Kramers are coming for dinner.
17. (disgust) What is that smell coming from the science lab?
18. (wonder) That was an amazing fireworks display!
19. (discovery) Now we see what you were trying to do.
20. (disbelief) I don't believe anyone would do that.

SPEAKING APPLICATION

With a partner, take turns talking about things that happen at school. Your partner should listen to each comment and respond with an interjection. For example, one person might say, "There is a test today," and the other might respond, "Ugh!"

WRITING APPLICATION

Write three sentences that include appropriate interjections. You can use interjections from Practice 5.2A and Practice 5.2B or from the list in the lesson.

Cumulative Review Chapters 1–5

PRACTICE 1 > Writing Sentences With Nouns

Write five sentences, each using one of the following kinds of nouns. Circle those nouns, and underline any other nouns you use.

1. a common noun that names a person
2. a proper noun that names a place
3. an abstract noun
4. a single-word compound noun
5. a collective noun

PRACTICE 2 > Identifying Pronouns

Read the sentences. Then, write the pronouns that each sentence contains. Label each pronoun *personal, reflexive, intensive, demonstrative, relative, interrogative,* or *indefinite.*

1. Uncle Rob, who lives in Spain, is visiting us.
2. Whose picture is this?
3. Jo herself had no idea that a party was planned.
4. Everyone likes this new invention of mine.
5. Sometimes I picture myself as a famous writer.
6. Why didn't anyone say that?
7. Who will the star himself take to the Oscars?
8. Jan, who is good in math, is our club's treasurer.
9. Something in the food gave me a stomachache.
10. Mom often talks to herself when she is happy.

PRACTICE 3 > Using Action and Linking Verbs

Write two sentences for each word below. In the first sentence, use the word as an action verb; in the second sentence, use it as a linking verb.

1. sound
2. grow
3. look
4. feel
5. appear

PRACTICE 4 > Identifying Helping Verbs and Main Verbs in Verb Phrases

Read the sentences. Write the complete verb phrase in each sentence. Then, label the parts of each verb phrase *helping* or *main.*

1. The twins have finished all their homework.
2. The train will arrive at 5:00 P.M.
3. I had been reading a short story.
4. She has worked hard for the medal.
5. The essay will be completed in twenty minutes.
6. Everyone can join in the chorus.
7. I will tell you a secret.
8. The game has been finished for some time now.
9. We had seen the rainbow yesterday.
10. I should have started my project sooner.

Continued on next page ▶

Cumulative Review Chapters 1–5

 PRACTICE 5 > **Revising Sentences With Adjectives and Adverbs**

Read the sentences. Then, rewrite each sentence by adding at least one adjective to modify a noun or a pronoun or one adverb to modify a verb, an adjective, or another adverb.

1. Inez lost her umbrella.
2. The boy rides his bicycle to school.
3. The child screams loudly.
4. A beautiful bird perched on the fence.
5. It was cloudy until noon.
6. The truck sped through the night.
7. Shadows fell on the mountainside.
8. Someone whispered in the back of the room.
9. The neon lights glowed like stars in the sky.
10. Have you seen an adventure film?

 PRACTICE 6 > **Writing Sentences With Prepositions and Adverbs**

Write ten sentences about running or runners. In your first five sentences, use the prepositional phrases in items 1–5. In your next five sentences, use the words in items 6–10 as adverbs.

1. before the race
2. inside the stadium
3. around the track
4. behind the others
5. up a hill
6. before
7. inside
8. around
9. behind
10. up

PRACTICE 7 > **Identifying Conjunctions**

Read the sentences. Then, identify each underlined word or pair of words as a *coordinating conjunction*, a *subordinating conjunction, correlative conjunctions*, or a *conjunctive adverb*.

1. My pet hamster escaped, <u>but</u> Mom found it.
2. We applauded wildly <u>when</u> the concert ended.
3. <u>Either</u> Pedro <u>or</u> Lucy will trade seats with me.
4. I play soccer; <u>however</u>, I rarely watch it on television.
5. My sister <u>and</u> brother walk to school with me.

PRACTICE 8 > **Revising to Include Interjections**

Rewrite the following dialogue, adding interjections to help show the speakers' emotions. Use either a comma or an exclamation mark after each interjection.

JUAN: Do you remember walking on the beach?

TARA: The sun was just beginning to set. It was so beautiful.

JUAN: Maybe we can go again next summer.

TARA: We'll see. But I sure wish it were summer now. I hate this cold weather.

JUAN: Be patient.

TARA: I guess you are right.

JUAN: It won't be long before we will be complaining that it is too hot.

CHAPTER 6

BASIC SENTENCE PARTS

Carefully select your subjects and verbs to create interesting and surprising sentences.

WRITE GUY *Jeff Anderson, M.Ed.*

WHAT DO YOU NOTICE?

Spot the subjects and verbs as you zoom in on these lines from the poem "The Walrus and the Carpenter" by Lewis Carroll.

MENTOR TEXT

> The Walrus and the Carpenter
>   Were walking close at hand:
> They wept like anything to see
>   Such quantities of sand ...

Now, ask yourself the following questions:

- Which two nouns form the compound subject in these lines?
- Which verbs show the subjects' actions?

The proper nouns *Walrus* and *Carpenter* form the compound subject. The verbs *were walking* and *wept* show their actions. You can tell that the proper nouns function as a compound subject because the conjunction *and* connects them, and they share the verb *were walking* and the verb *wept*.

Grammar for Writers Use a variety of conjunctions in your writing. The Walrus and the Carpenter are linked by *and*, but you can also use *or* to form a compound subject. For example, you could write, "Either my brother *or* my sister will make lunch today."

You and I share the same subjects at school.

That makes us a compound subject.

6.1 The Basic Sentence

There are many kinds of sentences. Some are short; others are long. Some are simple, and others are more complex. In order to be considered complete, a sentence must have two things: a subject and a verb.

The Two Basic Parts of a Sentence

Every sentence, regardless of its length, must have a subject and a verb.

RULE 6.1.1 ▷ A complete **sentence** contains a subject and a verb and expresses a complete thought.

The Subject
A sentence must have a **subject.** Most subjects are nouns or pronouns. The subject is usually, but not always, found near the beginning of the sentence.

RULE 6.1.2 ▷ The **subject** of a sentence is the word or group of words that names the person, place, thing, or idea that performs the action or is described. It answers the question *Who?* or *What?* before the verb.

EXAMPLES   The **cat** is hungry.

Mrs. Meow broke her dish.

She knows several tricks.

A **string** is her favorite toy.

The noun *cat* is the subject in the first sentence. It tells *what* is hungry. In the next sentence, the proper noun *Mrs. Meow* tells *who* broke her dish. The pronoun *she* in the third sentence tells *who* knows several tricks.

EL5

The Verb

As one of the basic parts of a sentence, the **verb** tells something about the subject.

> The **verb** in a sentence tells what the subject does, what is done to the subject, or what the condition of the subject is.

EXAMPLES

My cat **won** a ribbon.

The award **was given** in a big ceremony.

He **seems** tired now.

Won tells what *my cat* did. *Was given* explains what was done with *the award*. *Seems*, a linking verb, tells something about the condition of *he* by linking the subject to *tired*.

See Practice 6.1A

Using Subjects and Verbs to Express Complete Thoughts

Every basic sentence must express a complete thought.

> A sentence is a group of words with a subject and a verb that expresses a complete thought and can stand by itself and still make sense.

INCOMPLETE THOUGHT

in the basket in the hall

(This group of words cannot stand by itself as a sentence.)

This incomplete thought contains two prepositional phrases. The phrases can become a sentence only after *both* a subject and a verb are added to them.

COMPLETE THOUGHT

The **kittens** **are** in the basket in the hall.

subject   verb

(This group of words can stand by itself as a sentence.)

See Practice 6.1B

In grammar, incomplete thoughts are often called **fragments.**

PRACTICE 6.1A Finding Subjects and Verbs

Read the sentences. Write the subject and verb of each sentence.

EXAMPLE   Charlie watched the train go by.

ANSWER   *Charlie, watched*

1. The horses pulled the wagon.
2. We finished the assignment.
3. The hot sand burned our feet.
4. Your brother is very sick.
5. A crowd gathered around the guitar player.
6. Jake lives near a lake.
7. Volunteers collected donations.
8. She put the books back onto the shelf.
9. Mikhail came here from Russia.
10. Sondra was glad to be included.

PRACTICE 6.1B Recognizing Complete Thoughts

Read the following groups of words. If a group of words expresses a complete thought, write *complete*. If a group of words expresses an incomplete thought, write *incomplete*.

EXAMPLE   Outside, behind the barn.

ANSWER   *incomplete*

11. We enjoyed the baseball game.
12. Ducks near the pond.
13. In the evening, after sunset.
14. The storm came in quickly.
15. The garden in full bloom.
16. Leaving the doctor's office.
17. They went to the store.
18. Our cat ate the fish.
19. On the kitchen counter.
20. Everyone came home early.

SPEAKING APPLICATION

With a partner, take turns talking about an activity you enjoy. Your partner should listen for and name two subjects and two verbs.

WRITING APPLICATION

Write a short paragraph about your favorite class. Underline the subject in each sentence, and underline the verb twice.

6.2 Complete Subjects and Predicates

Have you ever seen tiles laid on a floor? First, a line is drawn in the center of the room. One tile is placed to the left of the line, and another is placed to the right. Then, more tiles are added in the same way: one to the left and one to the right.

Imagine that the first tile on the left is a subject and the first tile on the right is a verb. You would then have a subject and a verb separated by a vertical line, as shown in the example.

EXAMPLE   **Fur** | **flew** .

Now, in the same way that you would add a few more tiles if you were tiling a floor, add a few more words.

EXAMPLE   Ginger **fur** | **flew** through the air.

At this point, you could add still more words.

EXAMPLE   Oscar's long ginger **fur** | **flew** through the air in clumps and bunches.

EL8

The centerline is important in laying tiles. It is just as important in dividing these sentences into two parts. All the words to the left of the line in the preceding examples are part of the **complete subject.** The main noun in the complete subject, *fur*, is often called the **simple subject.**

> The **complete subject** of a sentence consists of the subject and any words related to it.

6.2.1 RULE

As in the examples above, the complete subject may be just one word—*fur*—or several words—*Oscar's ginger fur*.

Look at the example sentences again, plus one with new words added.

EXAMPLES   Ginger **fur** | **flew** through the air.

Oscar's ginger **fur** | **flew** through the air
in clumps.

Oscar's ginger **fur** | **had flown** through the air
during his grooming.

All the words to the right of the line in the preceding examples
are part of the **complete predicate.** The verb *flew*, or a verb
phrase such as *had flown*, on the other hand, is often called the
simple predicate.

See Practice 6.2A

> **The complete predicate** of a sentence consists of the verb
> and any words related to it.

EL8

As the examples show, a complete predicate may be just the verb
itself or the verb and several other words.

Many sentences do not divide so neatly into subject and
predicate. Look at the subjects and predicates in the following
sentences.

EXAMPLES   **After the picnic** , our **family** **went home** .

With the rising temperature , the **snow** **began
to melt** .

In these sentences, part of the predicate comes *before* the
subject, and the rest of the predicate follows the subject.

As you have seen, a complete simple sentence contains a simple
subject and a simple predicate. In addition, a complete simple
sentence expresses a complete thought.

See Practice 6.2B

PRACTICE 6.2A > **Identifying Complete Subjects and Predicates**

Read the sentences. Rewrite each sentence, and draw a vertical line between the complete subject and the complete predicate. Then, underline the subject once and the verb twice.

EXAMPLE   A few leaves remained on the tree.

ANSWER   *A few __leaves__ | __remained__ on the tree.*

1. The Russian ballerina twirled across the stage.

2. The second week of class seems more difficult.

3. Workers from the factory usually walk home for lunch.

4. My rusting old car needs a lot of work.

5. Our science teacher planned the next day's experiment.

6. The woman at the bakery sometimes gives me a sample of their bread.

7. The test results came back today.

8. My father told me I could go to the movies.

9. The white tiger is my favorite animal at the zoo.

10. Almost nobody went outside today.

PRACTICE 6.2B > **Writing Complete Sentences**

Read the items. Each item contains either a complete subject or a complete predicate. Rewrite each item along with the missing part to create complete sentences.

EXAMPLE   Flowers of every kind _____.

ANSWER   *Flowers of every kind crowded the gardens.*

11. _____ covered the ground completely.

12. That man in a suit _____.

13. _____ was on her way to the store.

14. The new movie theater _____.

15. _____ includes an instruction manual.

16. All the students from our school _____.

17. _____ usually carry their books in a backpack.

18. My favorite subject in school _____.

19. The firefighters _____.

20. The snow from yesterday's storm _____.

SPEAKING APPLICATION

With a partner, create sentences with complete subjects and complete predicates. Take turns talking about things that take place at school. One person offers a complete subject, and the other adds a complete predicate.

WRITING APPLICATION

Write three sentences about a favorite activity. Draw a vertical line between the complete subject and complete predicate of each sentence.

6.3 Compound Subjects and Compound Verbs

Some sentences have more than one subject. Some have more than one verb.

Recognizing Compound Subjects

A sentence containing more than one subject is said to have a **compound subject.**

RULE 6.3.1

> A **compound subject** is two or more subjects that have the same verb and are joined by a conjunction such as *and* or *or.*

EXAMPLES

Cats and kittens **are** popular as pets.
compound subject / verb

Cats, dogs, and other pets **can learn** to live together.
compound subject / verb

Recognizing Compound Verbs

A sentence with two or more verbs is said to have a **compound verb.**

RULE 6.3.2

> A **compound verb** is two or more verbs that have the same subject and are joined by a conjunction such as *and* or *or.*

EXAMPLES

The **project** **may succeed or fail**.
subject / compound verb

She **writes, performs, and directs** her plays.
subject / compound verb

Sometimes a sentence will have both a compound subject and a compound verb.

EXAMPLE

Jane and Sharon **sang and danced** on the stage.
compound subject / compound verb

See Practice 6.3A
See Practice 6.3B

PRACTICE 6.3A > **Recognizing Compound Subjects and Compound Verbs**

Read the sentences. Write the compound subject and/or the compound verb in each sentence.

EXAMPLE   My dog dashed out of the house, raced across the lawn, and happily rolled in the fallen leaves.

ANSWER   *dashed, raced, and rolled — compound verb*

1. My brother, sister, and I went out for dinner last night.

2. The old trees creaked and groaned as the temperature dropped.

3. Our softball teams practice and play on the community baseball diamond.

4. My sister and my brother made their beds, had breakfast, and headed for school.

5. The manager and supervisor discuss all job applicants and make a decision.

6. Before going to the store, my mom always checks the cupboard, looks in the refrigerator, and writes a shopping list.

7. Clarice, Juana, Bethany, and Valeria tried out for the part of Juliet in the school play.

8. The doctor and radiologist examined the X-rays, consulted a specialist, and planned possible treatments.

9. The spectators and the judges applauded the brilliant ice-skating routine during the Olympics.

10. As part of their community service, the boys picked up trash, trimmed bushes, and gathered cans and glass for recycling.

PRACTICE 6.3B ▶ **Combining Sentences With Compound Subjects and Compound Verbs**

Read the sentences. Combine each pair of sentences by using compound subjects or compound verbs.

EXAMPLE   Yesterday, I went to the store with my mom.

Yesterday, I also went to the post office with my mom.

ANSWER   *Yesterday, I went to the store and the post office with my mom.*

1. Today, my father will clean out the garage. Today, my father will also mow the lawn.

2. Last week, my aunt went to the movie theater for a special showing of old films. My mom went to the movie theater with her.

3. Exercising is good for your health. Eating a balanced diet is also good for your health.

4. Whenever I get the chance, I go through my mom's cookbooks. I choose recipes I would like to try.

5. Members of the soccer team often stay late after school to practice. Members of the baseball team also stay late after school to practice.

6. The new kittens were curious about their new surroundings. They explored every part of the house.

7. Fire trucks passed before the gathered crowds during the big parade. Floats, horses, and bands also passed before the gathered crowds during the big parade.

8. Sitting in the library, Larissa read a book to prepare for writing a report. Larissa took notes to prepare for writing a report.

9. My grandparents are going to eat at that new restaurant on the corner. My parents are going to go with them.

10. Many people take the train to work. Many people drive to work.

SPEAKING APPLICATION

With a partner, talk about a sport you enjoy playing or watching. Have compound subjects and/or compound verbs in your sentences. Your partner should listen for and identify sentences with compound subjects and/or compound verbs.

WRITING APPLICATION

Write two short sentences about something you do at school. Then, combine the two short sentences into one longer sentence that has a compound subject and/or compound verb.

6.4 Hard-to-Find Subjects

It can be difficult to identify simple subjects in certain sentences. These sentences do not follow **normal word order** in which the subject comes before the verb. Sometimes the subject will follow the verb or part of a verb phrase. This is called **inverted word order**. Questions are often presented in inverted word order.

NORMAL WORD ORDER

The **concert** **will begin** at 8:30 P.M.
   subject   verb

INVERTED WORD ORDER

When **will** the **concert** **begin**?
    verb   subject   verb

Sometimes the subject will not actually be stated in the sentence. It will be understood to be the pronoun *you*. This is often true in sentences that express commands or requests.

The Subject of a Command or Request

When a sentence commands or requests someone to do something, the subject is often unstated.

> The subject of a command or request is understood to be the pronoun *you*.

6.4.1 RULE

COMMANDS OR REQUESTS	HOW THE SENTENCES ARE UNDERSTOOD
Stop!	You stop!
Begin at once.	You begin at once.
Please come here.	You please come here.
Audrey, make a list.	Audrey, you make a list.
Bob, get the tickets.	Bob, you get the tickets.

See Practice 6.4A

Even though a command or request may begin with the name of the person spoken to, the subject is still understood to be *you*.

Finding Subjects in Questions

Questions are often presented in inverted word order. You will usually find the subject in the middle of the sentence.

In questions, the subject often follows the verb.

Some questions in inverted word order begin with the words *what, which, whom, whose, when, where, why,* and *how.* Others begin with the verb itself or with a helping verb.

EXAMPLES   How **are** the **kittens** today?

Did you feed them in the morning?

Have you found homes for all of them yet?

If you ever have trouble finding the subject in a question, use this trick: Change the question into a statement. The subject will then appear in normal word order before the verb.

QUESTIONS	REWORDED AS STATEMENTS
How are the pups today?	The pups are how today.
What did the doctor say?	The doctor did say what.
Were the labels ready?	The labels were ready.
Did she bring her camera with her?	She did bring her camera with her.

Not every question is in inverted word order. Some are in normal word order, with the subject before the verb. Questions beginning with *who, whose,* or *which* often follow normal word order.

EXAMPLES   **Who has** the camera?

Whose **story won** the writing contest?

Which **painting should win** the contest?   See Practice 6.4B

PRACTICE 6.4A Identifying Subjects in Commands or Requests

Read the sentences. Write the subject of each sentence.

EXAMPLE   Get the tools I left in the garage.

ANSWER   *you*

1. Get the clothes out of the washing machine.
2. Place the books onto the correct shelves.
3. Please, close the door.
4. Juwan, bring me that globe.
5. Don't forget to take an umbrella.
6. Come to the window so I can see you.
7. Jason and Keiko, put these boxes in the car.
8. For dessert, order whatever looks good.
9. Jena, get me five eggs from the refrigerator.
10. Bring the soup to a boil.

PRACTICE 6.4B Identifying Subjects in Questions

Read the questions. Write the subject of each question. If you have trouble finding the subject in a question, change the question into a statement.

EXAMPLE   Are the girls coming with us?

ANSWER   *girls*

11. Did you remember to lock the back door?
12. Are dogs allowed in your apartment?
13. Is it too late to buy tickets?
14. Will Daniel and Felicia be in the play?
15. Can Stefan bring his guitar?
16. Has everyone signed the petition?
17. Were the Donovans at the party?
18. Was Fernando ready for school?
19. Would your parents let you go to the dance?
20. Did the teacher explain the project to you?

SPEAKING APPLICATION

With a partner, take turns role-playing a coach or teacher getting players or students to do things. Your partner should listen for and identify commands and questions and name the subject.

WRITING APPLICATION

Write a short series of instructions for carrying out a task, such as making soup or turning on a computer. Include at least two command/ request sentences.

Finding the Subject in Sentences Beginning With *There* or *Here*

Sentences beginning with *there* or *here* are usually in inverted word order.

> **There or *here* is never the subject of a sentence.**

There or *here* can be used in two ways at the beginning of sentences. First, it can be used to start the sentence.

SENTENCE STARTER

There are two musicians from Texas in the band.

Here is where many fans who are not able to buy tickets will stand.

There or *here* can also be used as an adverb at the beginning of sentences. As adverbs, these two words point out *where* and modify the verbs.

ADVERB

There goes the famous rock star.

Here are the invitations to the party.

Be alert to sentences beginning with *there* and *here*. They are probably in inverted word order, with the verb appearing before the subject. If you cannot find the subject, reword the sentence in normal word order. If *there* is just a sentence starter, you can drop it from your reworded sentence.

SENTENCES BEGINNING WITH *THERE* OR *HERE*	REWORDED WITH SUBJECT BEFORE VERB
There is a mistake in the ad for the show.	A mistake is in the ad for the show.
Here comes the star of the show.	The star of the show comes here.

See Practice 6.4C

Finding the Subject in Sentences Inverted for Emphasis

Sometimes a subject is intentionally put after its verb to draw attention to the subject.

> In some sentences, the subject follows the verb in order to emphasize the subject, or make it stand out.

6.4.4 RULE

In the following examples, notice how the order of the words builds suspense by leading up to the subject.

EXAMPLES   In the midst of the crowd outside the theater

stood the **star**.
       verb   subject

Soaring high above the crowd **was** a huge
     verb   verb
bald eagle.
      subject

Hiding under the bedspread **were** my two
   verb   verb
orange **kittens**.
             subject

You can reword sentences such as these in normal word order to make it easier to find the subject.

INVERTED WORD ORDER	REWORDED WITH SUBJECT BEFORE VERB
In the midst of the crowd outside the theater stood the star.	The star stood in the midst of the crowd outside the theater.
Soaring high above the crowd was a huge bald eagle.	A huge bald eagle was soaring high above the crowd.
Hiding under the bedspread were my two orange kittens.	My two orange kittens were hiding under the bedspread.

See Practice 6.4D

| PRACTICE 6.4C | **Identifying Subjects in Sentences Beginning With *Here* or *There*** |

Read the sentences. Write the subject of each sentence.

EXAMPLE   Here is our library.

ANSWER   *library*

1. There goes the deliveryman.
2. Here is your jacket.
3. There is a fly near my soup.
4. Here are the guidebooks for our trip.
5. There were the Johnsons, in that car.
6. Here was a story to make you think.
7. There is a great musician playing on television.
8. Here comes the first rain of the month.
9. There lies the mystery behind this event.
10. Here is the information you requested.

| PRACTICE 6.4D | **Identifying Subjects in Sentences Inverted for Emphasis** |

Read the sentences. Write the subject of each sentence.

EXAMPLE   At the end of the road stood a crumbling house.

ANSWER   *house*

11. On the shores of the lake grew a magnificent tree.
12. In late August came the worst hurricane.
13. Right there in the driveway was the car I liked.
14. As I had feared, on the desk lay a math test.
15. In the carefully tended garden bloomed the most splendid roses.
16. In the middle of the Pacific Ocean are many islands.
17. Near the east coast of Australia lies a spectacular reef.
18. Behind the hedges waits the hunting fox.
19. By the side of the road was a strange sign.
20. On the stove simmers some stew.

SPEAKING APPLICATION

With a partner, take turns talking about a movie you saw. Be sure to start two or three sentences with *there* or *here*. Your partner should listen for and identify the subjects of the sentences.

WRITING APPLICATION

Write two sentences in normal word order. You may write on any topic that interests you. Then, rewrite the sentences in inverted order.

6.5 Complements

Often, a subject and verb alone can express a complete thought. For example, *Birds fly* can stand by itself as a sentence, even though it contains only two words, a subject and a verb. Other times, however, the thought begun by a subject and its verb must be completed with other words. For example, *Toni bought, The eyewitness told, Our mechanic is, Richard feels,* and *Marco won* all contain a subject and verb, but none expresses a complete thought. All these ideas need **complements**.

> **A complement** is a word or group of words that completes the meaning of a sentence.

 6.5.1 RULE

Complements are usually nouns, pronouns, or adjectives. They are located right after or very close to the verb. The complements are shown below in blue. The complements answer questions about the subject or verb in order to complete the sentence.

DIFFERENT KINDS OF COMPLEMENTS

Toni **bought** **cars** .
subject   verb   complement

The **eyewitness** **told** **us** the **story** .
   subject   verb   complements

Our **mechanic** **is** a **genius** .
   subject   verb   complement

Richard **feels** **sad** .
   subject   verb   complement

Marco **won** the **race** .
   subject   verb   complement

This section will describe three types of complements: **direct objects, indirect objects,** and **subject complements.** All complements add information about the subjects or verbs in the sentence. They paint a clearer picture that helps the reader understand the writer's thoughts.

Recognizing Direct Objects

Direct objects follow action verbs.

> A **direct object** is a noun or pronoun that receives the action of a verb.

You can find a direct object by asking *What?* or *Whom?* after an action verb.

EXAMPLES   My older **brother** **found** a grass **snake**.
                        subject   verb   direct object

I **called** **Ricky** early in the day.
subject verb   direct object

My dog **Champ** **likes** a good **scratch**
          subject   verb   direct object
on his belly.

Snake, Ricky, and *scratch* are the direct objects of the verbs in the examples. In the first sentence, *snake* answers the question *Found what?* In the second sentence, *Ricky* answers the question *Called whom?* In the third sentence, *scratch* answers the question *Likes what?*

Compound Direct Objects

Like subjects and verbs, direct objects can be compound. That is, one verb can have two or more direct objects.

EXAMPLES   The **lizard** **eats** **crickets** and other **bugs**.
                        subject   verb   direct object   direct object

The **committee** **chose** **Mrs. Franks**,
          subject   verb   direct object

Mr. Lynch, and **Ms. Chin** to organize the
direct object   direct object
reptile show.

See Practice 6.5A
See Practice 6.5B

PRACTICE 6.5A > **Recognizing Direct Objects**

Read the sentences. Write the direct object or the compound direct object in each sentence.

EXAMPLE   He loved building models.

ANSWER   *models*

1. Maria baked bread.
2. My friends brought gifts to the party.
3. Bears eat plants and meat.
4. The Carlisle twins raise rabbits.
5. Freddy strummed the guitar.
6. Mr. Sanchez speaks Spanish, English, and German.
7. The plant known as the Venus flytrap catches insects.
8. Sasha's older brother majored in math and science.
9. The female kangaroo carries her young in a pouch.
10. We all ordered salad, chicken, and potatoes.

PRACTICE 6.5B > **Adding Complements**

Read the sentences. Rewrite the sentences, and fill in the blanks with appropriate direct objects. Use both nouns and pronouns.

EXAMPLE   Marcus found his _____.

ANSWER   *Marcus found his key.*

11. Chandar saw _____ at the fair.
12. Estancia played the _____.
13. Jeffrey dug a _____.
14. The two boys visited _____.
15. Carly and Selene knitted _____.
16. I carefully watered _____ each morning.
17. Frankie asked _____ for a pencil .
18. Hey, Tommy, throw me that _____.
19. Michael's dad cooked a great _____.
20. Cecily scanned the _____.

SPEAKING APPLICATION

With a partner, discuss a hobby you have or would like to have. Your partner should listen for and name two direct objects.

WRITING APPLICATION

Write a short paragraph about packing for a trip. Make sure two or more sentences contain direct objects. Underline the direct object or direct objects in each sentence.

Distinguishing Between Direct Objects, Adverbs, and Objects of Prepositions

Not all action verbs have direct objects. Be careful not to confuse a direct object with an adverb or with the object of a preposition. If you are unsure if a word or phrase is a direct object, ask yourself who or what is receiving the action of the verb.

> **A direct object is never an adverb or the noun or pronoun at the end of a prepositional phrase.**

Compare the following examples. Notice that the action verb *drove* has a direct object in only the first sentence.

EXAMPLES
Joanne **drove** her new sports **car**.
subject · verb · direct object

Joanne **drove** **quickly**.
subject · verb · adverb

Joanne **drove** **through the town**.
subject · verb · prepositional phrase

Each example shows a very common sentence type. The first consists of a subject, a verb, and a direct object. The noun *car* is the direct object of the verb *drove*.

The second example consists of a subject, a verb, and an adverb. Nothing after the verb in the sentence answers the question *What?* so there is no direct object. *Quickly* modifies the verb and tells *how* Joanne drove.

The third example consists of a subject, a verb, and a prepositional phrase. Again, no noun or pronoun answers the question *What?* after the verb. The prepositional phrase tells *where* Joanne drove.

Notice also that a single sentence can contain more than one of these three parts.

EXAMPLE
Joanne drove her new sports **car** **quickly**
direct object · adverb
through the town.
prepositional phrase

See Practice 6.5C

Finding Direct Objects in Questions

In normal word order, a direct object follows a verb. In questions that are in inverted word order, however, the direct object often appears before the verb and subject.

> **A direct object in a question will sometimes be found before the verb.**

In the following chart, questions are paired with sentences reworded in normal word order. Direct objects are highlighted in pink, subjects are highlighted in yellow, and verbs are highlighted in orange. Compare the positions of the direct objects in each.

QUESTIONS	REWORDED IN NORMAL WORD ORDER
Did you hear the dog bark?	You did hear the dog bark.
What makes a great pizza?	A great pizza makes what.
What does a snake eat?	A snake does eat what.
Which T-shirt do you like, the purple one or the green striped one?	You do like which T-shirt, the purple one or the green striped one.
Whom did you meet in the cafeteria?	You did meet whom in the cafeteria.

In each of the five questions, the direct object appears before, rather than after, the verb. To locate the direct object in a question, put the sentence into normal word order with the subject appearing before the verb. Then, the direct object will be found in its usual position after the verb.

See Practice 6.5D

PRACTICE 6.5C Distinguishing Direct Object, Adverb, and Object of a Preposition

Read the sentences. Label each underlined word *DO* for direct object, *ADV* for adverb, or *OP* for object of a preposition.

EXAMPLE   Melissa walked through <u>town</u>.

ANSWER   *OP*

1. The jeweler polished the <u>bracelet</u>.
2. The squirrels ran up the <u>tree</u>.
3. Pedro carried the <u>groceries</u> into the house.
4. Tonight, the girls played <u>happily</u>.
5. The farmer walked into the <u>barn</u>.
6. The painter worked <u>quickly</u>.
7. Mr. Shapiro washed his <u>dog</u> today.
8. The willow tree swayed <u>gracefully</u>.
9. The children ran across the <u>field</u>.
10. The Nguyen family opened a new <u>restaurant</u>.

PRACTICE 6.5D Finding Direct Objects in Questions

Read the questions. Write the direct object in each question.

EXAMPLE   What will you wear tonight?

ANSWER   *What*

11. Whom did you talk to at the bank?
12. Did you ride the bus to school?
13. Which shoes should I take?
14. Whom did Dennis ask to the dance?
15. What will Kerri make for the bake sale?
16. Which class should I take first?
17. What did you throw out?
18. Whom will you be inviting to your party?
19. Which flavor do you like best?
20. What do squirrels do with the nuts they gather?

SPEAKING APPLICATION

With a partner, take turns asking questions about planning a party. Include at least two questions with direct objects. Your partner should listen for and name the direct objects.

WRITING APPLICATION

Use Practice 6.5C as a model, and write three sentences: one with a direct object following the verb, one with a prepositional phrase, and one with an adverb. As with the practice, write *DO*, *ADV*, or *OP* after each sentence.

Recognizing Indirect Objects

Sentences with a direct object may also contain another kind of complement, called an **indirect object.** A sentence cannot have an indirect object unless it has a direct object.

> An **indirect object** is a noun or pronoun that comes after an action verb and before a direct object. It names the person or thing to which something is given or for which something is done.

6.5.5 RULE

An indirect object answers the questions *To* or *for whom?* or *To* or *for what?* after an action verb. To find an indirect object, find the direct object first. Then, ask the appropriate question.

EXAMPLE   Shrini's **mom told them** the **story**.
                              indirect object   direct object

(Told *what?* [*story*])
(Told the story *to whom?* [*them*])

Keep in mind the following pattern: *Subject + Verb + Indirect Object + Direct Object.* An indirect object will almost always come between the verb and the direct object in a sentence.

Compound Indirect Objects

Like a subject, verb, or direct object, an indirect object can be compound.

EXAMPLES   **Dave painted** each **car and truck** a
              subject   verb   compound indirect object
             new **color**.
                  direct object

(Painted *what?* [*color*])
(Painted a color *to what?* [*car and truck*])

             Mom offered my sister and me sandwiches
             subject   verb   compound indirect object   compound direct object
             and milk.

(Offered *what?* [*sandwiches* and *milk*])
(Offered *sandwiches to whom?* [*my sister and me*])

See Practice 6.5E

Distinguishing Between Indirect Objects and Objects of Prepositions

Do not confuse an indirect object with the object of a preposition.

RULE 6.5.6

> **An indirect object never follows the preposition *to* or *for* in a sentence.**

Compare the following examples.

EXAMPLES   Father bought **him** a **car**.
                            indirect   direct
                            object   object

              Father bought a **car** for **him**.
                             direct   object of
                             object   preposition

In the first example above, *him* is an indirect object. It comes after the verb *bought* and before the direct object *car*. In the second example, *him* is the object of the preposition *for* and follows the direct object *car*.

EXAMPLES   Paul gave **Jerome** a **sandwich**.
                         indirect object   direct object

              Paul gave a **sandwich** to **Jerome**.
                          direct object   object of
                                             preposition

To find the indirect object in the first example above, you must first find the direct object. Ask yourself what Paul gave. He gave a sandwich, so *sandwich* is the direct object. Then, ask yourself to whom Paul gave the sandwich. He gave it to *Jerome*, so *Jerome* is the indirect object.

Use the same questions in the second example. Again, *sandwich* is the direct object of *gave*; however, *Jerome* is no longer the indirect object. Instead, it is the object of the preposition *to*.

See Practice 6.5F

PRACTICE 6.5E Recognizing Indirect Objects

Read the sentences. Write the indirect object in each sentence.

EXAMPLE   I brought Mom the paper.

ANSWER   *Mom*

1. Miguel threw Charlie the ball.
2. The Riveras got their dog a new collar.
3. Terry brought the kittens their dinner.
4. The company gave my dad a promotion.
5. Sheila bought her mother flowers.
6. Mom made us costumes for the play.
7. I gave my report a title page.
8. Kelly offered me money for my old bicycle.
9. The committee awarded the project a blue ribbon.
10. The park ranger gave the tourists directions.

PRACTICE 6.5F Distinguishing Indirect Object and Object of a Preposition

Read the sentences. Write whether the underlined word is an *indirect object* or an *object of a preposition*.

EXAMPLE   John threw the ball to <u>Ravi</u>.

ANSWER   *object of a preposition*

11. Johanna got a birthday card from her <u>grandmother</u>.
12. The baker brought <u>us</u> the bread we ordered.
13. Victoria gave the message to <u>Martina</u>.
14. Mom and I planned a party for <u>him</u>.
15. Our neighbor found <u>me</u> a job.
16. We fed the <u>seals</u> fish.
17. The artist showed her sketch to <u>me</u>.
18. Justin brought his <u>mother</u> a scarf.
19. Gina borrowed a dress from <u>me</u>.
20. My brother sent <u>me</u> a letter from camp.

SPEAKING APPLICATION

With a partner, talk about errands you or family members run regularly, such as trips to the store or library. Be sure to use indirect objects at least two times. Your partner should listen for and name the indirect objects.

WRITING APPLICATION

Write two sentences with indirect objects. Then, rewrite the sentences so that the indirect objects become objects of prepositions. Use the sentences in Practice 6.5F to help you with ideas.

Subject Complements

Both direct objects and indirect objects are complements used with action verbs. Linking verbs, however, have a different kind of complement called a **subject complement.** Like direct and indirect objects, subject complements add information to a sentence. However, subject complements give readers more information about the subject of the sentence, not the verb.

RULE 6.5.7

> A **subject complement** is a noun, pronoun, or adjective that follows a linking verb and provides important details about the subject.

Predicate Nouns and Pronouns

Both nouns and pronouns are sometimes used as subject complements after linking verbs.

RULE 6.5.8

> A **predicate noun** or **predicate pronoun** follows a linking verb and renames or identifies the subject of the sentence.

It is easy to recognize predicate nouns and predicate pronouns. The linking verb acts much like an equal sign between the subject and the noun or pronoun that follows the verb. Both the subject and the predicate noun or pronoun refer to the same person or thing.

EXAMPLES

Ronnie will be the **captain** of our team.
subject verb predicate noun

(The predicate noun *captain* renames the subject *Ronnie.*)

Ford's first **car was** the **Model A**.
subject verb predicate noun

(The predicate noun *Model A* identifies the subject *car.*)

The two **winners are they**.
subject verb predicate pronoun

(The predicate pronoun *they* identifies the subject *winners.*)   See Practice 6.5G

Predicate Adjectives
A linking verb can also be followed by a
predicate adjective.

> A **predicate adjective** follows a linking verb and describes
> the subject of the sentence.

6.5.9 RULE

A predicate adjective is considered part of the complete predicate
of a sentence because it comes after a linking verb. In spite of
this, a predicate adjective does not modify the words in the
predicate. Instead, it describes the noun or pronoun that serves as
the subject of the linking verb.

EXAMPLES   The **flight** to Houston **was** **swift**.
            subject   verb predicate adjective

(The predicate adjective *swift* describes the subject *flight*.)

The **salesperson** **seems** very **sensitive**
    subject   verb   predicate adjective
to the needs of customers.

(The predicate adjective *sensitive* describes the subject
salesperson.)

Compound Subject Complements
Like other sentence parts, subject complements can be
compound.

> A **compound subject complement** consists of two or
> more predicate nouns, pronouns, or adjectives joined by a
> conjunction such as *and* or *or*.

6.5.10 RULE

EXAMPLES   My two best **friends** **are** **Phil and Mark**.
                         subject   verb compound predicate noun

The **highway** **seems** **slick and icy**.
    subject   verb   compound predicate adjective

The **basket** **was** full of **apples and oranges**.
    subject   verb   compound predicate adjective

See Practice 6.5H

PRACTICE 6.5G > **Identifying Predicate Nouns and Predicate Pronouns**

Read the sentences. Write the predicate noun or predicate pronoun in each sentence.

EXAMPLE   My mom is a psychologist.

ANSWER   *psychologist*

1. The Komodo dragon is the largest lizard.
2. A loud voice announced, "It is I."
3. The man in the uniform was captain of the ship.
4. Rome is a city with a lot of history.
5. My favorite fruit is a peach.
6. That tree is a birch.
7. Margo is a good singer.
8. The caterpillar had become a butterfly.
9. The winner is he.
10. Even after his injury, Paco remained our best player.

PRACTICE 6.5H > **Identifying Predicate Adjectives**

Read the sentences. Write the predicate adjective in each sentence.

EXAMPLE   The mountains were really beautiful.

ANSWER   *beautiful*

11. Carla seems unhappy.
12. The backpack was heavy.
13. The girl's explanation sounded doubtful.
14. The breeze was gentle.
15. Jamal's new shoes seemed tight.
16. Those flowers smell wonderful.
17. The dresses were red.
18. That sweater looks warm.
19. Each day, the vegetables in the garden grow taller.
20. The thin ice looked dangerous.

SPEAKING APPLICATION

With a partner, talk about gardens, either ones you know or ones you can imagine. Use linking verbs to describe what happens and what is found in the garden. Your partner should listen for and name at least two predicate adjectives and two predicate nouns or predicate pronouns.

WRITING APPLICATION

Write a short paragraph about the changing seasons. Make sure that at least two sentences contain predicate adjectives and one contains a predicate noun or predicate pronoun.

CHAPTER 7

PHRASES *and* CLAUSES

Understanding how to build sentences using phrases and clauses will help add variety to your writing.

WRITE GUY *Jeff Anderson, M.Ed.*

WHAT DO YOU NOTICE?

Look for phrases as you zoom in on sentences from the play *The Phantom Toll Booth* by Susan Nanus, based on the book by Norton Juster.

MENTOR TEXT

> This is Dictionopolis, a happy kingdom, advantageously located in the foothills of Confusion and caressed by gentle breezes from the Sea of Knowledge. Today, by royal proclamation, is Market Day.

Now, ask yourself the following questions:

- What purpose does the appositive phrase *a happy kingdom* serve in the first sentence?
- What are the prepositional phrases in the first sentence?

The appositive phrase *a happy kingdom* provides readers with more information about Dictionopolis. The four prepositional phrases in the first sentence are *in the foothills, of Confusion, by gentle breezes,* and *from the Sea of Knowledge.*

Grammar for Writers Writers can use phrases to add more information to their sentences. Be sure to place phrases carefully in your sentences so that they modify the correct words.

Are phrases always short?

It depends on who their parents are.

7.1 Phrases

Sentences are usually built with more than just a subject and a predicate. **Phrases** play an important role in sentences by adding more information.

RULE 7.1.1

A **phrase** is a group of words that functions in a sentence as a single part of speech. Phrases do not contain a subject and a verb.

Prepositional Phrases

A **prepositional phrase** has at least two parts, a preposition and a noun or pronoun that is the object of the preposition.

EXAMPLES
near **airports**
prep   object

around **trees**
prep   object

The object of the preposition may be modified by one or more adjectives.

EXAMPLES
near busy urban **airports**
prep   adj   adj   object

around lovely green **trees**
prep   adj   adj   object

The object may also be a compound, consisting of two or more objects connected by a conjunction such as *and* or *nor*.

EXAMPLES
near busy urban **highways** and **airports**
prep   adj   adj   object   object

around lovely green **trees** and **grass**
prep   adj   adj   object   object

See Practice 7.1A

In a sentence, some prepositional phrases can act as adjectives that modify a noun or pronoun. Other prepositional phrases can act as adverbs that modify a verb, adjective, or adverb.

Using Prepositional Phrases That Act as Adjectives

A prepositional phrase that acts as an adjective in a sentence is called an **adjective phrase** or **adjectival phrase**.

> An **adjective phrase** or **adjectival phrase** is a prepositional phrase that modifies a noun or pronoun by telling *what kind* or *which one*.

7.1.2 RULE

Unlike one-word adjectives, which usually come before the nouns or pronouns they modify, adjectival phrases usually come after the nouns or pronouns they modify.

ONE-WORD ADJECTIVES	ADJECTIVAL PHRASES
The asphalt roadway began there.	The roadway with two lanes began there.
The angry rancher stopped us.	The rancher with the angry face stopped us.

Adjectival phrases answer the same questions as one-word adjectives do. *What kind* of roadway began there? *Which* rancher stopped us?

USES OF ADJECTIVAL PHRASES	
Modifying a Subject	The sound of the wind scared us.
Modifying a Direct Object	It rattled windows in the room.

When two adjectival phrases appear in a row, the second phrase may modify the object of the preposition in the first phrase or both phrases may modify the same noun or pronoun.

ADJECTIVAL PHRASES IN A ROW	
Modifying the Object of a Preposition	The weather vane on the roof of the barn spun wildly.
Modifying the Same Noun	There was a smell of rain in the air.

See Practice 7.1B

Using Prepositional Phrases That Act as Adverbs

A prepositional phrase that acts as an adverb modifies the same parts of speech as a one-word adverb does.

RULE 7.1.3

> An **adverbial phrase** or **adverb phrase** is a prepositional phrase that modifies a verb, an adjective, or an adverb. Adverbial phrases point out *where, when, in what way,* or *to what extent.*

Adverbial phrases are used in the same way as one-word adverbs, but they sometimes provide more precise details.

ONE-WORD ADVERBS	ADVERBIAL PHRASES
Bring your saddle here .	Bring your saddle to the barn .
The parade began early .	The parade began at exactly eleven o'clock .

Adverbial phrases can modify verbs, adjectives, and adverbs.

USES OF ADVERBIAL PHRASES	
Modifying a Verb	Raindrops fell in heavy torrents . (Fell *in what way?*)
Modifying an Adjective	The day was warm for December . (Warm *in what way?*)
Modifying an Adverb	The tornado struck suddenly, without warning . (Suddenly *to what extent?*)

Adverbial phrases, unlike adjectival phrases, are not always located near the words they modify in a sentence.

MODIFIES

EXAMPLE **During the storm** , ranchers chased the herd.

Two or more adverbial phrases can also be located in different parts of the sentence and still modify the same word.

MODIFIES MODIFIES

EXAMPLE **In an instant** , a tornado tore **through our house** . See Practice 7.1C
See Practice 7.1D

PRACTICE 7.1A Identifying Prepositional Phrases

Read the sentences. Then, write the prepositional phrase in each sentence and underline the object of the preposition. Then, write the function of the prepositional phrase (to convey *location*, *time*, or *direction*, or to provide *details*).

EXAMPLE   Stories of heroes exist in all societies.

ANSWER   *in all societies* — details

1. I found the professor in the chemistry lab.
2. Can you get my shirts from the cleaners?
3. She parked her bike in front of the store.
4. The advanced math concept was beyond his understanding.
5. They ran around the backyard.
6. The two baby girls were snug under the soft, warm, pink blanket.
7. I left the rake inside the tool shed.
8. The road runs between a forest and the river.
9. She read a history book during the first study period.
10. He backed his car into the neighbor's garage.

PRACTICE 7.1B Identifying Adjectival Phrases

Read the sentences. Then, write the adjectival phrase in each sentence. One sentence has two adjectival phrases.

EXAMPLE   The door to his office is locked.

ANSWER   *to his office*

11. The road toward the east is the one we will take.
12. Many of these books have great plots.
13. I want the one between the red and gray bicycles.
14. That's the birthday present from my grandmother.
15. The bed with the firm mattress was most comfortable.
16. The store at the corner has that magazine.
17. The sound of rushing water helped us find the waterfall.
18. I'm buying food for a friend with allergies.
19. This would be a great day for kite flying.
20. I bought a book about Booker T. Washington.

SPEAKING APPLICATION

With a partner, take turns talking about a trip to a store. Use at least two prepositional phrases (to convey *location*, *time*, or *direction*, or to provide *details*) and two adjectival phrases to describe something about the trip, such as where the store is, what it's like, or things you might buy there. Your partner should listen for and identify the prepositional phrases and adjectival phrases.

WRITING APPLICATION

Write a short paragraph about a trip into the country. Use prepositional phrases (to convey *location*, *time*, or *direction*, or to provide *details*) and adjectival phrases to describe the things you might see, hear, or experience.

PRACTICE 7.1C ▶ **Identifying Adverbial Phrases**

Read the sentences. Then, write the adverbial phrase in each sentence. One sentence has two adverbial phrases.

EXAMPLE   Mother worried about our safety.

ANSWER   *about our safety*

1. We crossed Lake Michigan on a ferry.
2. The glasses fell with a loud crash.
3. He stood in the rain.
4. The children spoke in hushed voices.
5. Carlotta plays on the soccer team.
6. In the morning, before sunrise, my mom starts making breakfast.
7. The ball rolled under the table.
8. Put those groceries in the cupboard.
9. The rain came down with increasing fury.
10. Craig and Aaron ran toward the cheering crowd.

PRACTICE 7.1D ▶ **Writing Adjectival and Adverbial Phrases**

Read the sentences. Then, rewrite the sentences by adding adjectival or adverbial phrases, as directed in parentheses.

EXAMPLE   Close the door. (adjectival phrase)

ANSWER   *Close the door* **to the basement.**

11. Many rivers flow. (adverbial phrase)
12. I would like a jacket. (adjectival phrase)
13. We went swimming. (adverbial phrase)
14. Jena works at the drugstore. (adverbial phrase)
15. The bicycle looks great. (adjectival phrase)
16. The forest is where we hike. (adjectival phrase)
17. The football team practices. (adverbial phrase)
18. I bought a wooden box. (adjectival phrase)
19. Some pieces are missing. (adjectival phrase)
20. We read the directions. (adverbial phrase)

SPEAKING APPLICATION

With a partner, discuss the climate where you live. Use at least one adjectival phrase and one adverbial phrase to describe different types of weather you experience. Your partner should listen for and identify the adjectival and adverbial phrases.

WRITING APPLICATION

Write a short paragraph about a visit to an amusement park. Use at least one adjectival phrase and one adverbial phrase to describe what you do and what you see.

Using Appositives and Appositive Phrases

Appositives, like adjectival phrases, give information about nouns or pronouns.

> An **appositive** is a noun or pronoun placed after another noun or pronoun to identify, rename, or explain the preceding word.

7.1.4 RULE

Appositives are very useful in writing because they give additional information without using many words.

MODIFIES

EXAMPLES   The conquistador **Francisco de Coronado** led an

expedition looking for gold.

MODIFIES

I admire the poet **Robert Frost** .

An appositive with its own modifiers creates an **appositive phrase.**

> An **appositive phrase** is a noun or pronoun with modifiers. It is placed next to a noun or pronoun and adds information or details.

7.1.5 RULE

The modifiers in an appositive phrase can be adjectives or adjectival phrases.

EXAMPLES   Uncle Jim, my **favorite** **uncle** , plays the piano.
                              adjective   noun

In the hall is a painting, a mural **in many bright colors** .
                                              adj phrase

Appositives and appositive phrases can also be a compound.

See Practice 7.1E
See Practice 7.1F

EXAMPLE   Volunteers, **boys** and **girls** , work together.
                              compound noun

PRACTICE 7.1E > Identifying Appositives and Appositive Phrases

Read the sentences. Then, write the appositive or appositive phrase in each sentence.

EXAMPLE   My cousin, Sarah Donnelly, is a veterinarian at our local zoo.

ANSWER   *Sarah Donnelly*

1. The Wright brothers, bicycle mechanics, built the first successful airplane.

2. I enjoy music written by the composer Mozart.

3. We took flowers to Mrs. Tran, our neighbor.

4. Alaska, the largest state in the nation, covers more than 500,000 square miles.

5. My mom's cousin, Misha, will be visiting.

6. Kanji, one of Japan's three alphabets, was adapted from Chinese characters.

7. Placido Domingo, the great Spanish singer, will be performing here next week.

8. America's Jazz Age, the 1920s, saw a growing appreciation of African American art and music.

9. This story was told by Isaac Asimov, the great science fiction writer.

10. Marsupials, animals that carry their young in pouches, include kangaroos and koalas.

PRACTICE 7.1F > Combining Sentences With Appositive Phrases

Read the sentences. Combine each pair of sentences by using an appositive phrase.

EXAMPLE   He won first prize. First prize is a trip to Hawaii.

ANSWER   *He won first prize, a trip to Hawaii.*

11. Samuel Adams was an American patriot. Samuel Adams entered Harvard at the age of 14.

12. Ancient Greeks played the lyre. The lyre is a stringed instrument.

13. Thistles are plants with purple flowers. The thistle is the national flower of Scotland.

14. Apples are members of the rose family. Apples have white and pink flowers.

15. Sequoyah was a Cherokee. Sequoyah invented an alphabet for the Cherokee people.

16. The fourth Thursday in November is Thanksgiving. It is a national holiday.

17. A diamond is the hardest mineral in the world. A diamond is a form of pure carbon.

18. Dr. Martin Luther King Jr. was a civil rights leader. Dr. King was a great speaker.

19. The pomegranate is a tart fruit. The pomegranate has many seeds.

20. The poem is about a gosling. A gosling is a young goose.

SPEAKING APPLICATION

With a partner, take turns telling about something you learned at school. Use two appositive phrases. Your partner should listen for and identify the appositive phrases.

WRITING APPLICATION

Write three sentences about a person or people you have studied. In each sentence, include an appositive phrase that adds information to the sentence.

Using Verbals and Verbal Phrases

A **verbal** is any verb form that is used in a sentence not as a verb but as another part of speech.

Like verbs, verbals can be modified by an adverb or adverbial phrase. They can also be followed by a complement. A verbal used with a modifier or a complement is called a **verbal phrase.**

Participles

Participles are verb forms with two basic uses. When they are used with helping verbs, they are verbs. When they are used alone to modify nouns or pronouns, they become adjectives.

EL6

> A **participle** is a form of a verb that is often used as an adjective.

7.1.6 RULE

There are two kinds of participles, **present participles** and **past participles.** Each kind can be recognized by its ending.

All present participles end in -*ing*.

EXAMPLES   talking   doing   eating   wanting

Most past participles end either in -*ed* or in -*d*.

EXAMPLES   opened   jumped   played   moved

Other past participles end in -*n*, -*t*, -*en*, or another irregular ending.

EXAMPLES   grown   felt   bought   eaten   held

Both present and past participles can be used in sentences as adjectives. They tell *what kind* or *which one*.

PRESENT PARTICIPLES	PAST PARTICIPLES
He arranged a walking tour.	Chilled fruit tastes good.
Talking quickly, she told her story.	He was, by then, a grown man.

See Practice 7.1G

Participle or Verb?

Sometimes, verb phrases (verbs with helping verbs) are confused with participles. A verb phrase always begins with a helping verb. A participle used as an adjective stands by itself and modifies a noun or pronoun.

VERB PHRASES	PARTICIPLES
The car was racing around the curve.	The racing car crashed into the wall.
Early settlers may have traveled on this road.	The traveled road led to the sea.

Participial Phrases

A participle can be expanded into a participial phrase by adding a complement or modifier.

RULE 7.1.7

> A **participial phrase** is a present or past participle and its modifiers. The entire phrase acts as an adjective in a sentence.

Participial phrases can be formed by adding an adverb, an adverbial phrase, or a complement to a participle.

EXAMPLES   The instructor, **speaking slowly**, explained the use of skis.

The esteemed poet, **honored by the award**, expressed his thanks.

The first participial phrase contains the adverb *slowly* added to the participle *speaking*. The second includes the adverbial phrase *by the award* added to the participle *honored*.

A participial phrase can also be placed at the beginning of a sentence. The phrase is usually followed by a comma.

EXAMPLE   **Honored by the award**, the esteemed poet expressed his thanks.

See Practice 7.1H
See Practice 7.1I
See Practice 7.1J

PRACTICE 7.1G ▷ Identifying Present and Past Participles

Read the sentences. Then, write the participle in each sentence and label it *present participle* or *past participle*.

EXAMPLE   Holding onto the railing, the toddler went down the stairs.

ANSWER   *Holding* — present participle

1. The rabbit, hopping across the yard, saw the cat.

2. The only people allowed in the classroom are students.

3. The actors, dressed in funny costumes, sprint across the stage.

4. Rushing down the hall, the doctor responds to an emergency.

5. Chess is a challenging game.

6. The picture drawn in charcoal wins first prize in the art contest.

7. The bird hurt in the storm couldn't return to its nest.

8. During the scavenger hunt, the best clue was the map hidden under the statue.

9. Neil's new running shoes were uncomfortable.

10. The laughter spreading through the audience almost brings the play to a halt.

PRACTICE 7.1H ▷ Distinguishing Verbs and Participles

Read the sentences. Then, write *verb* or *participle* for the underlined word in each sentence.

EXAMPLE   The woman <u>standing</u> in the corridor is the school principal.

ANSWER   *participle*

11. Those <u>participating</u> in the game were eager to start.

12. The airplane had <u>landed</u> twenty minutes early.

13. <u>Dripping</u> steadily, the leak filled the bucket in no time at all.

14. She was <u>learning</u> to play the guitar after school.

15. Greg <u>showed</u> up without any warning.

16. The plot of the mystery, <u>taken</u> from a recent news story, was familiar to everyone.

17. The trees <u>cleared</u> from the land were used to make wood for furniture.

18. The mayor is <u>defending</u> the new budget.

19. There were <u>varying</u> opinions on the success of the play.

20. The number of goals <u>scored</u> during the period was the highest of the season.

SPEAKING APPLICATION

With a partner, take turns describing a character in a book, movie, or television show. Use at least one present or past participle. Your partner should listen for and name the participle and tell whether it is present or past.

WRITING APPLICATION

Use sentence 13 as a model, and write one sentence with a participle. Then, use sentence 18 as a model, and write one sentence with a verb.

Identifying Participial Phrases

Read the sentences. Then, write the participial phrase in each sentence. Underline the participle.

EXAMPLE   Snakes found in South America are often poisonous.

ANSWER   *<u>found</u> in South America*

1. Told around the campfire, the stories seemed particularly exciting.
2. Letters sent by airmail arrive faster.
3. Saltwater crocodiles, measuring up to 25 feet in length, are the largest reptiles.
4. Originating in Africa, many folktales about animals are shared around the world.
5. Heading into the wind, the geese began their flight.
6. The pecans grown in Texas are some of the best.
7. The boys, ignoring all warnings, walked onto the ice-covered pond.
8. This plant, related to the lily, is easy to grow.
9. Climbing the tree, the camper had a better view of her surroundings.
10. Impressed by the student's interest, the teacher let him use the microscope.

Combining Sentences Using Participial Phrases

Read the sentences. Combine each pair of sentences by using a participial phrase.

EXAMPLE   Cassie was trusted by the students. She was elected class president.

ANSWER   *Trusted by the students, Cassie was elected class president.*

11. The weeds were growing quickly. The weeds soon overtook the small garden.
12. The students entered the auditorium. The principal followed the students.
13. The tulips were the first to bloom. The tulips were responding to the sunshine.
14. The music box was carved from wood. The music box created a warm, rich sound.
15. Everyone recognized the captain. The captain could not avoid the press.
16. Emma was laughing happily. Emma raced toward the ocean.
17. The kite was caught by the wind. The kite swooped and dove gracefully.
18. My mom shut the window. The noise outside annoyed her.
19. The critics praised the author's first book. The book sold well.
20. Carl stood silently watching the cheetah. Carl held his breath.

SPEAKING APPLICATION

With a partner, take turns talking positively about someone you know. Use two participial phrases. Your partner should listen for and identify the participial phrases.

WRITING APPLICATION

Write three sentences about an animal you have seen or read about. Include a participial phrase in each sentence to add information about the animal's appearance or behavior.

Gerunds

Like present participles, **gerunds** end in *-ing*. While present participles are used as adjectives, gerunds can be used as subjects, direct objects, predicate nouns, and objects of prepositions.

> A **gerund** is a form of a verb that acts as a noun.

USE OF GERUNDS IN SENTENCES	
Subject	Remodeling the building's style was a good idea.
Direct Object	Michael enjoys painting.
Predicate Noun	His favorite sport is fishing.
Object of a Preposition	Lucille never gets tired of singing country songs.

Gerund Phrases

Gerunds can also be part of a phrase.

> A **gerund phrase** is a gerund with modifiers or a complement, all acting together as a noun.

This chart shows how gerunds are expanded to form gerund phrases.

FORMING GERUND PHRASES	
Gerund With Adjectives	The loud, shrill howling continued all morning.
Gerund With Direct Object	Reading science fiction inspired many screenwriters.
Gerund With Prepositional Phrase	He helped the police by telling about his experience.
Gerund With Adverb and Prepositional Phrase	The dancers astound spectators by dancing skillfully across the stage in perfect symmetry.

See Practice 7.1K
See Practice 7.1L

Infinitives

Infinitives are verb forms that are used as nouns, adjectives, and adverbs. Like participles and gerunds, they can be combined with other words to form phrases.

> An **infinitive** is a verb form that can be used as a noun, an adjective, or an adverb. The word *to* usually appears before the verb.

EXAMPLES   It is important **to listen**.

He is the one **to ask**.

To stay calm can be difficult.

Infinitive Phrases

> An **infinitive phrase** is an infinitive with modifiers or a complement, all acting together as a single part of speech.

EXAMPLES   It is important **to listen carefully**.

It is not polite **to listen through a keyhole**.

They want **to give you a present**.

An **infinitive phrase** can be used in a sentence as a noun, an adjective, or an adverb. As a noun, an infinitive phrase can function as a subject, an object, or an appositive.

USES OF INFINITIVES	
Used as a Subject	To speak slowly is important.
Used as an Object	She tried to speak slowly.
Used as an Appositive	His suggestion, to speak slowly, was appreciated.
Used as an Adjective	It was her goal to speak slowly.
Used as an Adverb	It isn't always easy to speak slowly when you are excited.

See Practice 7.1M
See Practice 7.1N

PRACTICE 7.1K > **Identifying Gerund Phrases**

Read the sentences. Then, write the gerund phrase from each sentence, and underline the gerund. Remember to include all modifiers with the phrase.

EXAMPLE   The constant dripping began to bother me.

ANSWER   *The constant <u>dripping</u>*

1. Moving gracefully is important in women's gymnastics.
2. He gained confidence from his running.
3. Studying for the math exam took two hours.
4. The first step is buying the right equipment.
5. Rocking the crib might get the baby to sleep.
6. Chandra took off the bandages without considering the consequences.
7. Studying weather patterns helps scientists forecast the weather.
8. Use a sharp knife when cutting the vegetables.
9. The sweet, cheerful chirping of the birds told me spring was coming soon.
10. Counting your change is always a good idea.

PRACTICE 7.1L > **Writing Gerunds and Gerund Phrases**

Read the sentences. Then, rewrite each sentence, completing it with a gerund or gerund phrase.

EXAMPLE   In the summer, I do a lot of _____.

ANSWER   *In the summer, I do a lot of swimming.*

11. I enjoy _____ for bargains.
12. _____ helped prepare me for the English test.
13. It's important to use the right tools when _____.
14. My mom regretted _____ that dress.
15. The _____ could be heard for miles.
16. When the hikers returned, they told us about _____.
17. _____ can really mess up the kitchen.
18. He gained satisfaction from _____.
19. The most fun activity in the winter is _____.
20. _____ is the first step in making soup.

SPEAKING APPLICATION

With a partner, discuss activities you enjoy doing on weekends. Make sure to use at least two gerunds as you speak. Your partner should listen for and name two gerunds.

WRITING APPLICATION

Use gerund phrases and write three sentences about the summer. Vary the position of the gerund phrases; don't have them all at the beginning or the end of the sentences.

PRACTICE 7.1M ▷ **Identifying Infinitives and Infinitive Phrases**

Read the sentences. Then, write the infinitive phrase from each sentence, and underline the infinitive. Also write *noun, adjective,* or *adverb* to describe each infinitive phrase.

EXAMPLE   The easiest way to get there is through the woods.

ANSWER   <u>to get</u> there — adjective

1. To find the solution to the puzzle was Katrina's goal.

2. You can trust Miguel to hold the baby gently.

3. The Kim family came from North Korea to the United States to escape communism.

4. Sarai has a paper to write before Friday.

5. John's goal is to speak in front of a large group.

6. To see our grandmother smiling was reassuring.

7. Their plan to build a new house will be challenging.

8. My mom went to buy groceries.

9. We all wanted to go to the beach.

10. The project to raise money for hungry children was successful.

PRACTICE 7.1N ▷ **Writing Infinitives and Infinitive Phrases**

Read the sentences. Then, rewrite each sentence, completing it with an infinitive or an infinitive phrase.

EXAMPLE   Last summer we went _____ our favorite cousins.

ANSWER   *Last summer we went **to visit** our favorite cousins.*

11. His plan _____ was approved.

12. The class wanted _____ for Earth Day.

13. _____ is really unforgettable.

14. Marsha's dream is _____.

15. Why don't you ask your friends _____?

16. _____ was all that Clara had planned for the evening.

17. Don't you have a report _____?

18. The proposal _____ was put up for a vote.

19. _____ made everyone happy.

20. Grandfather wanted _____ after he retired.

SPEAKING APPLICATION

With a partner, take turns talking about school assignments. Use the sentences in Practice 7.1M as models to help you include two infinitive phrases. Your partner should listen for and identify the infinitive phrases.

WRITING APPLICATION

Use the sentences in Practice 7.1M as models, and write three sentences about everyday life that include infinitive phrases.

7.2 Clauses

Clauses are the basic structural unit of a sentence.

RULE 7.2.1

A **clause** is a group of words with its own subject and verb.

There are two basic kinds of clauses, **main** or **independent clauses** and **subordinate clauses.**

RULE 7.2.2

A **main** or **independent clause** has a subject and a verb and can stand by itself as a complete sentence.

As you can see in the examples below, a main clause can be long or short. All main clauses express a complete thought and can stand by themselves as complete sentences.

EXAMPLES

The **air** **vibrated** .
subject   verb

Early in the day, **he** **began** playing the cello.
subject   verb

RULE 7.2.3

A **subordinate clause,** also known as a dependent clause, has a subject and a verb but cannot stand by itself as a complete sentence. It is only part of a sentence.

SUBORDINATE CLAUSES

after **she** **performed** her solo
subject   verb

while the **band** **practiced** in the garage
subject   verb

After reading a subordinate clause, you will still need more information to have a complete sentence.

Subordinate clauses begin with **subordinating conjunctions or relative pronouns.**

Some subordinate clauses begin with **subordinating conjunctions,** such as *if, since, when, although, after, because,* and *while.* Others begin with **relative pronouns,** such as *who, which,* or *that.* These words are clues that the clause may not be able to stand alone. Notice how the addition of subordinating words changes the meaning of the main clauses in the examples below.

COMPARING TWO KINDS OF CLAUSES	
MAIN	SUBORDINATE
He arrives this morning.	*when* he arrives this morning
This mosque has a golden dome.	*because* the mosque has a golden dome
I planted the seeds	the seeds *that* I planted

In order to form a complete thought, a subordinate clause must be combined with a main clause.

EXAMPLES

After she performed her piece, Debbie felt
　　　　subordinate clause　　　　　　　　　　main clause

relieved.

The audience applauded **after Debbie performed**
　　　　main clause　　　　　　　　　subordinate clause

her piece .

It was Debbie **who was asked to perform first** .
　　main clause　　　　　　subordinate clause

When he arrives this morning , Tom needs to
　　subordinate clause　　　　　　　　　main clause

go right to the nurse.

See Practice 7.2A
See Practice 7.2B

PRACTICE 7.2A ▷ **Identifying Main and Subordinate Clauses**

Read the clauses. Then, write whether each clause is a *main clause* or a *subordinate clause*.

EXAMPLE   Because archaeology is a science.

ANSWER   *subordinate clause*

1. Where many seashells are found.
2. The rules of the game are easy.
3. After the third person walked across the hall.
4. Which meant someone had to call for help immediately.
5. Until the storm finally passed.
6. The team listened intently to the coach's words
7. He worked hard.
8. That was hiding in plain sight on the lowest bookshelf in the library.
9. Whose paper was about to rip apart.
10. It seemed unbelievable to most listeners.

PRACTICE 7.2B ▷ **Identifying and Using Main and Subordinate Clauses**

Read the clauses. Write *main clause* or *subordinate clause* for each clause. Then, expand each subordinate clause into a complete sentence by adding a main clause.

EXAMPLE   Since the snowstorm ended.

ANSWER   *subordinate clause*
We have been shoveling the driveway since the snowstorm ended.

11. When you are ready.
12. Every day is a new opportunity.
13. Although it was hot and sunny outside.
14. If the trumpet solo is easy enough to learn.
15. Jumping over a hurdle is difficult.
16. All the mail arrived safely.
17. After he arrived.
18. Ambulance driving is dangerous.
19. Even babies respond to smiles.
20. Who worked every weekend for a month.

SPEAKING APPLICATION

With a partner, take turns saying a subordinate clause. Your partner should expand the subordinate clause into a complete sentence by adding a main clause.

WRITING APPLICATION

Write three complete sentences about what you did at school today. Include a main clause and a subordinate clause. Circle the main clause and underline the subordinate clause in each sentence.

Adjectival Clauses

A subordinate clause will sometimes act as an adjective in a sentence. An adjectival clause or adjective clause is a dependent clause and can not stand on its own.

RULE 7.2.5

> An **adjectival clause** or **adjective clause** is a subordinate clause that modifies a noun or a pronoun.

Like one-word adjectives and adjectival phrases, **adjectival clauses** tell *what kind* or *which one*.

WHAT KIND?

EXAMPLES   clothes **that are bright and colorful**

WHICH ONE?

the city **where I was born**

Recognizing Adjectival Clauses

Most adjectival clauses begin with the words *that, which, who, whom,* and *whose*. Sometimes an adjectival clause begins with a subordinating conjunction, such as *since, where,* or *when*. In the chart below, the adjectival clauses are hightlighted in pink.

ADJECTIVAL CLAUSES
The teacher whom I asked for help stayed after school to work with me. (*Which* teacher?)
The talent show, which was advertised in the local paper, is tomorrow. (*Which* talent show?)
In the years since she started playing, Maia has become an accomplished pianist. (*Which* years?)
I hid my treasure box in the small closet where no one usually goes. (*Which* closet?)
We visited the museum that honors veterans of World War II. (*Which* museum?)
The museum whose exhibits include aircraft carriers is located in our town. (*Which* museum?)

See Practice 7.2C

Combining Sentences With Adjectival Clauses

Two sentences can be combined into one sentence by changing one of them into an adjectival clause. Sometimes you will need to add a relative pronoun or subordinating conjunction to make the sentence read correctly. In the sentences below, the adjectival clauses are highlighted in pink.

TWO SENTENCES	COMBINED WITH AN ADJECTIVAL CLAUSE
My history teacher has written books on the American Revolution. My history teacher is a famous scholar.	My history teacher, who has written books on the American Revolution, is a famous scholar.
We visited the history museum. The history museum is Tori's favorite museum.	We visited the history museum, which is Tori's favorite.
We decided to shop in Don's Grocery. We usually get the best bargains there.	We decided to shop in Don's Grocery, where we usually get the best bargains.
Paula visited her cousin last summer. Paula's cousin lives on a farm in Kansas.	Paula visited her cousin, who lives on a farm in Kansas, last summer.
Elizabeth goes to a camp every summer. Her camp is on a beautiful lake.	Elizabeth goes to a camp every summer that is on a beautiful lake.

See Practice 7.2D

PRACTICE 7.2C ▷ **Identifying Adjectival Clauses**

Read the sentences. Then, write the adjectival clause in each sentence. One sentence has two adjectival clauses.

EXAMPLE   The book, which my sister lent me, was totally engrossing.

ANSWER   *which my sister lent me*

1. The fish that Sam saw at the aquarium were incredibly colorful.

2. The movie scared my cousin, who asked if we could leave.

3. Your dog, whose bark is loud, is actually a nice dog, isn't he?

4. Heather's neighbors, whom she had not seen in many days, had been away on vacation.

5. The violinist who will be the soloist tonight is originally from Poland.

6. Jerry's great-grandmother, whom he never met, was the person who named him.

7. She had a strong preference for recipes that were easy to follow.

8. The path, which no one ever took, was overgrown and almost impassable.

9. The house where the playwright was born is now a tourist site.

10. Until now, the era when technological innovation was the greatest was the Industrial Revolution.

PRACTICE 7.2D ▷ **Combining Sentences Using Adjectival Clauses**

Read the sentences. Combine the pairs of sentences by changing one of them into an adjectival clause.

EXAMPLE   Kyle and Marcus ran indoors. They were dying of thirst.

ANSWER   *Kyle and Marcus, who were dying of thirst, ran indoors.*

11. The middle school held a science fair. The science fair was a great success.

12. The thunderstorm ruined the picnic. The picnic was for the softball team.

13. Tarik's cousin was visiting from Louisiana. Tarik hosted a Fourth of July party.

14. The dentist examined my teeth. The dentist was happy I had no cavities.

15. A snake startled me. The snake was slithering in the grass.

16. The babies' mothers leave the room. Babies often start crying.

17. Adam ran his eighth marathon last year. Adam is in good shape.

18. The firehouse was just rebuilt. The firehouse is ready to house a new engine.

19. Talia was the last to arrive. Talia did not know anyone.

20. The letter was waiting for him at home. The letter was an acceptance letter.

SPEAKING APPLICATION

With a partner, take turns describing something in the classroom. Use at least one adjectival clause. Your partner should listen for and identify the adjectival clause.

WRITING APPLICATION

Use the sentences in Practice 7.2D as models, and write two pairs of sentences. Then, for each pair, combine the sentences by changing one of them into an adjectival clause.

Adverbial Clauses

Subordinate clauses can also be used as adverbs. Adverbial clauses or adverb clauses are dependent clauses.

> An **adverbial clause** or **adverb clause** is a subordinate clause that modifies a verb, an adjective, or an adverb.

7.2.6 RULE

Adverbial clauses can answer any of the following questions about the words they modify: *Where? When? In what manner? To what extent? Under what conditions?* or *Why?*

ADVERBIAL CLAUSES	
Modifying Verbs	Put the package wherever you find room. (Put *where?*)
	The concert will begin when the conductor enters. (Will begin *when?*)
	Leo spoke as if he were frightened. (Spoke *in what manner?*)
	I will have lemonade if you do too. (Will have *under what conditions?*)
Modifying an Adjective	I am tired because I have been chopping wood all day. (Tired *why?*)
Modifying an Adverb	She knows more than the other engineers do. (More *to what extent?*)

Recognizing Adverbial Clauses

> A **subordinating conjunction** introduces an adverbial clause.

7.2.7 RULE

A **subordinating conjunction** always introduces an adverbial clause. In a sentence, the conjunction will usually appear in one of two places—either at the beginning, when the adverbial clause begins the sentence, or in the middle, connecting the independent clause to the subordinate clause. In the examples on the next page, the subordinating conjunctions are highlighted in purple.

EXAMPLES   **Because** you will get home late, I will prepare dinner.

I will prepare dinner **because** you will get home late.

Whenever you are late, I expect you to call.

I expect you to call **whenever** you are late.

Common Subordinating Conjunctions

Here are the most common subordinating conjunctions. Knowing them can help you recognize adverbial clauses.

COMMON SUBORDINATING CONJUNCTIONS		
after	even though	unless
although	if	until
as	in order that	when
as if	since	whenever
as long as	so that	where
because	than	wherever
before	though	while

Elliptical Adverbial Clauses

In certain adverbial clauses, words are left out. These clauses are said to be elliptical.

RULE 7.2.8

In an **elliptical adverbial clause,** the verb or the subject and verb are understood rather than stated.

Many elliptical adverbial clauses are introduced by one of two subordinating conjunctions, *as* or *than*. In the following examples, the understood words have been added in parentheses. The first elliptical adverbial clause is missing a verb; the second is missing a subject and a verb.

EXAMPLES   My brother can eat as much **as I** (can eat).

I liked this book more **than** (I liked) **that one**.

See Practice 7.2E
See Practice 7.2F

Identifying Adverbial Clauses and Recognizing Elliptical Adverbial Clauses

Read the sentences. Then, write the adverbial clauses. For any of the adverbial clauses that are elliptical, add the understood words in parentheses.

EXAMPLE   I enjoyed Barcelona more than Madrid.

ANSWER   *than (I enjoyed) Madrid*

1. Not all countries have the same laws as the United States.

2. David wore boots so that his feet would not get wet in the rain.

3. Christine will not see her family again until after New Year's Day.

4. As long as the weather is good, we can have our picnic!

5. I liked this book more than that one.

6. China's population is larger than Japan's.

7. As the years go by, my aunt's eyesight worsens.

8. Carmen spent more time in France than in Germany.

9. When she arrived at the station, Sherri phoned.

10. Because I was tired, I didn't mind that everyone went home.

Combining Sentences With Adverbial Clauses

Read the sentences. Combine each pair of sentences by changing one of them into an adverbial clause. Use an appropriate subordinating conjunction, and drop or change words as necessary.

EXAMPLE   I want to keep walking. My feet hurt.

ANSWER   *I want to keep walking even though my feet hurt.*

11. We watched a movie. We ate dinner.

12. We stayed home. There was a blizzard.

13. Jorge put a gate across the door. His puppy could not get into the kitchen.

14. Many people celebrated. The new president was inaugurated.

15. I will do the cooking. The dishes get washed and put away.

16. This book is interesting. It describes the history of baseball.

17. The carpenter began working. The oak boards had not yet been delivered.

18. Jeremy left the meeting. It was still going on.

19. Monica recognized her uncle. She had not seen him in five years.

20. I wanted to stay. I could continue to take notes.

SPEAKING APPLICATION

With a partner, take turns discussing two books that you read. Use Sentence 5 as a model, and say which book you liked more than the other. Your partner should listen for and identify the adverbial clause.

WRITING APPLICATION

Use the sentences in Practice 7.2F as models, and write two pairs of sentences. For each pair, combine the two sentences by changing one of them into an adverbial clause using an appropriate subordinating conjunction.

7.3 Classifying Sentences by Structure

All sentences can be classified according to the number and kinds of clauses they contain.

The Simple Sentence

The **simple sentence** is the most common type of sentence structure.

RULE 7.3.1

> **A simple sentence** consists of a single independent clause.

Simple sentences vary in length. Some are quite short; others can be several lines long. All simple sentences, however, contain just one subject and one verb. They may also contain adjectives, adverbs, complements, and phrases in different combinations.

Simple sentences can also have various compound parts. They can have a compound subject, a compound verb, or both. Sometimes, they will also have other compound elements, such as a compound direct object or a compound phrase.

All of the following sentences are simple sentences.

TYPES OF SIMPLE SENTENCES	
With One Subject and Verb	The rain came.
With a Compound Subject	Rain and snow are common.
With a Compound Verb	The door squeaked and rattled.
With a Compound Subject and Compound Verb	My mother and father said good-bye and left on vacation.
With a Compound Direct Object	He opened the letter and the box. direct object direct object
With a Compound Prepositional Phrase	It can rain from the east or from the west. prep phrase prep phrase

A simple sentence never has a subordinate clause, and it never has more than one main or independent clause.

The Compound Sentence

A **compound sentence** is made up of more than one simple sentence.

> A **compound sentence** consists of two or more main or independent clauses.

In most compound sentences, the main or independent clauses are joined by a comma and a coordinating conjunction (*and, but, for, nor, or, so,* or *yet*). They may also be connected with a semicolon (;) or a colon (:).

EXAMPLES   **Jamal organized** a two-day music festival**, and** eight **bands agreed** to play.

All the bands **performed** on the first day**; two were missing** the second day

See Practice 7.3A

See Practice 7.3B

Notice in both of the preceding examples that there are two separate and complete main clauses, each with its own subject and verb. Like simple sentences, compound sentences never contain subordinate clauses.

The Complex Sentence

Complex sentences contain subordinate clauses, which can be either adjectival clauses or adverbial clauses.

> A **complex sentence** consists of one main or independent clause and one or more subordinate clauses.

In a complex sentence, the independent clause is often called the **main clause.** The main clause has its own subject and verb, as does each subordinate clause.

In a complex sentence, the main clause can stand alone as a simple sentence. The subordinate clause cannot stand alone as a sentence.

EXAMPLES **January 26, 1947, is the day** **that India won its**
main clause   subordinate clause

independence .

Because the day is so important, **many of the**
                    subordinate clause

festivities are official .
                    main clause

In some complex sentences, the main clause is split by a subordinate clause that acts as an adjective.

EXAMPLE **Schoolchildren** , **who have the day**

off , **participate in an exciting parade** .

The two parts of the main clause form one main clause: *Schoolchildren participate in an exciting parade.*

See Practice 7.3C
See Practice 7.3D

The Compound-Complex Sentence

A **compound-complex sentence,** as the name indicates, contains the elements of both a compound sentence and a complex sentence.

RULE 7.3.4

A **compound-complex sentence** consists of two or more main or independent clauses and one or more subordinate clauses.

EXAMPLE **As he was leaving for school** ,
                    subordinate clause

Larry remembered to take his lunch , but
                    main clause

he forgot the report **that he had finished the**
          main clause   subordinate clause

night before .

PRACTICE 7.3A **Distinguishing Simple and Compound Sentences**

Read the sentences. Then, write *simple* or *compound* for each sentence.

EXAMPLE   Students will perform the school musical at the end of March.

ANSWER   *simple*

1. The parrots flew out of the forest.

2. The lions and tigers were in separate cages, but they ate at the same time.

3. My mom went on a business trip to San Francisco, so I did not see her.

4. The train puffed and chugged up the hill.

5. The Pony Express carried mail across the West.

6. My grandfather and my dad measured the wall, yet the refrigerator did not quite fit.

7. My brother mowed Mrs. Clausen's lawn and trimmed her hedges.

8. Last night's snowstorm kept us from going to school today, but we should be back in school tomorrow.

9. My sister and her friends wanted to go to a museum, so they planned a trip for next Tuesday.

10. The plane arrived ten minutes early.

PRACTICE 7.3B **Combining Simple Sentences to Form Compound Sentences**

Read the sentences. Combine the pairs of simple sentences to form compound sentences.

EXAMPLE   The sun was hot. The water was cold.

ANSWER   *The sun was hot, but the water was cold.*

11. Dad found a worm in the apple. He threw out the apple.

12. The snow was falling. The children were catching the snowflakes.

13. Eva cried and stamped her feet. Dad still would not let her see that movie.

14. Johnny and Carlos ran to school. The twins followed them.

15. My sister wanted to live in a warmer climate. She moved to Texas.

16. We must fix the roof. The rain will get in.

17. Latisha and Samuel finished their homework. They may go out to play.

18. The rain began to come down. I opened my umbrella.

19. We tried to get tickets for the play. The box office was closed.

20. Mrs. Baez just arrived for dinner. I heard her car door close.

SPEAKING APPLICATION

With a partner, take turns talking about chores you do around your house. Use one compound sentence. Your partner should listen for and identify two main clauses.

WRITING APPLICATION

Write three compound sentences about activities you do after school. Underline the main clauses.

PRACTICE 7.3C > Recognizing Complex Sentences

Read the sentences. Then, label each sentence *complex* or *not complex*.

EXAMPLE   Kim had never had a pet, so her parents gave her one for her birthday.

ANSWER   *not complex*

1. Before she entered a room, the nurse checked to see that she had everything.

2. Mom sent me to the store to buy noodles and celery.

3. Until the Johnsons get home, Marcie is caring for their cats.

4. We had better hurry, or we will miss the train.

5. I did not pass the test, which means I have to take it over.

6. Janine trained hard for the race, though she did not expect to win.

7. Last week we visited five cities in three states.

8. Because Celine was celebrating her birthday, we all brought gifts.

9. If you get an *A* on the test, you may go to the fair.

10. We should have reached Grandmother's house by now.

PRACTICE 7.3D > Distinguishing Compound and Complex Sentences

Read the sentences. Then, label each sentence *compound* or *complex*.

EXAMPLE   When the bird landed on the branch, Shelby took a photograph.

ANSWER   *complex*

11. I went to the grocery store, and Dad went to the hardware store.

12. Cory chose to write about Australia, because he wanted to learn about kangaroos.

13. If we find we are running late, we can call a taxi.

14. Loraine and Brandon enjoy basketball, and they play often.

15. While Mom and Aunt Grace fixed dinner, Dad and Uncle Sal fixed the television set.

16. Felicia is very good at math, and she wants to study math in college.

17. Juwan enjoys fishing, and he often goes fishing with his brothers.

18. When I have enough money for a new bicycle, I will give you the old one.

19. Because clouds were gathering, Mom made us go inside.

20. We took photographs of the waterfall; we wanted to remember its beauty.

SPEAKING APPLICATION

With a partner, take turns discussing a movie you saw recently. Use at least two complex sentences to show the relationships between events. Your partner should listen for and identify two subordinate clauses.

WRITING APPLICATION

Write a brief summary of a story you recently read. Include at least two complex sentences to show how events or actions are related.

CHAPTER 8

EFFECTIVE SENTENCES

Using a variety of sentences will add interest to your writing and help it flow smoothly.

WRITE GUY *Jeff Anderson, M.Ed.*

WHAT DO YOU NOTICE?

Check out different types of sentences as you zoom in on these lines from the poem "April Rain Song" by Langston Hughes.

MENTOR TEXT

> Let the rain beat upon your head with silver liquid drops.
> Let the rain sing you a lullaby.
>
> The rain makes still pools on the sidewalk.
> The rain makes running pools in the gutter.

Now, ask yourself the following questions:

- Which sentences give a command or an order?
- Which sentences state or declare a fact or an idea?

The first and second sentences are imperative; they command the reader to do something. The third and fourth sentences are declarative; they state a fact. Both imperative and declarative sentences usually end with a period.

Grammar for Writers Writers use different types of sentences to say what they really mean. Effective sentences give readers a strong sense of the writer's voice and message.

I look great today.

How very declarative of you to say so.

8.1 Classifying the Four Functions of a Sentence

Sentences can be classified according to what they do. Some sentences present facts or information in a direct way, while others pose questions to the reader or listener. Still others present orders or directions. A fourth type of sentence expresses strong emotion.

These four types of sentences are called **declarative, interrogative, imperative,** and **exclamatory.** As well as having a different purpose, each type of sentence is constructed in a different way.

The type of sentence you are writing determines the punctuation mark you use to end the sentence. The three end marks are the **period (.),** the **question mark (?),** and the **exclamation mark (!).**

The **declarative sentence** is the most common type of sentence. It is used to state, or "declare," facts.

RULE 8.1.1

A **declarative sentence** states, or declares, an idea and ends with a period.

DECLARATIVE   Soccer is a team sport.

Golf is a sport that can be played throughout a lifetime.

Although most schools fund team sports, many students choose to participate in individual sports.

Interrogative means "asking." An **interrogative sentence** is a question. Interrogative sentences often begin with *who, what, when, why, how,* or *how many.* They end with a question mark.

> **An interrogative sentence asks a question and ends with a question mark.**

8.1.2 RULE

INTERROGATIVE	What is your time in the half-mile run?
	Where is the county track meet being held?
	Who is the fastest runner on the track team?

> **An imperative sentence gives an order, or command, or a direction and ends with either a period or an exclamation mark.**

8.1.3 RULE

EL8

The word *imperative* comes from the Latin word that means "commanding." **Imperative sentences** are commands or directions. Most imperative sentences start with a verb. In this type of sentence, the subject is understood to be *you*.

IMPERATIVE	Follow my instructions carefully.
	Run as hard as you can!

Notice the punctuation at the end of these examples. In the first sentence, the period suggests that a mild command is being given in an ordinary tone of voice. The exclamation mark at the end of the second sentence suggests a strong command, one given in a loud voice.

> **An exclamatory sentence conveys strong emotion and ends with an exclamation mark.**

8.1.4 RULE

Exclaim means "to shout out." **Exclamatory sentences** are used to "shout out" emotions such as happiness, fear, delight, or anger.

See Practice 8.1A
See Practice 8.1B
See Practice 8.1C
See Practice 8.1D

EXCLAMATORY	She's going to crash into that hurdle!
	What an outstanding runner she is!

Identifying Four Types of Sentences

Read the sentences. Then, identify each type of sentence by writing *declarative*, *interrogative*, *imperative*, or *exclamatory*.

EXAMPLE The blue whale is the largest animal on Earth.

ANSWER *declarative*

1. Cashews originated in South America.
2. How much does an elephant eat every day?
3. Clarence Birdseye invented a method for freezing foods.
4. Jupiter is absolutely immense!
5. Put your luggage on the conveyor belt.
6. Where do birds go in the winter?
7. When the island Krakatoa exploded, it was heard more than 2,000 miles away!
8. More people drink water than drink milk.
9. When will the next storm occur?
10. Please read the sign out front.

Punctuating Four Types of Sentences

Read the sentences. Then, rewrite each sentence, adding the correct end punctuation.

EXAMPLE Where is the post office

ANSWER *Where is the post office?*

11. Are there any peaches today
12. He looked at the stars
13. I can't believe you did that
14. How will we get to school
15. Tell us about the Arctic
16. Is that the right answer
17. That's terrible
18. Don't forget your coat
19. When will they get here
20. I sing in the school chorus

SPEAKING APPLICATION

With a partner, take turns talking about something that surprised you. Include at least three different types of sentences in your discussion. Your partner should listen for and identify the three types of sentences.

WRITING APPLICATION

Write four sentences on any topics you wish. Make one declarative, one exclamatory, one interrogative, and one imperative. Be sure to punctuate them correctly.

PRACTICE 8.1C ▷ **Writing Four Types of Sentences**

Read the topics. For each topic, write the type of sentence specified in parentheses. Be sure to use the appropriate end punctuation.

EXAMPLE   weather (exclamatory)

ANSWER   *The weather is so cold!*

1. sun (declarative)
2. bicycle (interrogative)
3. door (imperative)
4. astronaut (declarative)
5. whales (exclamatory)
6. vacation (interrogative)
7. books (imperative)
8. forest (declarative)
9. solar eclipse (exclamatory)
10. restaurant (interrogative)

PRACTICE 8.1D ▷ **Revising Four Types of Sentences**

Read the sentences. Rewrite each sentence, changing it to the type of sentence specified in parentheses. Be sure to use the appropriate end punctuation.

EXAMPLE   You can watch a caterpillar. (interrogative)

ANSWER   *Can you watch a caterpillar?*

11. Can you go to the library? (declarative)
12. That mountain is so high! (interrogative)
13. Don't clouds sometimes look like cotton balls? (declarative)
14. Are elephants really big? (exclamatory)
15. Dad went to the hardware store. (interrogative)
16. Why don't you look where you're going? (imperative)
17. Those are her favorite shoes. (interrogative)
18. Would you please close the window? (imperative)
19. Is summer vacation starting soon? (declarative)
20. Is that ice dangerously thin? (exclamatory)

SPEAKING APPLICATION

With a partner, take turns giving orders, as if you were a coach. Give at least two orders each, using imperative sentences. Then, turn the orders into requests, using interrogative sentences.

WRITING APPLICATION

Write a short paragraph about something in nature that you find interesting. Begin with a question. Then, answer the question with at least one declarative and one exclamatory sentence.

8.2 Combining Sentences

Good writing should include sentences of varying lengths and complexity to create a flow of ideas. One way to achieve sentence variety is to combine sentences to express two or more related ideas or pieces of information in a single sentence.

Look at the example below. Then, look at how the ideas are combined in different ways.

EXAMPLE   We went to the zoo. We saw monkeys.

COMBINED   We went to the zoo and saw monkeys.

We saw monkeys when we went to the zoo.

Combining Sentence Parts

Sentences can be combined by using a compound subject, a compound verb, or a compound object.

EXAMPLE   Moira enjoyed watching the monkeys.

Tom enjoyed watching the monkeys.

COMPOUND   **Moira** and **Tom** enjoyed watching the
SUBJECT   monkeys.

EXAMPLE   Lisa played the game.

Lisa won a stuffed animal.

COMPOUND   Lisa **played** the game and **won** a stuffed
VERB   animal.

EXAMPLE   Scott rode the roller coaster.

Scott rode the Ferris wheel.

COMPOUND   Scott rode the **roller coaster** and the
OBJECT   **Ferris wheel** .

Joining Clauses

A **compound sentence** consists of two or more main or independent clauses. (See Chapter 7 for more information about clauses.) Use a compound sentence when combining related ideas of equal weight.

To create a compound sentence, join two main clauses with a comma and a coordinating conjunction. Common conjunctions include *and, but, nor, for, so, or,* and *yet.* You can also link the two sentences with a semicolon (;) if they are closely related.

> Sentences can be combined by joining two main clauses to create a **compound sentence.**

8.2.2 RULE

EXAMPLE	The wind whipped against our faces. The screams of other riders excited us.
COMPOUND SENTENCE	The wind whipped against our faces, and the screams of other riders excited us.
EXAMPLE	The ride lasted just a few minutes. My stomach churned for several hours.
COMPOUND SENTENCE	The ride lasted just a few minutes, but my stomach churned for several hours.
EXAMPLE	The roller coaster is such fun. It's very popular.
COMPOUND SENTENCE	The roller coaster is such fun; it's very popular.
EXAMPLE	I'm so tired when I leave the amusement park. I can't wait to come back again.
COMPOUND SENTENCE	I'm so tired when I leave the amusement park, yet I can't wait to come back again.

See Practice 8.2A
See Practice 8.2B

Sentences can be combined by changing one of them into a subordinate clause.

A **complex sentence** consists of one **main** or **independent clause** and one or more **subordinate clauses.** (See Chapter 7 for more information about clauses.) Combine sentences into a complex sentence to emphasize that one of the ideas in the sentence depends on the other. A subordinating conjunction will help readers understand the relationship. Common subordinating conjunctions are *after, although, because, before, since,* and *unless.* Generally no punctuation is required when a main and a subordinate clause are combined. When the subordinate clause comes first, a comma is needed. (See Chapter 13 for more information on punctuation.)

EXAMPLE   We were frightened. The ride went so fast.

COMBINED   We were frightened because the ride went

so fast.

See Practice 8.2C

Sentences can be combined by changing one of them into a phrase.

When combining sentences in which one of the sentences simply adds details, change one of the sentences into a **phrase.**

EXAMPLE   My family is leaving to go on vacation.
We are leaving in the morning.

COMBINED   My family is leaving in the morning to go on

vacation.

EXAMPLE   My mother packed a picnic basket.
It was filled with sandwiches.

COMBINED   My mother packed a picnic basket filled with

sandwiches.

See Practice 8.2D

PRACTICE 8.2A ▷ Combining Sentences Using Compound Subjects, Verbs, and Objects

Read the sentences. Combine the sentences in each group into a single sentence. Identify each combination as *compound subject, compound verb,* or *compound object.*

EXAMPLE   Tanner went to the drugstore. Marcie went to the drugstore, too.

ANSWER   *Tanner and Marcie went to the drugstore.* — compound subject

1. Claudio typed his report. Claudio also printed out his report.

2. Paul tried out for the play. Liam tried out for the play. Rubin tried out for the play.

3. Sari wrote a poem. Sari wrote a short story.

4. Yesterday my grandmother called. She invited me to visit for the weekend.

5. Jordan plays golf. Shelly plays golf, too.

6. My sister likes fruit. She also likes vegetables.

7. I need to paint the model cars. I need to paint the model planes, too.

8. The bake sale raised a lot of money. The car wash raised a lot of money, too.

9. My dog chased the ball. My dog caught the ball.

10. My mom is planning our trip to the museum. My dad is helping her.

PRACTICE 8.2B ▷ Combining Sentences Using Main Clauses

Read the sentences. Combine each pair into a compound sentence using the coordinating conjunction in parentheses. Be sure to use correct punctuation for compound sentences.

EXAMPLE   Penguins look awkward on land. They are graceful in the water. (but)

ANSWER   *Penguins look awkward on land, but they are graceful in the water.*

11. I went to the department store. I found the outfit I needed for band. (and)

12. We needed milk. I went to the store. (so)

13. My sister really likes math. My brother does not like math. (but)

14. In this recipe, we add peppers to the sauce. This makes the sauce spicy. (;)

15. We could go to the movies. We could go to the dance. (or)

16. A tadpole grows legs. Its tail disappears. (and)

17. We missed the bus. We took a taxi. (so)

18. My brother is feeling better. It will still be a while before he is well. (but)

19. Our class came in from recess. It was time for lunch. (;)

20. The flowers are beginning to come up. The trees are turning green. (and)

SPEAKING APPLICATION

With a partner, take turns talking about foods you like. Your partner should listen for and name three conjunctions you use.

WRITING APPLICATION

Write three sentences about the kinds of stories you most enjoy reading. Make sure your sentences combine main clauses or contain a compound verb, subject, or object.

Practice   131

PRACTICE 8.2C > **Combining Sentences Using Subordinate Clauses**

Read the sentences. Combine each pair by changing one sentence into a subordinate clause, using the subordinating conjunction in parentheses. Be sure to use the correct punctuation for complex sentences.

EXAMPLE   Cleo is going to the game. Then, she is going to Sue's house. (after)

ANSWER   *After Cleo goes to the game, she is going to Sue's house.*

1. I need to get the house cleaned. Mom comes home tonight. (before)
2. The doctor told Rory he should not run. Rory decided to enter the race. (although)
3. Dad went to the hardware store. We needed batteries. (because)
4. I have to stay inside. I have to get my homework done. (until)
5. The birds start building nests. We know it's spring. (when)
6. Liana took extra science classes. She can get into the advanced class. (so that)
7. You finish your chores. You may leave. (if)
8. Stefan got an *A* on the test. He studied very hard. (because)
9. I'm baking potatoes. I'm making soup. (while)
10. Pedro got the soccer ball. A game of soccer started. (after)

PRACTICE 8.2D > **Combining Sentences Using Phrases**

Read the sentences. Combine each pair of sentences by changing one into a phrase.

EXAMPLE   Mrs. Shankar led the class through the museum. Mrs. Shankar is a dinosaur expert.

ANSWER   *Mrs. Shankar, a dinosaur expert, led the class through the museum.*

11. Ann plays the flute. She plays in the band.
12. Today, we meet Mr. Beale. He is the coach.
13. Jun took his model plane to the park. He wanted to see it fly.
14. Frank Lloyd Wright was a famous architect. He designed this house.
15. We wanted to pick the flowers. The flowers covered the meadow.
16. Everyone knew Shelby. Shelby could not go anywhere without seeing friends.
17. The dog was eager for its dinner. It ran to its bowl.
18. The paper's travel section is interesting. The section is edited by Mr. Keller.
19. The children were laughing excitedly. The children played on the swings.
20. The actress walked toward the stage. Her costar followed her.

SPEAKING APPLICATION

With a partner, take turns talking about something you saw on television. Use at least three subordinating conjunctions. Your partner should listen for and name the conjunctions.

WRITING APPLICATION

Write three sentences about a place you visited recently (a museum, park, or friend's house). In each sentence, use a phrase (any kind) to add information.

8.3 Varying Sentences

When you vary the length and form of the sentences you write, you are able to create a rhythm, achieve an effect, or emphasize the connections between ideas.

There are several ways you can introduce variety into the sentences you write.

> **Varying the length of sentences makes writing lively and interesting to read.**

8.3.1 RULE

Varying Sentence Length

Reading too many long sentences in a row can be just as uninteresting as reading too many short sentences in a row. When you want to emphasize a point or surprise a reader, insert a short, direct sentence to interrupt the flow of several long sentences.

EXAMPLE   Otters are expert swimmers and divers, swimming at an average speed of seven miles per hour and staying underwater for up to two minutes. Unlike muskrats or beavers, otters barely make a ripple when swimming or a splash when diving. **Otters are even waterproof.** When they are underwater, a flap of skin covering their ears and nose closes to keep them watertight.

You can also break some longer sentences into shorter sentences. If the longer sentence contains two or more ideas, you can break up the ideas into separate sentences. However, if a longer sentence contains only one main idea, you should not break it apart.

LONGER SENTENCE   Many animals in the world fear snakes, but the mongoose does not.

TWO SENTENCES   Many animals in the world fear snakes. The mongoose does not.

See Practice 8.3A

Varying Sentence Beginnings

Another way to create variety is by changing from the usual subject–verb order in a sentence.

> Sentence beginnings can also be varied by reversing the traditional subject–verb order or starting the sentence with an adverb or a phrase.

EXAMPLES

The **bus** **is** **here** .
subject verb adverb

Here **is** the **bus** .
adverb verb subject

The **ship** **sailed** **into the bay** .
subject verb prepositional phrase

Into the bay **sailed** the **ship** .
prepositional phrase verb subject

We **left** the **island** **quickly** .
subject verb direct object adverb

Quickly , **we** **left** the **island** .
adverb subject verb direct object

Another way to vary your sentences is to begin them in different ways. For instance, you can start sentences with different parts of speech.

See Practice 8.3B

WAYS TO VARY SENTENCE BEGINNINGS	
Start with a noun.	**Birdhouses** , surprisingly, are not difficult to make.
Start with an adverb.	**Surprisingly** , birdhouses are not difficult to make.
Start with an infinitive.	**To make birdhouses** is, surprisingly, not difficult.
Start with a gerund.	**Making birdhouses is** , surprisingly, not difficult.
Start with a prepositional phrase.	**For a skilled carpenter** , making birdhouses is not difficult.

PRACTICE 8.3A **Varying Sentence Length**

Read the sentences. Rewrite each long compound sentence as two or more shorter sentences.

EXAMPLE   During vacation, we went to the circus, and we also swam, and we visited a museum.

ANSWER   *During vacation, we went to the circus. We also swam, and we visited a museum.*

1. We could not stop the dripping, nor could we turn off the water, so we put a bucket under the leak.

2. Australia has many interesting animals, such as wombats and koalas, and they carry their young in pouches.

3. My sister went to summer camp, and my brother went to summer school, and I am going to make money mowing lawns.

4. In the movie, the hero captures the bad guy, but at the end the bad guy escapes, so I think there will be another movie.

5. Bethany came to the United States from England, and she speaks with an English accent.

PRACTICE 8.3B **Varying Sentence Beginnings**

Read the sentences. Rewrite each sentence, changing the beginning as specified in parentheses. If there are two sentences, combine them, using one of the sentences to help you create the specified beginning.

EXAMPLE   Repairing the bike will cost money. It is unfortunate. (Begin with an adverb)

ANSWER   *Unfortunately,* repairing the bike will cost money.

6. It takes a lot of practice to learn how to swim well. (Begin with a gerund.)

7. I found the wallet I lost during our hike. That was lucky. (Begin with an adverb.)

8. The film star strutted into the room. (Reverse the subject-verb order.)

9. Modern car engines can be confusing for anyone who does not know the cars. (Begin with a prepositional phrase.)

10. When you are planning a big project like this, you need lots of advice. (Begin with an infinitive.)

SPEAKING APPLICATION

With a partner, read aloud two of the long sentences in Practice 8.3A. Then, read the way you broke up the long sentences. Tell your partner why you think it was good to break up the sentences.

WRITING APPLICATION

Write three sentences about people you know. Vary the sentence beginnings, or use inverted order. You may look at Practice 8.3B to remind you of how sentence beginnings can be varied.

8.4 Avoiding Sentence Problems

Recognizing problems with sentences will help you avoid and fix any problems in your writing.

Correcting Fragments

Some groups of words—even though they have a capital letter at the beginning and a period at the end—are not complete sentences. They are **fragments.**

RULE
8.4.1

A **fragment** is a group of words that does not express a complete thought.

A fragment can be a group of words that includes a possible subject but no verb. A fragment could also be a group of words that includes a possible verb but no subject. It can even be a group of words that contains no subject and no verb. Fragments can be turned into complete sentences by adding a subject, a verb, or both.

FRAGMENTS	COMPLETE SENTENCES
felt happy and relaxed	**I** felt happy and relaxed. (A subject is added.)
the train around the bend	The train **was coming** around the bend. (A verb is added.)
in the early evening	The **flight** **arrived** in the early evening. (A subject and verb are added.)

See Practice 8.4A

Correcting Phrase Fragments A **phrase fragment** cannot stand alone because it does not have both a subject and a verb.

RULE
8.4.2

A **phrase fragment** should not be capitalized and punctuated as if it were a sentence.

A phrase fragment can be corrected in one of two ways: (1) by adding it to a nearby sentence or (2) by adding whatever is needed to make it a complete sentence.

PHRASE FRAGMENT	The travelers rode camels. **on the morning of March 4**
ADDED TO OTHER SENTENCE	The travelers rode camels **on the morning of March 4** .
PHRASE FRAGMENT	They rode the camels for hours. **parched by the hot sun**
COMPLETE SENTENCES	They rode the camels for hours. They were **parched by the hot sun** .

CHANGING PHRASE FRAGMENTS INTO SENTENCES	
PHRASE FRAGMENT	COMPLETE SENTENCE
in the ancient tomb	The treasure was found **in the ancient tomb** .
laughing at her father's jokes	Helen enjoyed **laughing at her father's jokes** .
to play soccer	Elana learned **to play soccer** .

See Practice 8.4B

Correcting Clause Fragments

All clauses have subjects and verbs, but some cannot stand alone as sentences.

> **A subordinate clause** should not be capitalized and punctuated as if it were a sentence.

RULE 8.4.3

Subordinate clauses do not express complete thoughts. Although a subordinate adjective or adverb clause has a subject and a verb, it cannot stand by itself as a sentence. (See Chapter 7 for more information about subordinate clauses and the words that begin them.)

Like phrase fragments, **clause fragments** can usually be corrected in either of two ways: (1) by attaching the fragment to a nearby sentence or (2) by adding whatever words are needed to turn the fragment into a sentence.

CLAUSE FRAGMENT	The audience left the concert hall. **after the band finished playing**
COMPLETE SENTENCE	**After the band finished playing** , the audience left the concert hall.
CLAUSE FRAGMENT	The class enjoyed the poem. **that I recited to them as part of my oral report on horses**
COMPLETE SENTENCE	The class enjoyed the poem **that I recited to them as part of my oral report on horses** .
CLAUSE FRAGMENT	I'll give my report today. **as long as you give yours, too**
COMPLETE SENTENCE	I'll give my report today **as long as you give yours, too** .

To change a clause fragment into a sentence by the second method, you must add an independent clause to the fragment.

CHANGING CLAUSE FRAGMENTS INTO SENTENCES	
CLAUSE FRAGMENT	**COMPLETE SENTENCE**
that you requested	I returned the book **that you requested** . The book **that you requested** has been returned.
when he began shouting	I looked up in surprise **when he began shouting.** **When he began shouting** , I looked up in surprise.
what she was thinking	I could not figure out **what she was thinking** .

See Practice 8.4C

See Practice 8.4D

PRACTICE 8.4A > **Recognizing Fragments**

Read the groups of words. Then, write whether each group of words is a *sentence* or a *fragment*.

EXAMPLE   In the swimming pool.

ANSWER   *fragment*

1. When you arrive.
2. Dad went to work.
3. Because of the rain.
4. A really good idea.
5. Tomorrow is a new day.
6. Mom washed the dog.
7. Cat in a tree.
8. Spring always returns.
9. Without your raincoat.
10. The car is turning.

PRACTICE 8.4B > **Changing Phrase Fragments Into Sentences**

Read the phrase fragments. Then, use each fragment in a sentence.

EXAMPLE   to the library

ANSWER   *I need to go to the library.*

11. at the zoo
12. to open the box
13. around the school
14. finding my books
15. to build that model
16. after the ride
17. taking the bird food
18. in the classroom
19. to climb that tree
20. trading baseball cards

SPEAKING APPLICATION

With a partner, take turns creating phrases. Your partner should listen to the phrase and then turn the phrase into a sentence.

WRITING APPLICATION

Write three sentences about what the yard of your home or school is like and what is found there. Use at least two phrases. Underline the phrases in the sentences.

PRACTICE 8.4C Changing Clause Fragments Into Sentences

Read the clause fragments. Then, use each fragment in a sentence.

EXAMPLE   that we bought yesterday

ANSWER   *Bring me the magazine* that we bought yesterday.

1. as soon as you finish your work
2. while my little brother played
3. even though he was tired
4. because they usually get lost
5. as long as you are here
6. before the sun rises
7. until Dad gets home
8. unless it rains
9. although it seemed late
10. whenever Grandmother visits

PRACTICE 8.4D Changing Fragments Into Sentences

Read the groups of words. If a group of words is a fragment, use it in a sentence. If a group of words is already a sentence, write *sentence*.

EXAMPLE   Looking for their dog.

ANSWER   *I saw the neighbors* looking for their dog.

11. When the bell rings.
12. To find a dress.
13. We found good seats.
14. To finish the project.
15. The snow melted.
16. Eating the leftovers.
17. The library has magazines.
18. We could go with them.
19. To draw a picture.
20. The stairs creaked.

SPEAKING APPLICATION

With a partner, take turns choosing two clause fragments from Practice 8.4D. Read the clause fragment out loud, changing one word in the fragment. Your partner should reply with a sentence using the changed fragment.

WRITING APPLICATION

Write a short paragraph about the plot or action of a movie or book you enjoyed. Include at least two clause fragments as you relate what happened. Then, exchange papers with a partner. Your partner should identify and underline the clause fragments.

Run-on Sentences

A fragment is an incomplete sentence. A **run-on,** on the other hand, is two or more complete sentences that are punctuated as though they were one sentence.

> A **run-on** is two or more complete sentences that are not properly joined or separated.

8.4.4 RULE

Run-ons are usually the result of carelessness. Check your sentences carefully to see where one sentence ends and the next one begins.

Two Kinds of Run-ons

There are two kinds of run-ons. The first one is made up of two sentences that are run together without any punctuation between them This is called a **fused sentence.**

The second type of run-on consists of two or more sentences separated by only a comma. This type of run-on is called a **comma splice.**

FUSED SENTENCES	I flew out of my bed I ran into the hall.
	The Lions ran for two touchdowns they won the game.
COMMA SPLICE	Everyone in the house was up, the smoke alarm had gone off.
	The Lions have a great offensive team, they also have a great defensive team.

See Practice 8.4E

A good way to distinguish between a run-on and a sentence is to read the words aloud. Your ear will tell you whether you have one or two complete thoughts and whether you need to make a complete break between the thoughts.

Three Ways to Correct Run-ons

There are three ways to correct run-on sentences. You can use end marks, commas and coordinating conjunctions, or semicolons.

Using End Marks
Periods, question marks, and exclamation marks are useful to fix run-on sentences.

> **Use an end mark to separate a run-on sentence into two sentences.**

Sometimes the best way to correct a run-on is to use an end mark to split the run-on into two shorter but complete sentences. End marks help your reader pause and group your ideas more effectively.

RUN-ON	On Saturday Jill plays softball, Luis has band practice.
CORRECTED	On Saturday Jill plays softball. Luis has band practice.
RUN-ON	Hurry up we don't want to be late.
CORRECTED	Hurry up! We don't want to be late.
RUN-ON	Are you going to the game I'll meet you there.
CORRECTED	Are you going to the game? I'll meet you there.
RUN-ON	Where have you been, I've been waiting for you for two hours!
CORRECTED	Where have you been? I've been waiting for you for two hours!

Using Commas and Coordinating Conjunctions
Sometimes the two parts of a run-on are related and should be combined into a compound sentence.

> Use a **comma** and a **coordinating conjunction** to combine two independent clauses into a compound sentence.

To separate the clauses properly, use both a comma and a coordinating conjunction. The most common coordinating conjunctions are *and, but, or, for, nor,* and *yet.* Before you separate a sentence into parts, though, be sure each part expresses a complete thought.

RUN-ON	I want to buy some new shoes, I need more money.
CORRECTED	I want to buy some new shoes, but I need more money.
RUN-ON	The shoes I have are too tight, their heels are worn out.
CORRECTED	The shoes I have are too tight, and their heels are worn out.

Using Semicolons
You can sometimes use a semicolon to connect the two parts of a run-on into a correct sentence.

> Use a **semicolon** to connect two closely related ideas into one sentence.

Use a semicolon only when the ideas in both parts of the sentence are closely related.

RUN-ON	The first train to Houston leaves at 6:05, the express doesn't leave until an hour later.
CORRECTED	The first train to Houston leaves at 6:05; the express doesn't leave until an hour later.

See Practice 8.4F

PRACTICE 8.4E ▷ Recognizing Run-ons

Read the groups of words. Then, write whether each group is a *sentence* or a *run-on*.

EXAMPLE   Rachel Carson was a biologist she wrote about nature.

ANSWER   *run-on*

1. George Washington is called the Father of Our Country he was our first president.

2. Many people visit Italy because there is so much art, history, and good food there.

3. Elsa was an African lion, she became famous because of the book *Born Free*.

4. Isadora Duncan was a dancer, she danced in many countries.

5. Ruth Streeter was the first woman to hold the rank of major in the Marine Corps.

6. Squanto was a Native American who helped the Pilgrims he spoke English.

7. When Columbus first tasted hot chile peppers, he called them "violent fruit."

8. Cashews are related to poison ivy, they originally came from Brazil.

9. Benjamin Carson liked learning about science, he became a leading surgeon.

10. Grace Hopper was one of the world's first software engineers.

PRACTICE 8.4F ▷ Correcting Run-ons

Read the sentences. Rewrite each run-on sentence to correct the problem.

EXAMPLE   The shepherd led the sheep he took them to a grassy field.

ANSWER   *The shepherd led the sheep. He took them to a grassy field.*

11. The herb rosemary is good in food it is also used as a symbol of remembrance.

12. Booker T. Washington wrote *Up from Slavery*, it is a book about his early life.

13. Gus and Romero are good friends they go everywhere together.

14. Quito is the capital of Ecuador, it is in the northern half of the country.

15. We hurried to the train station we were late.

16. Alaska is our largest state, Rhode Island is our smallest state.

17. Bananas are green when they are shipped they turn yellow as they ripen.

18. Shandra and Lacey went to the school carnival they had a lot of fun.

19. On Memorial Day, the nation honors its heroes it recalls their bravery.

20. James Naismith invented basketball in 1891, he used peach baskets for the game.

SPEAKING APPLICATION

With a partner, take turns reading the run-ons in Practice 8.4F out loud. Talk about how speaking the run-ons out loud helps you hear where the sentences should end.

WRITING APPLICATION

Choose two run-ons from Practice 8.4F, and rewrite them. This time, feel free to reverse the order of the clauses or add more words. Be sure you don't have any run-ons when you're done.

EL7

Properly Placing Modifiers

If a phrase or clause acting as an adjective or adverb is not placed near the word it modifies, it may seem to modify a different word. Then the sentence may seem unclear or odd.

> A **modifier** should be placed as close as possible to the word it describes.

8.4.8 RULE

A modifier placed too far away from the word it describes is called a **misplaced modifier**.

MISPLACED MODIFIER
We rented a boat at the lake **with an outboard motor**.

The misplaced phrase *with an outboard motor* makes it seem as though the lake has an outboard motor.

PROPERLY PLACED MODIFIER
At the lake, we rented a boat **with an outboard motor**.

Below is a different type of misplaced modifier that is sometimes called a **dangling modifier.** A dangling modifier at the beginning of a sentence causes the sentence to be unclear.

DANGLING MODIFIER
Walking on the beach, the sand felt hot under our feet.

In this sentence, *walking on the beach* should modify a person or people. Instead, it incorrectly modifies *sand*.

See Practice 8.4G
See Practice 8.4H

CORRECTED
Walking on the beach, we felt the hot sand under our feet.

PRACTICE 8.4G ▷ Revising to Correct Misplaced Modifiers

Read the sentences. Then, rewrite each sentence to correct the underlined misplaced modifier.

EXAMPLE   A woman was walking a dog <u>in a blue dress</u>.

ANSWER   *A woman in a blue dress was walking a dog.*

1. I found the book after looking in three rooms <u>that I need for class</u>.

2. The boy is my brother <u>in the red shirt</u>.

3. The shopping list seemed long <u>that Dad wrote</u>.

4. <u>Crushed at the bottom of the box</u>, Eileen saw her hat.

5. The bottle fell and broke <u>full of perfume</u>.

6. We knew the music would be played <u>that we liked</u>.

7. Ari's report was fascinating <u>about reptiles</u>.

8. We left our car at the shop <u>with a flat tire</u>.

9. The purse was lost <u>that had her wallet</u>.

10. <u>On the top shelf</u>, my sister found her favorite book.

PRACTICE 8.4H ▷ Recognizing and Correcting Misplaced Modifiers

Read the sentences. If a sentence has a misplaced modifier, rewrite the sentence so the modifier is properly placed. If a sentence is correct, write *correct*.

EXAMPLE   Covered in flowers, Marilyn admired the hillside.

ANSWER   *Marilyn admired the hillside covered in flowers.*

11. My sister found a sweater in the closet that does not belong to her.

12. Running across the yard, the grass tickled our bare feet.

13. Carrying the luggage outside, Dad began to pack the car for our trip.

14. Sizzling on the grill, Carlos smells the food.

15. Please discuss the information that is enclosed with your friends.

16. I like the car with leather seats.

17. My neighbors have a fence behind the house with a gate.

18. Trying three different keys, the front door was finally unlocked.

19. Leaving his book unfinished, the writer decided to write a short story.

20. Hopping beside the lake I saw a frog.

SPEAKING APPLICATION

With a partner, take turns describing a place you have studied or seen in a movie. Use modifiers to add detail. Your partner should listen for and identify modifiers and what they modify.

WRITING APPLICATION

Write a short paragraph about clothes that are currently in style. Include at least two modifiers to add detail, taking care to properly place the modifiers.

Avoiding Double Negatives

Negative words, such as *nothing* and *not*, are used to deny or to say *no*. Some people mistakenly use **double negatives**—two negative words—when only one is needed.

> **Avoid writing sentences that contain double negatives.**

8.4.9 RULE

In the following examples, negative words are highlighted. The first sentence in each example contains double negatives. The corrected sentences show two ways to correct each double-negative sentence.

DOUBLE NEGATIVES	The lightning **didn't** damage **nothing**.
CORRECTED SENTENCES	The lightning **didn't** damage anything.
	The lightning damaged **nothing**.
DOUBLE NEGATIVES	I **haven't no** time now.
CORRECTED SENTENCES	I **haven't** any time now.
	I have **no** time now.
DOUBLE NEGATIVES	She **never** told us **nothing** about the storm.
CORRECTED SENTENCES	She **never** told us anything about the storm.
	She told us **nothing** about the storm.
DOUBLE NEGATIVES	A few clouds **don't** bother **no one**.
CORRECTED SENTENCES	A few clouds **don't** bother anyone.
	A few clouds bother **no one**.
DOUBLE NEGATIVES	Janice **didn't** invite **nobody**.
CORRECTED SENTENCES	Janice **didn't** invite anybody.
	Janice invited **nobody**.

See Practice 8.4I
See Practice 8.4J

PRACTICE 8.4I ▷ **Using Negatives Correctly**

Read the sentences. Then, write the word in parentheses that makes each sentence negative without creating a double negative.

EXAMPLE   The coach (can, can't) find no one to be quarterback.

ANSWER   *can*

1. The new box of pencils wasn't (anywhere, nowhere) in my room.

2. Maria (has, hasn't) said nothing about her visit to her grandmother's.

3. Henry didn't know (nobody, anybody) at the party.

4. I don't like (none, any) of the television shows this season.

5. I (would, wouldn't) do nothing to hurt my little brother.

6. Our house (is, isn't) nowhere near the grocery store.

7. This magazine doesn't have (anything, nothing) about the parade.

8. We (had, hadn't) never thought that my sister would get a poem published.

9. No one (can, can't) get into our clubhouse.

10. They didn't (never, ever) go away on vacation.

PRACTICE 8.4J ▷ **Revising to Correct Double Negatives**

Read the sentences. Then, rewrite each sentence to correct the double negative.

EXAMPLE   I don't have no interest in that.

ANSWER   *I have no interest in that.*

11. We don't want nobody to go in there.

12. Mom can't find her rolling pin nowhere.

13. I didn't have nothing to do with it.

14. My brother can't never remember his password for that Web site.

15. My sister didn't take none of her books to school.

16. You haven't said nothing about your band concert.

17. The movie stars didn't want to pose for no photographers.

18. We didn't tell nobody about the secret room.

19. I can't find no one to go to the store with me.

20. She didn't go nowhere near the place.

SPEAKING APPLICATION

With a partner, take turns talking about things that should not happen, such as breaking rules at home or failing to take safety precautions. Your partner should listen for and identify negatives and whether they are used correctly.

WRITING APPLICATION

Write two negative sentences about things you have seen happen—or not happen. Be sure to use the negatives correctly.

Avoiding Common Usage Problems

This section contains fifteen common usage problems in alphabetical order. Some are expressions that you should avoid in both your speaking and your writing. Others are words that are often confused because of similar spellings or meanings.

(1) accept, except   Do not confuse the spelling of these words. *Accept*, a verb, means "to take what is offered" or "to agree to." *Except*, a preposition, means "leaving out" or "other than."

VERB   She **accepted** the gift generously.

PREPOSITION   She gave everyone a gift **except** me.

(2) advice, advise   Do not confuse the spelling of these related words. *Advice*, a noun, means "an opinion." *Advise*, a verb, means "to give an opinion."

NOUN   My friend gave me **advice** about hotels in Rome.

VERB   My friend **advised** me to find a good guide.

(3) affect, effect   *Affect*, a verb, means "to influence" or "to cause a change in." *Effect*, usually a noun, means "result."

VERB   The sandstorm **affected** my eyes.

NOUN   What is the **effect** of getting sand in your ears?

(4) at   Do not use *at* after *where*.

INCORRECT   Do you know **where** he is **at**?

CORRECT   Do you know **where** he is?

(5) because   Do not use *because* after *the reason*. Eliminate one or the other.

INCORRECT   **The reason** I am sad is **because** our trip was canceled.

CORRECT   I am sad **because** our trip was canceled.

                     The **reason** I am sad is **that** our trip was canceled.

(6) beside, besides   These two prepositions have different meanings and cannot be interchanged. *Beside* means "at the side of" or "close to." *Besides* means "in addition to."

EXAMPLES   We picnicked **beside** the Mississippi River.

No one **besides** us had blankets to sit on.

(7) different from, different than   *Different from* is preferred over *different than.*

EXAMPLE   The monkeys were **different from** what I had expected.

(8) farther, further   *Farther* is used to refer to distance. *Further* means "additional" or "to a greater degree or extent."

EXAMPLES   We walked much **farther** than he did.

After he raised his voice, I listened no **further**.

(9) in, into   *In* refers to position. *Into* suggests motion.

POSITION   The tourists are **in** the history museum.

MOTION   They walked **into** the room of famous documents.

(10) kind of, sort of   Do not use *kind of* or *sort of* to mean "rather" or "somewhat."

INCORRECT   This CD of jazz music is **sort of** new.

CORRECT   This CD of jazz music is **rather** new.

(11) like   *Like*, a preposition, means "similar to" or "in the same way as." It should be followed by an object. Do not use *like* before a subject and a verb. Use *as* or *that* instead.

PREPOSITION   The pyramids looked **like** giant triangles.

INCORRECT   This stew doesn't taste **like** it should.

CORRECT   This stew doesn't taste **as** it should.

(12) that, which, who   *That* and *which* refer to things. *Who* refers only to people.

THINGS	The photograph **that** I took won first prize.
PEOPLE	The dancer **who** performed is my cousin.

(13) their, there, they're   Do not confuse the spelling of these three words. *Their*, a possessive adjective, always modifies a noun. *There* is usually used as a sentence starter or as an adverb. *They're* is a contraction of *they are*.

POSSESSIVE ADJECTIVE	The tourists boarded **their** bus.
SENTENCE STARTER	**There** are many tours available.
ADVERB	The tour guide is standing over **there** .
CONTRACTION	**They're** trying to board the bus now.

(14) to, too, two   Do not confuse the spelling of these words. *To* plus a noun creates a prepositional phrase. *To* plus a verb creates an infinitive. *Too* is an adverb and modifies adjectives and other adverbs. *Two* is a number.

PREPOSITION	**to** the house	**to** Florida
INFINITIVE	**to** meet	**to** hide
ADVERB	**too** sad	**too** quickly
NUMBER	**two** clouds	**two** dolphins

(15) when, where, why   Do not use *when*, *where*, or *why* directly after a linking verb such as *is*. Reword the sentence.

INCORRECT	To see the Alamo is **why** we came to Texas.
CORRECT	We came to Texas to see the Alamo.
INCORRECT	In the evening is **when** I walk my dog.
CORRECT	I walk my dog in the evening.

See Practice 8.4K
See Practice 8.4L
See Practice 8.4M
See Practice 8.4N

Choosing the Correct Usage

Read the sentences. Then, write the word in parentheses that best completes each sentence.

EXAMPLE   When the shipment arrived, I (accepted, excepted) the package.

ANSWER   *accepted*

1. The neighbors invited us to (their, they're) house.
2. I thought Mom would be the best one to (advise, advice) me on the science project.
3. It is (to, too) cold to go out without a coat.
4. The news did not seem to (affect, effect) my sister as much as I thought it would.
5. When it is sunny, my cat loves to sleep (beside, besides) the window.
6. Our team hiked two miles (further, farther).
7. Anita is the only one (that, who) knows the combination to the lock.
8. Moisha followed Juan (into, in) the hall.
9. Everyone is here (accept, except) Lisa.
10. The football player carried the ball for only (to, two) yards.

Recognizing and Correcting Usage Problems

Read the sentences. If the underlined word is used correctly, write *correct*. If the word is incorrect, write the correct word.

EXAMPLE   The moonlight had a lovely <u>affect</u> on the scene.

ANSWER   *effect*

11. The results of the experiment were different <u>than</u> what I expected.
12. I would like to have your <u>advise</u> on this issue.
13. My sister does not know how to <u>except</u> a compliment.
14. My dog loves sleeping <u>beside</u> the fireplace.
15. This food is <u>kind of</u> good.
16. The milk did not smell <u>like</u> it should.
17. I want to discuss this <u>further</u>.
18. I called Derek and Carlos, and <u>their</u> bringing food for the party.
19. This is the friend <u>that</u> went with me to the concert.
20. The stars that night looked <u>like</u> diamonds on black velvet.

SPEAKING APPLICATION

With a partner, choose four sentences from Practice 8.4K. Take turns making up new sentences that correctly use the word that *was not* the right choice in the practice. Your partner should listen and confirm that the word was used correctly.

WRITING APPLICATION

Write a short paragraph about an event in your life that was a surprise. Correctly use at least three words from Practice 8.4K and Practice 8.4L in your paragraph.

PRACTICE 8.4M ▷ **Recognizing and Correcting Usage Problems**

Read the sentences. Then, if a sentence has a usage problem, rewrite it to correct the problem. If a sentence is correct, write *correct*.

EXAMPLE   Your sandwich is different than mine.

ANSWER   *Your sandwich is different from mine.*

1. Maybe this police officer can tell us where we are at.

2. The reason I want to go is because I'll see Mark.

3. The restaurant was farther away than I thought.

4. This book is kind of interesting.

5. The costumes we rented do not fit like they should.

6. To try out for the play is why I came.

7. The woman who interviewed me is named Carlotta.

8. Five o'clock is when we are supposed to arrive.

9. Grandma and Grandpa invited me to stay at they're house.

10. I loved the special affects in that movie.

PRACTICE 8.4N ▷ **Avoiding Usage Problems**

Read the pairs of words. For each pair of words, write two sentences that are related in meaning.

EXAMPLE   there, their

ANSWER   *My friends invited me to **their** party. I put my gift over **there**.*

11. accept, except

12. there, they're

13. advise, advice

14. two, too

15. affect, effect

16. beside, besides

17. farther, further

18. who, that

19. into, in

20. like, as

SPEAKING APPLICATION

With a partner, talk about a place you would like to visit. Use two or three words from Practice 8.4M and Practice 8.4N to include in your discussion. Your partner should listen for words and say whether they were used correctly.

WRITING APPLICATION

Write a very brief story (three or four sentences) about a cat or dog. Choose four "problem" words or phrases from Practice 8.4M and Practice 8.4N, and use them correctly in the story.

Using Complete Subjects and Predicates

Each item below contains only a complete subject or a complete predicate. Rewrite each item, making a sentence by adding the missing part indicated in parentheses.

1. The set for the school play (add a predicate).
2. (add a subject) played three songs at halftime.
3. The substitute teacher (add a predicate).
4. Was (add a subject) hard to fix?
5. My favorite science project (add a predicate).
6. (add a subject) ran through the streets.
7. The local library (add a predicate).
8. (add a subject) left an enormous mess.
9. The girl and her family (add a predicate).
10. (add a subject) competed in the tournament.

PRACTICE 2 **Using Direct Objects**

Rewrite each incomplete sentence, supplying a direct object where indicated in parentheses. You may also include the article *a*, *an*, or *the* or another modifier along with the direct object.

1. Lions eat (direct object).
2. The workers are building (direct object).
3. On a clear night, Jill studies (direct object).
4. Nick designs (direct object) for a living.
5. Brianna put (direct object) in the refrigerator.
6. I asked (direct object) for a ride home.
7. We saw (direct object) at the street fair.
8. Yesterday, Dan met (direct object) at the zoo.
9. Our teacher gave us (direct object).
10. Who put (direct object) on the chessboard?

PRACTICE 3 **Identifying Indirect Objects**

Read the sentences. Then, write the indirect object in each sentence. If there is no indirect object, write *none*.

1. The police officer gave the driver a ticket.
2. I told them the story.
3. My father bought himself a new suit.
4. Nadia saved money for a new camera.
5. Please bring me a glass of water.
6. The magician showed us a new trick.
7. Miranda offered the concert tickets to Jake.
8. I wish you a happy birthday.
9. The interviewer asked Jon several questions.
10. Who gave her the new umbrella?

PRACTICE 4 **Identifying Subject Complements**

Read the sentences. Then, write the subject complement in each sentence. Also indicate whether it is a *predicate noun*, *predicate pronoun*, or *predicate adjective*.

1. The bus ride to the museum seemed long.
2. Maya Angelou is a famous poet.
3. The girls looked unhappy about the situation.
4. Pete will be the president of our class.
5. The person with the highest score is you.
6. She has been mayor for more than six years.
7. Of all the singers, the most talented one is you.
8. Please do not be upset with me.
9. That loud boom was not really anything.
10. Are we late for our piano lessons?

Read the sentences. Then, rewrite each sentence, supplying the type of prepositional phrase indicated in parentheses.

1. The team practiced. (Add an adjectival phrase.)
2. Jojo flew a kite. (Add an adverbial phrase.)
3. The odor was strong. (Add an adjectival phrase.)
4. Mom baked bread. (Add an adverbial phrase.)
5. She twirled her baton. (Add an adverbial phrase.)

Read the sentences. Then, write whether the underlined phrase in each sentence is an *appositive phrase*, a *participial phrase*, a *gerund phrase*, or an *infinitive phrase*.

1. Perry loves <u>singing in the choir</u>.
2. <u>Frightened by the noise</u>, the bull charged.
3. We went to the roof <u>to gaze at the stars</u>.
4. The storm, <u>a strong hurricane</u>, devastated the city of Galveston.
5. The birds <u>flocking to the trees</u> were all crows.
6. The coach needs <u>to find another strategy</u>.
7. <u>A Missouri native</u>, Mark Twain in later life lived in Connecticut.
8. <u>Cooking Mexican food</u> is just one of my many interests.
9. <u>Running swiftly</u>, Jesse won the race.
10. Bev wants <u>to find a good hiking trail</u>.

Read the sentences. Then, write and label the *main clause* and the *subordinate clause* in each sentence.

1. After he stayed up all night, Nick yawned all morning.
2. Nobody answered when I rang the bell at the front door.
3. Judge Levy, who lives down the road, always invites us to his annual summer barbecue.
4. Because she sews so well, Mrs. Sanchez helped with the costumes for the school play.
5. Over the winter, moths attacked the wool sweater that I bought last year.

Read the sentences. Combine each pair of sentences by turning one into a subordinate clause. Then, underline the subordinate clause, and indicate whether it is an *adjectival clause* or an *adverbial clause*.

1. My brother works late at the radio station. He gets home after midnight.
2. My sister is in the second grade. She is the youngest member of my family.
3. I searched the library shelves. I finally found an interesting book.
4. The town pool opens in June. It has a lifeguard staff of high school students.
5. My head aches. Toby is playing the trumpet again.

Continued on next page ▶

Cumulative Review Chapters 6–8

 Writing Sentences

For each item, write the indicated type of sentence, using the words provided.

1. Write a compound sentence using *the athlete* as one of the subjects.

2. Write a declarative sentence using *a flower* as the subject.

3. Write a complex sentence using *was tired* as one of the verbs.

4. Write an exclamatory sentence using the word *exciting*.

5. Write an imperative sentence using *wait* as the verb.

 Combining Sentences

Read the sentences. Combine each pair of sentences by using compound structures. Indicate whether your sentence contains a *compound subject*, a *compound verb*, or a *compound object*, or whether it is a *compound sentence*.

1. Gregory plays the guitar. Mackenzie also plays the guitar.

2. I add milk to my cereal. I add fruit to my cereal too.

3. Barb wanted a new bicycle for her birthday. Her mom gave her a new sweater instead.

4. The painter chooses his paints carefully. He mixes them carefully as well.

5. We may travel to Dallas by train. We may travel to Dallas by bus.

PRACTICE 11 > **Revising to Correct Fragments and Run-ons**

Read each group of words. If it is a fragment, use it in a sentence. If it is a run-on, correct the run-on. If it is a sentence that needs no correction, write *correct*.

1. The bank teller standing at her window.

2. The soup was pretty tasteless, I ate it anyway.

3. Aunt Meg pays for my dance classes.

4. The color is wrong you need a paler blue.

5. Unless you have the package delivered.

PRACTICE 12 > **Revising to Correct Common Usage Problems**

Read the sentences. Then, rewrite each sentence to correct misplaced modifiers, double negatives, and other usage problems.

1. Everyone accept Thomas went on the class trip.

2. The medical researchers studied the affects of the new treatment.

3. Twinkling overhead, I thought the stars looked awesome.

4. Many years ago, my grandmother gave me some good advise.

5. I didn't learn nothing new at the meeting.

6. The reason I am so cranky is because I had too little sleep last night.

7. Our teacher told us about earthquakes and volcanoes in our science class.

8. Their doing they're homework in the kitchen.

9. Did anyone beside you and me volunteer to help with the decorations?

10. The trees should be planted further apart.

CHAPTER 9

USING VERBS

Knowing how to use verb tenses will help you convey the correct timing of actions in your writing.

WRITE GUY *Jeff Anderson, M.Ed.*

WHAT DO YOU NOTICE?

Take a snapshot of the verbs as you zoom in on these sentences from the story "The Circuit" by Francisco Jiménez.

MENTOR TEXT

> I was completely soaked in sweat and my mouth felt as if I had been chewing on a handkerchief. I walked over to the end of the row, picked up the jug of water we had brought, and began drinking.

Now, ask yourself the following questions:

- What about the verbs *soaked*, *walked*, and *picked* shows that the action takes place in the past?
- How are the verbs *was*, *felt*, and *began* different from *soaked*, *walked*, and *picked*?

The *-ed* ending on the regular verbs *soak*, *walk*, and *pick* shows that the action takes place in the past. The irregular verbs *was*, *felt*, and *began* also show action that takes place in the past. However, these irregular verbs are spelled differently from their present tenses: *am*, *feel*, and *begin*.

Grammar for Writers Using carefully chosen verbs and their correct tenses helps a writer convey when actions happen. Be sure to use correct tenses of regular and irregular verbs.

I felt all mixed up this morning, but now I feel fine.

And your irregular verbs are in good shape, too!

9.1 The Four Principal Parts of Verbs

Verbs have different tenses to express time. The tense of the verb *walk* in the sentence "They *walk* very fast" expresses action in the present. In "They *walked* too far from home," the tense of the verb shows that the action happened in the past. In "They *will walk* home from school," the verb expresses action in the future. These forms of verbs are known as **tenses**.

A verb's **tense** shows the time of the action or state of being that is being described. To use the tenses of a verb correctly, you must know the **principal parts** of the verb.

EL5

EL6

RULE
9.1.1 > A verb has four **principal parts:** the **present**, the **present participle**, the **past**, and the **past participle**.

THE FOUR PRINCIPAL PARTS OF *WALK*			
PRESENT	PRESENT PARTICIPLE	PAST	PAST PARTICIPLE
walk	(am) walking	walked	(have) walked

The first principal part, called the present, is the form of a verb that is listed in a dictionary. The present participle and the past participle must be combined with helping verbs before they can be used as verbs in sentences. The result will always be a verb phrase.

EXAMPLES He **walks** toward us in a hurry.

June **was walking** behind us a minute ago.

They **walked** to the park.

We **have walked** three miles in the last hour.

The way the past and past participle of a verb are formed shows whether the verb is **regular** or **irregular.**

158   Using Verbs

Using Regular Verbs

Most verbs are **regular,** which means that their past and past participle forms follow a standard, predictable pattern.

> The past and past participle of a **regular verb** are formed by adding **-ed** or **-d** to the present form.

9.1.2 RULE

To form the past and past participle of a regular verb such as *chirp* or *hover*, you simply add *-ed* to the present. With regular verbs that already end in *e*—verbs such as *move* and *charge*—you simply add *-d* to the present.

PRINCIPAL PARTS OF REGULAR VERBS			
PRESENT	PRESENT PARTICIPLE	PAST	PAST PARTICIPLE
call	(am) calling	called	(have) called
change	(am) changing	changed	(have) changed
charge	(am) charging	charged	(have) charged
chirp	(am) chirping	chirped	(have) chirped
contain	(am) containing	contained	(have) contained
describe	(am) describing	described	(have) described
fix	(am) fixing	fixed	(have) fixed
hover	(am) hovering	hovered	(have) hovered
jump	(am) jumping	jumped	(have) jumped
lift	(am) lifting	lifted	(have) lifted
look	(am) looking	looked	(have) looked
move	(am) moving	moved	(have) moved
play	(am) playing	played	(have) played
save	(am) saving	saved	(have) saved
serve	(am) serving	served	(have) served
ski	(am) skiing	skied	(have) skied
talk	(am) talking	talked	(have) talked
type	(am) typing	typed	(have) typed
visit	(am) visiting	visited	(have) visited
walk	(am) walking	walked	(have) walked

See Practice 9.1A
See Practice 9.1B

PRACTICE 9.1A **Identifying the Principal Parts of Regular Verbs**

Read the sentences. Then, label each underlined verb *present*, *present participle*, *past*, or *past participle*.

EXAMPLE   I enjoy seeing a full moon.

ANSWER   *present*

1. When Dad has time, he <u>walks</u> to the train station.
2. My grandmother has <u>lived</u> in the same house for 70 years.
3. Our dog is <u>chasing</u> snowflakes in the backyard.
4. The teacher <u>assigned</u> three pages of homework.
5. The baseball players have <u>used</u> the same equipment for three seasons now.
6. Katrina <u>wants</u> a new microscope.
7. At a Chinese restaurant, I <u>tasted</u> shrimp for the first time.
8. Band members are <u>washing</u> cars to raise money.
9. I have never <u>climbed</u> a tree that tall.
10. My brother is always <u>looking</u> for a new hobby.

PRACTICE 9.1B **Supplying the Principal Parts of Regular Verbs**

Read the verbs. Write and label the four principal parts of each verb. Use a form of the helping verb *be* with the present participle and a form of the helping verb *have* with the past participle.

EXAMPLE   rely

ANSWER   *rely* — present
          is relying — present participle
          relied — past
          has relied — past participle

11. drop
12. hurry
13. ask
14. move
15. search
16. flap
17. serve
18. knock
19. close
20. divide

SPEAKING APPLICATION

With a partner, take turns talking about current events. Use at least three of the principal verb parts as you talk. Your partner should listen for and name the principal parts of at least three of the verbs you use.

WRITING APPLICATION

Write a short paragraph about friends or family members. Use all four principal verb parts in your sentences.

Using Irregular Verbs

While most verbs are regular, many very common verbs are **irregular**—their past and past participle forms do not follow a predictable pattern.

> The past and past participle of an **irregular verb** are not formed by adding *-ed* or *-d* to the present tense form.

IRREGULAR VERBS WITH THE SAME PAST AND PAST PARTICIPLE			
PRESENT	PRESENT PARTICIPLE	PAST	PAST PARTICIPLE
bring	(am) bringing	brought	(have) brought
build	(am) building	built	(have) built
buy	(am) buying	bought	(have) bought
catch	(am) catching	caught	(have) caught
fight	(am) fighting	fought	(have) fought
find	(am) finding	found	(have) found
get	(am) getting	got	(have) got *or* (have) gotten
hold	(am) holding	held	(have) held
lay	(am) laying	laid	(have) laid
lead	(am) leading	led	(have) led
lose	(am) losing	lost	(have) lost
pay	(am) paying	paid	(have) paid
say	(am) saying	said	(have) said
sit	(am) sitting	sat	(have) sat
sleep	(am) sleeping	slept	(have) slept
spin	(am) spinning	spun	(have) spun
stand	(am) standing	stood	(have) stood
stick	(am) sticking	stuck	(have) stuck
swing	(am) swinging	swung	(have) swung
teach	(am) teaching	taught	(have) taught
win	(am) winning	won	(have) won

Check a dictionary whenever you are in doubt about the correct form of an irregular verb.

IRREGULAR VERBS WITH THE SAME PRESENT, PAST, AND PAST PARTICIPLE

PRESENT	PRESENT PARTICIPLE	PAST	PAST PARTICIPLE
bid	(am) bidding	bid	(have) bid
burst	(am) bursting	burst	(have) burst
cost	(am) costing	cost	(have) cost
hurt	(am) hurting	hurt	(have) hurt
put	(am) putting	put	(have) put
set	(am) setting	set	(have) set

IRREGULAR VERBS THAT CHANGE IN OTHER WAYS

PRESENT	PRESENT PARTICIPLE	PAST	PAST PARTICIPLE
arise	(am) arising	arose	(have) arisen
be	(am) being	was	(have) been
bear	(am) bearing	bore	(have) borne
beat	(am) beating	beat	(have) beaten
begin	(am) beginning	began	(have) begun
blow	(am) blowing	blew	(have) blown
break	(am) breaking	broke	(have) broken
choose	(am) choosing	chose	(have) chosen
come	(am) coming	came	(have) come
do	(am) doing	did	(have) done
draw	(am) drawing	drew	(have) drawn
drink	(am) drinking	drank	(have) drunk
drive	(am) driving	drove	(have) driven
eat	(am) eating	ate	(have) eaten
fall	(am) falling	fell	(have) fallen
fly	(am) flying	flew	(have) flown
forget	(am) forgetting	forgot	(have) forgotten
freeze	(am) freezing	froze	(have) frozen

IRREGULAR VERBS THAT CHANGE IN OTHER WAYS (CONTINUED)			
PRESENT	PRESENT PARTICIPLE	PAST	PAST PARTICIPLE
give	(am) giving	gave	(have) given
go	(am) going	went	(have) gone
grow	(am) growing	grew	(have) grown
know	(am) knowing	knew	(have) known
lie	(am) lying	lay	(have) lain
ride	(am) riding	rode	(have) ridden
ring	(am) ringing	rang	(have) rung
rise	(am) rising	rose	(have) risen
run	(am) running	ran	(have) run
see	(am) seeing	saw	(have) seen
shake	(am) shaking	shook	(have) shaken
sing	(am) singing	sang	(have) sung
sink	(am) sinking	sank	(have) sunk
speak	(am) speaking	spoke	(have) spoken
spring	(am) springing	sprang	(have) sprung
strive	(am) striving	strove	(have) striven
swear	(am) swearing	swore	(have) sworn
swim	(am) swimming	swam	(have) swum
take	(am) taking	took	(have) taken
tear	(am) tearing	tore	(have) torn
throw	(am) throwing	threw	(have) thrown
wear	(am) wearing	wore	(have) worn
weave	(am) weaving	wove	(have) woven
write	(am) writing	wrote	(have) written

See Practice 9.1C
See Practice 9.1D
See Practice 9.1E
See Practice 9.1F

As you can see, there are many irregular verbs. For most of these verbs, you should memorize the different forms. Whenever you are not sure of which form of an irregular verb to use, check a dictionary.

Supplying the Principal Parts of Irregular Verbs

Read the verbs. Write and label the four principal parts of each verb. Use a form of the helping verb *be* with the present participle and a form of the helping verb *have* with the past participle.

EXAMPLE stick

ANSWER *stick* — present
is sticking — present participle
stuck — past
have stuck — past participle

1. hold
2. spin
3. cost
4. grow
5. sing
6. write
7. bring
8. lead
9. sit
10. swim

Choosing the Correct Form of Irregular Verbs

Read the sentences. Then, choose and write the form of the verb in parentheses that correctly completes each sentence.

EXAMPLE I have (tore, torn) the paper in half.

ANSWER *torn*

11. Sheila (brung, brought) fruit to the picnic.
12. Which one (cost, costed) the most?
13. We wanted to see the sunrise, so everyone had (arose, arisen) while it was still dark.
14. Carlos (choosed, chose) to perform a difficult piece of music.
15. The water was cool, and we (drank, drunk) our fill.
16. Celeste had never (flew, flown) in a plane before.
17. The town (builded, built) a new government office.
18. If we had (knew, known) then what we know now, things would have been different.
19. They have (sank, sunk) the toy boats.
20. You have (wore, worn) that same shirt three days in a row.

SPEAKING APPLICATION

With a partner, choose two irregular verbs from Practice 9.1C. Take turns using the different parts of the verb in sentences. Your partner should listen for and name which principal part of a verb you have used.

WRITING APPLICATION

Choose one of the irregular verbs from Practice 9.1C and 9.1D. Write four sentences, each one with a different principal part of the verb you selected.

PRACTICE 9.1E Using Irregular Verbs

Read the sentences. Rewrite each sentence, using the form of the verb in parentheses that correctly completes the sentence.

EXAMPLE   I wish I had (know) you were coming.

ANSWER   I wish I had *known* you were coming.

1. My mom (teach) math for ten years.
2. It (hurt) more yesterday than it does today.
3. Because the wind had (blow) all night, there were no leaves left on the trees.
4. My great-grandfather (fly) a plane in World War II.
5. The potted plants would have (freeze) if we had left them out last night.
6. The carpenters (build) a stage for the spring play.
7. What I should have (say) is, "Please."
8. Grandmother had (write) a letter, and she wanted me to mail it for her.
9. I (see) a four-leaf clover yesterday.
10. My cousin had (drive) all night to join us for Thanksgiving dinner.

PRACTICE 9.1F Revising for Irregular Verbs

Read the sentences. Then, if the underlined verb is in the correct form, write *correct*. If it is not, rewrite the sentence with the correct verb form.

EXAMPLE   We wished we could have <u>layed</u> there in the sun all day.

ANSWER   We wished we could have *lain* there in the sun all day.

11. They <u>knowed</u> I was coming.
12. My little sister has <u>grew</u> three inches since her last birthday.
13. When the baseball hit the window, the glass <u>broke</u>.
14. The bell at the fire department <u>ringed</u>.
15. We <u>ate</u> dinner at a restaurant near the park.
16. We should have <u>took</u> an extra blanket.
17. We had <u>shaken</u> all the sand out of the blanket before packing it.
18. My brother <u>catched</u> the fly ball.
19. My teacher had <u>spoke</u> to me about the project before class began.
20. My sister <u>swore</u> not to tell anyone about the surprise party.

SPEAKING APPLICATION

With a partner, take turns saying irregular verbs from Practice 9.1E. Your partner should then state one of the other principal parts of the verb and use it in a sentence.

WRITING APPLICATION

Write three or four sentences about what last autumn was like where you live. Use the past and past participle of two or three irregular verbs in your sentences. You may scan the list of words in Practice 9.1E and 9.1F for ideas.

9.2 The Six Tenses of Verbs

In English, verbs have six **tenses**: the **present**, the **past**, the **future**, the **present perfect**, the **past perfect**, and the **future perfect**.

EL6

The **tense** of a verb shows the time of the action or state of being.

Every tense has both **basic** forms and **progressive** forms.

Identifying the Basic Forms of the Six Tenses

The chart below shows the **basic** forms of the six tenses, using *begin* as an example. The first column gives the name of each tense. The second column gives the basic form of *begin* in all six tenses. The third column gives the principal part needed to form each tense. Only three of the four principal parts are used in the basic forms: the present, the past, and the past participle.

BASIC FORMS OF THE SIX TENSES OF *BEGIN*		
TENSE	BASIC FORM	PRINCIPAL PART USED
Present	I begin.	Present
Past	I began.	Past
Future	I will begin.	Present
Present Perfect	I have begun.	Past Participle
Past Perfect	I had begun.	Past Participle
Future Perfect	I will have begun.	Past Participle

Study the chart carefully. First, learn the names of the tenses. Then, learn the principal parts needed to form them. Notice also that the last four tenses need helping verbs.

As you have already learned, some verbs form their tenses in a regular, predictable pattern. Other verbs use an irregular pattern. *Begin* is an example of an irregular verb.

See Practice 9.2A

Conjugating the Basic Forms of Verbs

A helpful way to become familiar with all the forms of a verb is by **conjugating** it.

> A **conjugation** is a list of the singular and plural forms of a verb in a particular tense.

Each tense in a conjugation has six forms that fit with first-, second-, and third-person forms of the personal pronouns. These forms may change for each personal pronoun, and they may change for each tense.

To conjugate any verb, begin by listing its principal parts. For example, the principal parts of the verb *go* are *go, going, went,* and *gone.* The following chart shows the conjugation of all the basic forms of *go* in all six tenses. Notice that the forms of the helping verbs may also change for each personal pronoun and tense.

CONJUGATION OF THE BASIC FORMS OF GO		
TENSE	**SINGULAR**	**PLURAL**
Present	I go. You go. He, she, or it goes.	We go. You go. They go.
Past	I went. You went. He, she, or it went.	We went. You went. They went.
Future	I will go. You will go. He, she, or it will go.	We will go. You will go. They will go.
Present Perfect	I have gone. You have gone. He, she, or it has gone.	We have gone. You have gone. They have gone.
Past Perfect	I had gone. You had gone. He, she, or it had gone.	We had gone. You had gone. They had gone.
Future Perfect	I will have gone. You will have gone. He, she, or it will have gone.	We will have gone. You will have gone. They will have gone.

See Practice 9.2B

Conjugating *Be*

The verb *be* is an important verb to know how to conjugate. It is both the most common and the most irregular verb in the English language. You have already seen how to use forms of *be* with the perfect tenses. You will also use the basic forms of *be* when you conjugate the progressive forms of verbs later in this section.

EL6

PRINCIPAL PARTS OF *BE*			
PRESENT	PRESENT PARTICIPLE	PAST	PAST PARTICIPLE
be	being	was	been

Once you know the principal parts of *be*, you can conjugate all of the basic forms of *be*.

CONJUGATION OF THE BASIC FORMS OF *BE*		
TENSE	SINGULAR	PLURAL
Present	I am. You are. He, she, or it is.	We are. You are. They are.
Past	I was. You were. He, she, or it was.	We were. You were. They were.
Future	I will be. You will be. He, she, or it will be.	We will be. You will be. They will be.
Present Perfect	I have been. You have been. He, she, or it has been.	We have been. You have been. They have been.
Past Perfect	I had been. You had been. He, she, or it had been.	We had been. You had been. They had been.
Future Perfect	I will have been. You will have been. He, she, or it will have been.	We will have been. You will have been. They will have been.

See Practice 9.2C
See Practice 9.2D

PRACTICE 9.2A > **Identifying Present, Past, and Future Tenses of Verbs**

Read the sentences. Then, label each underlined verb *present*, *past*, or *future*.

EXAMPLE   Storm clouds <u>linger</u> above the mountains.

ANSWER   *present*

1. Tomorrow we <u>will wash</u> the car.
2. My brother just <u>swept</u> the driveway yesterday.
3. I <u>check</u> my e-mail every day after school.
4. Chandra <u>touched</u> the rabbit's soft fur.
5. After this winter, we <u>will welcome</u> spring.
6. Miguel <u>brought</u> two friends to the party.
7. The bells <u>ring</u> each morning.
8. This summer I <u>will learn</u> how to swim.
9. This bucket <u>holds</u> five gallons.
10. The weather <u>will turn</u> cool this weekend.

PRACTICE 9.2B > **Identifying Perfect Tenses of Verbs**

Read the sentences. Then, write the verb in each sentence, and label it *present perfect*, *past perfect*, or *future perfect*.

EXAMPLE   The end of summer had come so much faster than I expected.

ANSWER   *had come* — past perfect

11. I wish I had known there was a test today.
12. By this time next year, Kendra will have finished high school.
13. We have bought a copy of my favorite author's new book.
14. My mom has started a new job.
15. I had brought a salad to the luncheon.
16. Carly had planted the flowers in the window.
17. Our town has benefited from recycling.
18. By 10 P.M., the kids will have come home from the school dance.
19. The days had begun to get longer.
20. The Jacksons have built a porch on the back of their house.

SPEAKING APPLICATION

With a partner, take turns talking about school. Talk about something you did last year, something you are doing now, and something you hope to do next year. Your partner should listen for and name one past-, one present-, and one future-tense verb.

WRITING APPLICATION

Write a short paragraph about a hobby or interest you have had for a while. Write about what you have been doing with it and what you hope you will be doing in the future. Use a perfect tense verb at least once.

PRACTICE 9.2C ▷ Forming Verb Tenses

Read the sentences, which are all in the present tense. Then, rewrite each sentence, changing it to the tense indicated in parentheses.

EXAMPLE   My sister holds the kitten. (past perfect)

ANSWER   My sister **had held** the kitten.

1. The teacher gives homework. (future)

2. The painters put the final coat of paint on the house. (present perfect)

3. We bring Aunt Shelby to every concert. (past)

4. The Boy Scout troop begins the service project. (future perfect)

5. We drink the juice. (past perfect)

6. You eat dinner with your family. (past)

7. Carlo completes the assignment. (future perfect)

8. They run in a marathon. (future)

9. Maureen chooses a science class. (past perfect)

10. Some say history repeats itself. (present perfect)

PRACTICE 9.2D ▷ Using Verb Tenses Correctly

Read the sentences. Then, write the verb in parentheses that correctly completes each sentence.

EXAMPLE   Tomorrow (will be, was) another day.

ANSWER   *will be*

11. By this time next year, Geo (will complete, will have completed) his degree.

12. Everything would change, now that Jill (chose, had chosen) to stay.

13. Rafael (will bring, will have brought) his brother to the party tonight.

14. We (ate, will eat) lunch at Grandma's yesterday.

15. They (had drunk, drink) all the milk by the time we got there.

16. The teacher said that everyone (has done, does) well this week.

17. Cooking (existed, exists) before people began recording history.

18. My mom (writes, had written) a note to my dad every morning.

19. I (will come, have come) to your party this afternoon.

20. My brother (carries, carried) the groceries in for my aunt when she came home.

SPEAKING APPLICATION

With a partner, take turns talking about holidays you celebrate. Talk about what you have done for past holidays, what you might be planning, and what you hope to do in the future. Your partner should listen for and name three verbs in perfect tenses.

WRITING APPLICATION

Write three sentences about school. One sentence should use a verb in the past perfect tense; one, a verb in the present perfect tense; and one, a verb in the future perfect tense.

Recognizing the Progressive Tense of Verbs

The six tenses of *go* and *be* in their basic forms were shown in the charts earlier in this section. Each of these tenses also has a progressive tense or form. The progressive form describes an event that is in progress. In contrast, the basic forms of a verb describe events that have a definite beginning and end.

EL6

> The **progressive tense,** or form, of a verb shows an action or condition that is ongoing.

9.2.3 RULE

All six of the progressive tenses of a verb are made using just one principal part: the present participle. This is the principal part that ends in *-ing*. Then, the correct form of *be* is added to create the progressive tense or form.

Progressive Tenses of *Sing*

PROGRESSIVE TENSE = be + present participle

PRESENT
I **am** **singing** in the chorus.
be present participle

PAST
I **was** **singing** in practice all last week.
be present participle

FUTURE
I **will be** **singing** in this weekend's concert.
be   present participle

PRESENT PERFECT
I **have been** **singing** since I was a young child.
      be   present participle

PAST PERFECT
I **had been** **singing** only in the chorus, but now
    be   present participle
I also sing solos.

FUTURE PERFECT
I **will have been** **singing** in the chorus for ten
        be   present participle
years by the time I graduate.

Conjugating Progressive Tenses

To create the progressive tenses or forms of a verb, you must know the basic forms of *be*.

> **RULE 9.2.4**
>
> To conjugate the **progressive** forms of a verb, add the present participle of the verb to a conjugation of the basic forms of *be*.

A complete conjugation of the basic forms of *be* is shown earlier in this section. Compare that conjugation with the following conjugation of the progressive forms of *go*. You will notice that, even though the present participle form of the verb does not change, the form of the helping verb does change. It is the form of *be* that tells you whether the action or condition is taking place in the past, present, or future.

CONJUGATION OF THE PROGRESSIVE FORMS OF *GO*		
TENSE	SINGULAR	PLURAL
Present Progressive	I am going. You are going. He, she, it is going.	We are going. You are going. They are going.
Past Progressive	I was going. You were going. He, she, it was going.	We were going. You were going. They were going.
Future Progressive	I will be going. You will be going. He, she, it will be going.	We will be going. You will be going. They will be going.
Present Perfect Progressive	I have been going. You have been going. He, she, it has been going.	We have been going. You have been going. They have been going.
Past Perfect Progressive	I had been going. You had been going. He, she, it had been going.	We had been going. You had been going. They had been going.
Future Perfect Progressive	I will have been going. You will have been going. He, she, it will have been going.	We will have been going. You will have been going. They will have been going.

See Practice 9.2E
See Practice 9.2F

PRACTICE 9.2E ▷ **Identifying the Progressive Tenses of Verbs**

Read the sentences. Then, write whether the underlined verb tense in each sentence is *present progressive, past progressive, future progressive, present perfect progressive, past perfect progressive,* or *future perfect progressive.*

EXAMPLE   The wind <u>was blowing</u> across the prairie.

ANSWER   *past progressive*

1. The sun <u>is rising</u> over the ocean.
2. Jenny and Charlotte <u>were watching</u> the younger children play.
3. That movie <u>will be showing</u> at a theater next week.
4. I <u>had been looking</u> for a watch just like that.
5. The sky <u>was turning</u> from pink to orange.
6. I <u>have been cooking</u> all day.
7. The jet soon <u>will be soaring</u> high above Earth.
8. The students <u>had been practicing</u> their parts in the play for weeks.
9. Celia <u>is bringing</u> her cousin.
10. By next Wednesday, they <u>will have been dancing</u> together for two years!

PRACTICE 9.2F ▷ **Using Progressive Tenses of Verbs**

Read the sentences. Then, rewrite each one as a complete sentence, using the tense of the verb in parentheses.

EXAMPLE   Candace _____ her vacation. (*plan,* present progressive)

ANSWER   *Candace is planning her vacation.*

11. Meta's story _____ more exciting. (*become,* present progressive)
12. José _____ the architecture. (*admire,* past progressive)
13. Liana _____ in New Mexico. (*live,* present perfect progressive)
14. They _____ while they study. (*eat,* future progressive)
15. Mr. Jung _____ before the alarm went off. (*sleep,* past perfect progressive)
16. I _____ for 12 hours by the time I reach China. (*fly,* future perfect progressive)
17. The author _____ her new book. (*sign,* past progressive)
18. Rosa _____ the sunshine. (*enjoy,* present progressive)
19. Dwayne _____ lawns since he was ten. (*mow,* present perfect progressive)
20. My puppy _____ on the bed. (*sleep,* past perfect progressive)

SPEAKING APPLICATION

With a partner, take turns talking about current events. Use progressive tenses of verbs. Your partner should listen for and name two progressive tense verbs.

WRITING APPLICATION

Write a brief summary of a story or book you enjoyed. Use progressive tenses of verbs in at least two sentences of the summary.

Identifying Active and Passive Voice

Just as verbs change tense to show time, they may also change form to show whether or not the subject of the verb is performing an action.

> **The voice** of a verb shows whether or not the subject is performing the action.

In English, most verbs have two **voices: active,** to show that the subject is performing an action, and **passive,** to show that the subject is having an action performed on it.

> A verb is in the **active voice** when its subject performs the action.

ACTIVE VOICE

Sharon **plays** the piano.

Bob **photographed** the debate team.

In each example above, the subject performs the action, so it is said to be in the active voice.

> A verb is in the **passive voice** when its subject does not perform the action.

PASSIVE VOICE

The piano **is being played** by Sharon.

The debate team **was photographed** by Bob.

In each example above, the person doing the action becomes the object of the preposition *by* and is no longer the subject. Both subjects—*piano* and *team*—are receivers rather than performers of the action. When the subject is acted upon, the verb is said to be in the passive voice.

See Practice 9.2G

Forming the Tenses of Passive Verbs

A passive verb always has two parts.

> A **passive verb** is always a verb phrase made from a form of *be* plus a past participle.

The following chart shows a conjugation of the passive forms of the verb *report* with the pronoun *it*.

CONJUGATION OF THE PASSIVE FORMS OF *REPORT*	
TENSE	PASSIVE FORM
Present	It is reported.
Past	It was reported.
Future	It will be reported.
Present Perfect	It has been reported.
Past Perfect	It had been reported.
Future Perfect	It will have been reported.

While there are uses for the passive voice, most writing is more lively when it is in the active voice. Think about how to change each sentence below to the active voice. Follow the pattern in the first two examples.

PASSIVE It **is decided** to bring the car.

ACTIVE We **have decided** to bring the car.

PASSIVE It **was decided** to bring the car.

ACTIVE We **decided** to bring the car.

PASSIVE It **will be decided** Tuesday if we should bring the car.

It **has been decided** to bring the car.

It **had been decided** that we will need the car.

It **will have been decided** if we need the car.

Using Active and Passive Voices

Each of the two voices has its proper use in English.

RULE 9.2.9

> **Use the active voice whenever possible.**

Sentences with active verbs are less wordy and more forceful than those with passive verbs. Compare, for example, the following sentences. Notice the different number of words each sentence needs to report the same information.

ACTIVE   Students **conducted** a taste test.

PASSIVE   A taste test **was conducted** by students.

Although you should aim to use the active voice in most of your writing, there will be times when you will need to use the passive voice.

RULE 9.2.10

> **Use the passive voice to emphasize the receiver of an action rather than the performer of an action.**

In the following example, the receiver of the action is the subject *candidate*. It is the *voters* (the direct object) who are actually performing the action.

EMPHASIS ON RECEIVER   The candidate **was supported** by the voters.

The passive voice should also be used when there is no performer of the action.

RULE 9.2.11

> **Use the passive voice to point out the receiver of an action when the performer is unknown or not named in the sentence.**

PERFORMER UNKNOWN   The secret research **was ordered** sometime last year.

See Practice 9.2H

PRACTICE 9.2G > **Distinguishing Active and Passive Voice**

Read the sentences. Then, write *AV* if the underlined verb is in active voice or *PV* if the verb is in passive voice.

EXAMPLE   The ball <u>was thrown</u> to first base.

ANSWER   *PV*

1. Sondra <u>opened</u> the door for Mrs. Santos.
2. Jason said that the book <u>was dropped</u> by Celia.
3. The event <u>is being covered</u> by a rookie reporter.
4. I <u>juggled</u> two jobs while studying for my college exams.
5. Christine <u>was awakened</u> by her alarm clock at 6:00 A.M.
6. The kitten <u>lapped</u> up the spilled milk.
7. Lexie quickly <u>drank</u> three glasses of water.
8. The results of the election <u>pleased</u> the candidate.
9. The baby <u>was comforted</u> by its mother's voice.
10. Janet <u>helped</u> her little brother with his chores.

PRACTICE 9.2H > **Revising to Use Active Voice**

Read the sentences. Then, rewrite each sentence that is in passive voice so that it is in active voice. If the sentence is already in active voice, write *active*.

EXAMPLE   This song was written by Jackie.

ANSWER   *Jackie wrote this song.*

11. I found a hat that I like.
12. The movie was made by a French director.
13. I went bowling yesterday.
14. The actors were applauded by the audience.
15. The snake warmed itself in the sun.
16. Sammy and Keisha were helped by Richard.
17. The show continued without further interruption.
18. The computer was fixed by the technician.
19. Ten items were scanned by the cashier.
20. Madison jogged around the park.

SPEAKING APPLICATION

With a partner, take turns saying one sentence in active voice and one sentence in passive voice. Use the sentences in Practice 9.2H as models to create your sentences. Your partner should listen to the two sentences and identify which sentence is in active voice and which is in passive voice.

WRITING APPLICATION

Write at least two sentences in passive voice about an activity you enjoy. Then, rewrite the sentences so they are in active voice.

Moods of Verbs

Verbs in English also use **mood** to describe the status of an action.

> There are three moods for English verbs: the **indicative mood,** the **subjunctive mood**, and the **imperative mood.**

The **indicative mood** indicates, or states, something. It is also used to ask questions. The **subjunctive mood** describes a wish or a condition that may be contrary to fact.

INDICATIVE MOOD	SUBJUNCTIVE MOOD
Melanie **is** in my class.	I wish Joanna **were** in my class.
Jared **has** a new telescope.	If he **had brought** it to camp, we could have looked at the stars.
I **would** like to be president of the debating club.	If I **were** president of the debating club, I would be fair to everyone.

The subjunctive mood can be used to describe situations that are unlikely to happen or not possible. It is often used in clauses that begin with *if* or *that*. In these cases, use the plural form of the verb.

EXAMPLES   If I **were** you, I would leave for home after the

rain stops.
(I am not you, so the situation is not possible.)

Mary wishes that she **were** on vacation now.
(She is not going until next month, so the situation is not possible.)

The **imperative** mood states a request or command and always uses the present tense. A mild imperative is followed by a period; a strong imperative is followed by an exclamation point.

EXAMPLES   **Call** me after school. Please **don't** forget.

Watch out, that window is broken!

Notice that the subject, *you*, is understood but omitted.

EL8

See Practice 9.2I
See Practice 9.2J

PRACTICE 9.2I > **Identifying Moods of Verbs**

Read the sentences. Then, write *indicative, subjunctive,* or *imperative* for the mood of the underlined verb in each sentence.

EXAMPLE   Please <u>close</u> the door.

ANSWER   *imperative*

1. I wish I <u>were</u> taller.
2. Lisa <u>is bringing</u> the popcorn tonight.
3. <u>Don't forget</u> your gloves.
4. If I <u>were</u> you, I would think carefully about your choice.
5. Mom and Dad <u>are going</u> out for dinner.
6. <u>Come in</u> for dinner now.
7. If it <u>were</u> up to me, we would take a different path.
8. Carla <u>has</u> a new bicycle.
9. I wish Dad <u>were</u> here now.
10. <u>Send</u> your grandmother a thank-you note.

PRACTICE 9.2J > **Writing Sentences to Express Mood**

Read the verbs. Then, write sentences using the different moods of verbs as indicated below.

EXAMPLE   drink (imperative)

ANSWER   *Please drink some water.*

11. were (subjunctive)
12. will bring (indicative)
13. open (imperative)
14. went (indicative)
15. had been (subjunctive)
16. put (imperative)
17. ran (indicative)
18. could hear (subjunctive)
19. are leaving (indicative)
20. finish (imperative)

SPEAKING APPLICATION

With a partner, take turns talking about what you might like to do if things were different. Your partner should confirm whether you are using the subjunctive mood correctly.

WRITING APPLICATION

Write a short paragraph about what you would like to do if you were older. Use the subjunctive mood at least twice.

9.3 Troublesome Verbs

The following verbs cause problems for many speakers and writers of English. Some of the problems involve using the principal parts of certain verbs. Others involve learning to distinguish between the meanings of certain confusing pairs of verbs.

(1) ain't *Ain't* is not considered standard English. Avoid using it in speaking and in writing.

INCORRECT   He **ain't** the first to explore this island.

CORRECT   He **isn't** the first to explore this island.

(2) did, done Remember that *done* is a past participle and can be used as a verb only with a helping verb such as *have* or *has*. Instead of using *done* without a helping verb, use *did*.

INCORRECT   I already **done** my history project.

CORRECT   I already **did** my history project.

I **have** already **done** my history project.

See Practice 9.3A

(3) dragged, drug *Drag* is a regular verb. Its principal parts are *drag, dragging, dragged,* and *dragged. Drug* is never correct as the past or past participle of *drag*.

INCORRECT   The sailor **drug** the heavy box.

CORRECT   The sailor **dragged** the heavy box.

(4) gone, went *Gone* is the past participle of *go* and can be used as a verb only with a helping verb such as *have* or *has. Went* is the past of *go* and is never used with a helping verb.

INCORRECT   Jean and Frank **gone** to the museum.

We **should have went** along with them.

CORRECT   Jean and Frank **went** (or **have gone**) to the museum.

We **should have gone** along with them.

(5) *have, of* The words *have* and *of* often sound very similar. Be careful not to write *of* when you mean the helping verb *have* or its contraction *'ve*.

INCORRECT   Columbus should **of** continued on.

CORRECT   Columbus should **have** (or **should've**) continued on.

(6) *lay, lie* These verbs look and sound almost alike and have similar meanings. The first step in distinguishing between *lay* and *lie* is to memorize the principal parts of both verbs.

PRINCIPAL PARTS			
lay	laying	laid	laid
lie	lying	lay	lain

Lay usually means "to put (something) down" or "to place (something)." It is almost always followed by a direct object. *Lie* means "to rest in a reclining position" or "to be situated." This verb is used to show the position of a person, place, or thing. *Lie* is never followed by a direct object.

EXAMPLES   The captain **lays** his glasses on the desk.

The sailors must **lie** down in bunks.

Pay special attention to the past tense of *lay* and *lie*. *Lay* is the past tense of *lie*. The past tense of *lay* is *laid*.

PRESENT TENSE OF *LAY*   I **lay** the map on the table.

PAST TENSE OF *LAY*   The sailors **laid** their uniforms on their bunks.

PAST TENSE OF *LIE*   The sailor **lay** down on his bunk.

See Practice 9.3B

(7) *leave, let* *Leave* means "to allow to remain." *Let* means "to permit." Do not reverse the meanings.

INCORRECT   **Leave** me think in peace! **Let** the poor dog alone!

CORRECT   **Let** me think in peace! **Leave** the poor dog alone!

(8) *raise, rise* *Raise* can mean "to lift (something) upward," "to build (something)," or "to increase (something)." It is usually followed by a direct object. *Rise* is not usually followed by a direct object. This verb means "to get up," "to go up," or "to be increased."

EXAMPLES   **Raise** the anchor so we can cast off.

The sailors must **rise** before five in the morning.

(9) *saw, seen* *Seen* is a past participle and can be used as a verb only with a helping verb such as *have* or *has*.

INCORRECT   I **seen** that exhibit last year.

CORRECT   I **saw** that exhibit last year.

(10) *says, said* A common mistake in reporting what someone said is to use *says* (present tense) rather than *said* (past tense).

INCORRECT   The captain **says**, "I need to sit down."

CORRECT   The captain **said**, "I need to sit down."

(11) *set, sit* The first step in learning to distinguish between *set* and *sit* is to become thoroughly familiar with their principal parts.

PRINCIPAL PARTS			
set	setting	set	set
sit	sitting	sat	sat

Set means "to put (something) in a certain place or position." It is usually followed by a direct object. *Sit* usually means "to be seated" or "to rest." It is usually not followed by a direct object.

EXAMPLES   He **set** the cup on the coaster.

We **have set** the plants safely in the cargo bay.

Mona **sat** in the captain's chair.

The parrot **has sat** on the perch since it ate.

See Practice 9.3C
See Practice 9.3D

PRACTICE 9.3A > Using *Did* and *Done*

Read the sentences. Then, for each sentence, if *did* or *done* is used correctly, write *correct*. If it is not, write *incorrect*.

EXAMPLE   My brother done something really dangerous.

ANSWER   *incorrect*

1. We did all our homework.

2. We have did what we could to help.

3. Mom has done enough work for today.

4. I done a good job washing the car.

5. Celeste will have done everything necessary.

6. My little brother did his homework without my help.

7. Getting exercise done a lot to improve my health.

8. We have done all our shopping for the party.

9. Carmen has already did the painting.

10. We did invite Michelle and Carlos.

PRACTICE 9.3B > Using *Lay* and *Lie*

Read the sentences. Then, choose and write the correct form of the verb from the pair in parentheses.

EXAMPLE   Our cats love (lain, lying) near the heater.

ANSWER   *lying*

11. He carefully (laid, laying) the tray on the table.

12. Why don't you (lying, lie) down for a while?

13. They were (laying, laid) out their clothes for the next day.

14. You have (lay, lain) there all day!

15. She should (lie, lay) down on the couch to rest.

16. Most chickens (laid, lay) an egg every day.

17. There is a book (lying, laid) on my desk.

18. Yesterday, I (lay, lie) on the lawn, enjoying the smell of cut grass.

19. Jamal isn't feeling well and is (lying, lain) on the bed in the nurse's office.

20. The snow (lay, laid) thick and deep on the field last week.

SPEAKING APPLICATION

With a partner, take turns talking about activities that you do around your home. Use at least two of the verbs practiced on this page. Your partner should confirm whether the verbs were used correctly.

WRITING APPLICATION

Write three sentences about chores you do around your home. In your sentences, use *did* or *done* (you may use both), as well as at least one tense of *lay*.

PRACTICE 9.3C > Using *Set* and *Sit*

Read the sentences. Then, choose and write the correct form of the verb from the pair in parentheses.

EXAMPLE   I'll just (set, sit) right here until you come back.

ANSWER   *sit*

1. You can just (set, setting) it on the table.

2. If you (sat, sit) very still, you may see birds at the feeder.

3. Dad was (sitting, setting) the bags of sand in the truck when his back started to hurt.

4. The students (sat, set) in silence, waiting for the concert to begin.

5. I left the shopping list (setting, sitting) on the counter.

6. Cassie (set, sat) the books on the cart.

7. This weekend, we will be (sitting, setting) the cornerstone for the new library.

8. Our dog loves to (set, sit) on the sofa.

9. The waiter (sit, set) the bowl of soup down carefully.

10. My little brother (sit, sat) happily in the middle of the pile of toys.

PRACTICE 9.3D > Using Troublesome Verbs

Read the sentences. If the underlined verb is used correctly, write *correct*. If it is not, rewrite the sentence using the correct verb.

EXAMPLE   I <u>seen</u> a good place for a picnic.

ANSWER   I *saw* a good place for a picnic.

11. Mom <u>dragged</u> my brother to the barber for a haircut.

12. Have you <u>did</u> the research for your social studies project?

13. My sister wants to <u>raise</u> vegetables this summer.

14. The coach should <u>has</u> sent in a different player.

15. <u>Leave</u> that cut alone, or it won't heal.

16. The teacher gave us an assignment, and then he <u>says</u> it's due tomorrow.

17. Justin and Cleo <u>gone</u> to the zoo with their friends.

18. We <u>seen</u> someone riding an elephant.

19. <u>Leave</u> me sit here for a while.

20. You should have <u>gone</u> on the class trip.

SPEAKING APPLICATION

With a partner, take turns describing an exciting event. Use at least two of the troublesome verbs. Your partner should confirm whether you are using the verbs correctly.

WRITING APPLICATION

Write a short paragraph about a visit to a zoo (real or imagined). Use at least two of the troublesome verbs in your paragraph.

CHAPTER 10

USING PRONOUNS

Using the correct types of pronouns will help make your writing flow smoothly.

WRITE GUY *Jeff Anderson, M.Ed.*

WHAT DO YOU NOTICE?

Focus on the pronouns as you zoom in on these sentences from the speech "Stage Fright" by Mark Twain.

> **MENTOR TEXT**
>
> My knees were shaking so that I didn't know whether I could stand up. If there is an awful, horrible malady in the world, it is stage fright—and seasickness. They are a pair.

Now, ask yourself the following questions:

- In the first sentence, how do the pronouns *my* and *I* help you figure out whose knees were shaking?
- In the third sentence, how can you tell what the pronoun *they* refers to?

In the first sentence, the pronoun *I* shows that the text is written in the first person. Therefore, the pronoun *my* shows that the narrator is describing his own knees. The pronoun *they* in the third sentence is plural. In the previous sentence, the author says there is one horrible malady, stage fright. Then he adds seasickness. Therefore, *they* refers to both *stage fright* and *seasickness*.

Grammar for Writers Writers use pronouns to avoid awkward repetition. For example, it sounds clumsy to say, "Dave forgot Dave's homework, so Dave's mother brought it to school for Dave." Instead you could say, "Dave forgot *his* homework, so *his* mother brought it to school for *him*."

I'd like to share my pronouns with you.

Thanks! That would make them ours.

10.1 Recognizing Cases of Personal Pronouns

In Chapter 1, you learned that personal pronouns can be arranged in three groups: first person, second person, and third person. Pronouns can also be grouped by their **cases.**

RULE 10.1.1

English has three cases: **nominative, objective,** and **possessive.**

The chart below shows the personal pronouns grouped according to the three cases. The case shows whether a pronoun is being used as a subject, an object, or a possessive.

THE THREE CASES OF PERSONAL PRONOUNS	
NOMINATIVE CASE	**USE IN A SENTENCE**
I, we, you, he, she, it, they	subject of a verb predicate pronoun
OBJECTIVE CASE	**USE IN A SENTENCE**
me, us, you, him, her, it, them	indirect object object of a preposition direct object
POSSESSIVE CASE	**USE IN A SENTENCE**
my, mine, our, ours, your, yours, his, her, hers, its, their, theirs	to show ownership

SUBJECT OF A VERB	**We** wanted badly to see the game.
PREDICATE PRONOUN	The winner is **she** .
INDIRECT OBJECT	Please give **me** the ball.
OBJECT OF A PREPOSITION	Please show the photograph to **me** .
DIRECT OBJECT	A basketball hit **him** on the head.
TO SHOW OWNERSHIP	That is **my** jacket, not **yours** .

See Practice 10.1A

See Practice 10.1B

PRACTICE 10.1A **Identifying Cases of Personal Pronouns**

Read the sentences. Then, identify the case of each underlined personal pronoun by writing *nominative*, *objective*, or *possessive*.

EXAMPLE   <u>They</u> wanted to go to the store.

ANSWER   *nominative*

1. Celeste offered <u>me</u> a chair.
2. Stanley made <u>his</u> way to the back of the bus.
3. <u>We</u> tried to get tickets for that concert.
4. Why did you invite <u>them</u>?
5. The person at the door announced, "It is <u>I</u>."
6. I grabbed my purse, and Mom grabbed <u>hers</u>.
7. Did you give the boxes to <u>him</u>?
8. I reminded Jena and Phil to bring <u>their</u> notebooks.
9. <u>He</u> went to the movies.
10. We can do it; just leave it to <u>us</u>.

PRACTICE 10.1B **Identifying Pronoun Cases and Uses**

Read the sentences. Write the case of each underlined pronoun. Then, label it *subject of a verb*, *predicate pronoun*, *direct object*, *indirect object*, or *object of a preposition*.

EXAMPLE   Ravi gave <u>her</u> the signed permission slip.

ANSWER   *objective, indirect object*

11. Carlos grabbed the ball and threw <u>it</u> to first base.
12. <u>She</u> carried the bottles to the recycling bin.
13. It was <u>they</u> who built the snow fort.
14. <u>Mine</u> was the first one picked.
15. Melanie handed the pile of papers to <u>me</u>.
16. After the tornado, <u>we</u> went outside to check for damage.
17. Chandra passed <u>him</u> the list.
18. My grocery cart ran into <u>his</u>.
19. The guide sent <u>them</u> to the information desk.
20. I wondered if it was <u>he</u> who had fixed the window.

SPEAKING APPLICATION

With a partner, take turns talking about things you do with your friends or classmates. Your partner should listen for and name at least two different cases of pronouns.

WRITING APPLICATION

Write three sentences about your family or friends. Use the nominative case in one sentence, the objective in one, and the possessive in one.

The Nominative Case

Personal pronouns in the nominative case have two uses.

> **Use the nominative case for (1) the subject of a verb and (2) a predicate pronoun.**

Note that predicate pronouns follow linking verbs. Pronouns that follow linking verbs should be in the nominative case. The linking verbs are highlighted in orange in the examples below.

SUBJECTS	**She** hopes to be on our team.
	Excitedly, **they** prepared for the game.
PREDICATE PRONOUNS	It **was** **I** who suggested a picnic.
	The best players **are** **she** and Mark.

Checking for Errors in the Nominative Case

People seldom forget to use the nominative case for a pronoun that is used by itself as a subject. Problems sometimes arise, however, when the pronoun is part of a compound subject.

INCORRECT	John and **me** played jacks.
CORRECT	John and **I** played jacks.

To make sure you are using the correct case of the pronoun in a compound subject, isolate the pronoun and the verb in the sentence. *Me played jacks* is obviously wrong, so the nominative case *I* should be used instead.

If the sentence is in verb–subject order, rearrange it into subject–verb order, and then isolate the pronoun and verb.

INCORRECT	Are you and **her** going to the dance?
REARRANGED	You and **?** are going to the dance.
CORRECT	Are you and **she** going to the dance?

See Practice 10.1C

The Objective Case

Personal pronouns in the objective case have three uses.

> Use the **objective** case for (1) a direct object, (2) an indirect object, and (3) the object of a preposition.

DIRECT OBJECT

Frank's comment on the game upset **me**.

The referee penalized **her**.

INDIRECT OBJECT

Tell **her** the good news.

My friend gave **me** highlights of the game.

OBJECT OF PREPOSITION

Our team captain voted for **him**.

The players swarmed around **me**.

Checking for Errors in the Objective Case

As with the nominative case, people seldom forget to use the objective case for a pronoun that is used by itself as a direct object, indirect object, or object of a preposition. Problems may arise, however, when the pronoun is part of a compound object.

INCORRECT   The players swarmed around Lucy and **I**.

CORRECT   The players swarmed around Lucy and **me**.

To make sure you are using the correct case of the pronoun in a compound object, use only the pronoun with the rest of the sentence. *The players swarmed around I* is obviously wrong, so the objective case *me* should be used instead.

If the sentence is in verb–subject order, rearrange it into subject–verb order.

INCORRECT   Did my mother give Toby and **she** a drink?

REARRANGED   My mother gave Toby and **?** a drink.

See Practice 10.1D   **CORRECT**   Did my mother give Toby and **her** a drink?

The Possessive Case

Personal pronouns in the possessive case show ownership of one sort or another.

RULE
10.1.4

Use the **possessive** case of personal pronouns before nouns to show possession. In addition, certain personal pronouns may also be used by themselves to indicate possession.

BEFORE NOUNS

The team won **its** game.

Chris held **my** baseball glove.

BY THEMSELVES

Is this marble **yours** or **mine**?

Hers was the best score.

Checking for Errors in the Possessive Case

Personal pronouns in the possessive case are never written with an apostrophe because they already show ownership. Keep this in mind, especially with possessive pronouns that end in *s*.

INCORRECT

These seats are **our's**, not **their's**.

CORRECT

These seats are **ours**, not **theirs**.

When the pronoun *it* is followed by an apostrophe and an *s*, the word becomes *it's*, which is a contraction of *it is*. The possessive pronoun *its* does not have an apostrophe.

CONTRACTION

It's going to rain.

POSSESSIVE PRONOUN

The team loves **its** uniform.

To check if you need the contraction *it's* or the possessive pronoun *its*, substitute *it is* and reread the sentence.

INCORRECT

My sweater has lost **it's** button.

CORRECT

My sweater has lost **its** button.

See Practice 10.1E

See Practice 10.1F

PRACTICE 10.1C **Identifying Nominative Case Pronouns**

Read the sentences. Write the correct pronoun from the choices in parentheses. Then, label the pronoun *subject of a verb* or *predicate pronoun*.

EXAMPLE   It was (them, they) who brought the food.

ANSWER   *they* — predicate pronoun

1. Justin and (me, I) went to the soccer game.
2. It was (she, her) who finished first.
3. I saw the twins, and (they, them) were headed for home.
4. I asked Pedro if it was Bill and (him, he) who found the lost dog.
5. Either Tonya or (her, she) will come to get you.
6. Weren't you and (they, them) trying out for basketball?
7. It was (we, us) who came up with the idea.
8. (He, Him) and I wanted to find a new game.
9. The Steins and (us, we) are going to see a play.
10. It is (I, me) who drew the winning picture.

PRACTICE 10.1D **Using Objective Case Pronouns**

Read the sentences. Write an objective pronoun to correctly complete each sentence. Then, label each pronoun *direct object, indirect object,* or *object of a preposition.*

EXAMPLE   Jonas sat beside _____.

ANSWER   *her* — object of a preposition

11. Ali handed _____ the book.
12. The guide directed _____ to the entrance.
13. From the plane, I gazed down at the land under _____.
14. I recommended _____ for the job.
15. Dad gave _____ gift certificates.
16. I sent a letter to _____.
17. My grandmother bought _____ the book I wanted.
18. Tina got in line in front of _____.
19. Mom made _____ costumes for the play.
20. We found _____ in the basement.

SPEAKING APPLICATION

With a partner, take turns talking about a movie or television show you enjoyed. Your partner should listen for and name at least two objective and two nominative pronouns.

WRITING APPLICATION

Write three sentences about the characters in a book you have read. Use at least one pronoun in each sentence. Underline each pronoun and write above it *N* if it's nominative and *O* if it's objective.

PRACTICE 10.1E › **Using Possessive Case Pronouns**

Read the sentences. Write the correct pronoun from the choices in parentheses.

EXAMPLE   That backpack is (my, mine).

ANSWER   *mine*

1. My brother and I gathered (our, ours) books.

2. A bird builds (it's, its) nest in the spring.

3. The Corrigans invited us to (their, theirs) house.

4. Those dresses are (her's, hers).

5. It's (your, yours) turn to play.

6. Sandra brought her DVDs, and the twins brought (their, theirs).

7. The teacher pointed to (my, mine) project.

8. It turned out those shoes weren't (ours, our's).

9. I could tell the dog was friendly because it wagged (it's, its) tail.

10. My brother asked if I had seen (him, his) baseball glove.

PRACTICE 10.1F › **Revising to Correct Pronoun Errors**

Read the sentences. For each sentence with a pronoun error, write the incorrect pronoun. Then, rewrite the sentence with the correct pronoun. If a sentence has no pronoun error, write *correct*.

EXAMPLE   It was us who won the contest.

ANSWER   *us;* It was *we* who won the contest.

11. Claudia and him went to the museum.

12. A chick has to peck it's way out of the egg.

13. It was he who reached the top of the hill first.

14. Mom gave my sister and I our lunches.

15. Our class thought the prize was our's.

16. I sent you and she a letter.

17. My dad took the Johnsons and us to the movies.

18. Was it them who decorated the room?

19. I thought it was mine, but Jena said it was her.

20. John and me went to the game.

SPEAKING APPLICATION

With a partner, talk about things you or your family members own. Your partner should listen for and name three possessive pronouns you used.

WRITING APPLICATION

Write three sentences. In each sentence, use compound subjects or compound objects that include only pronouns. Check to make sure that both pronouns in a compound subject or object are correct.

Cases of *Who* and *Whom* The pronouns *who* and *whom* are often confused. *Who* is a nominative case pronoun, and *whom* is an objective case pronoun. *Who* and *whom* have two common uses in sentences: They can be used in questions or to begin subordinate clauses in complex sentences.

> Use **who** for the subject of a verb. Use **whom** for (1) the direct object of a verb and (2) the object of a preposition.

 10.1.5 RULE

You will often find *who* used as the subject of a question. *Who* may also be used as the subject of a subordinate clause in a complex sentence.

SUBJECT IN A QUESTION	**Who** hit the most home runs?
SUBJECT IN A SUBORDINATE CLAUSE	I admire the player **who** hit the most home runs.

The following examples show *whom* used in questions.

DIRECT OBJECT	**Whom** did he see at the game?
OBJECT OF PREPOSITION	From **whom** is she getting the new softball?

Questions that include *whom* are generally in inverted word order, with the verb appearing before the subject. If you reword the first example in subject–verb word order, you will see that *whom* is the direct object of the verb *did see: He did see whom?* In the second example, *whom* is the object of the preposition *from: She is getting the new softball from whom?*

Subordinate clauses that begin with *whom* will always be in verb–subject word order. To check the case of the pronoun, reword the clause into subject–verb word order.

VERB–SUBJECT ORDER	From **whom** had she received a ball?
SUBJECT–VERB ORDER	She had received a ball from **whom**?

See Practice 10.1G
See Practice 10.1H

PRACTICE 10.1G **Identifying the Correct Use of Who and Whom**

Read the sentences. Write the pronoun in parentheses that correctly completes each sentence.

EXAMPLE   With (who, whom) are you going?

ANSWER   *whom*

1. (Who, Whom) brought the potato salad?

2. They told me (who, whom) it was at the door.

3. Anna is the one from (who, whom) I got this book.

4. The ball rolled toward (who, whom)?

5. (Who, whom) are you?

6. I met the friend (who, whom) you brought to the party.

7. You and (who, whom) else are going tonight?

8. Jeff is the one from (who, whom) I heard the news.

9. That is the coach (who, whom) will lead us to victory.

10. The teacher introduced (who, whom) to the class?

PRACTICE 10.1H **Revising to Correct Who and Whom**

Read the sentences. Then, if a sentence uses *who* or *whom* incorrectly, rewrite the sentence with the correct pronoun form. If a sentence has no pronoun error, write *correct*.

EXAMPLE   I wondered to who I should give it.

ANSWER   *I wondered to whom I should give it.*

11. May I ask whom is calling?

12. That's the aunt from whom I get my sense of humor.

13. You mailed a letter to who?

14. That is the person who I met yesterday.

15. If you don't come to the meeting, who will?

16. Besides Mom, whom else is bringing salad?

17. The teacher sent who to the principal's office?

18. With whom were you dancing last night?

19. Whom is at the door?

20. The books were given to him and who else?

SPEAKING APPLICATION

With a partner, take turns asking questions about giving and receiving (for example, "Who gave you that?"). Your partner should listen for and confirm whether you used *who* or *whom* correctly.

WRITING APPLICATION

Write two or three sentences about planning a party. Use *who* in one sentence and *whom* in one sentence.

MAKING WORDS AGREE

Making subjects agree with verbs and pronouns with the words for which they stand will help you write clear sentences.

WRITE GUY *Jeff Anderson, M.Ed.*

WHAT DO YOU NOTICE?

Pay attention to agreement as you zoom in on these lines from the poem "Wilbur Wright and Orville Wright" by Rosemary and Stephen Vincent Benét.

MENTOR TEXT

> —And kingdoms may forget their kings
> And dogs forget their bites,
> But, not till Man forgets his wings,
> Will men forget the Wrights.

Now, ask yourself the following questions:

- How can you tell that the verb *forget* agrees with the subject *kingdoms* in the first line?
- Why do the poets use the pronouns *their* and *his* in the second and third lines?

Because *kingdoms* is a plural subject and *forget* is a plural verb, they agree with each other. While nouns ending in *-s* or *-es* are usually plural, verbs without *-s* or *-es* endings are usually plural. The poets use the plural pronoun *their* to indicate that the bites belong to the dogs. Because *dogs* is a plural noun, *their* is used instead of *its*. The poets use the singular pronoun *his* to indicate that the wings belong to Man. Because *Man* is a masculine noun, *his* is used instead of *her*.

Grammar for Writers Sentences flow smoothly when subjects and verbs agree and when pronouns match the words for which they stand.

How can you help subjects and verbs to agree?

You always give them the same number.

11.1 Subject-Verb Agreement

For a sentence to be correct, its subject and verb must match each other, or agree. Subject–verb agreement has one main rule.

The subject and verb in a sentence must agree in number.

In grammar, the concept of **number** is simple. The number of a word can be either **singular** or **plural.** A singular word indicates *one.* A plural word indicates *more than one.* In English, only nouns, pronouns, and verbs have number.

Singular and Plural Subjects

Most of the time, it is easy to tell whether a simple subject, such as a noun or pronoun, is singular or plural. That is because most nouns are made plural by adding *-s* or *-es* to their singular form.

EXAMPLES	custom	custom **s**
	bell	bell **s**
	box	box **es**
	tax	tax **es**

Some nouns form plurals in irregular ways.

EXAMPLES	knife	**knives**
	mouse	**mice**
	child	**children**
	goose	**geese**

Pronouns also have different forms to indicate singular and plural. For example, the pronouns *I, he, she, it,* and *this* are singular. *We, they,* and *these* are plural. *You, who,* and *some* can be either singular or plural.

Singular and Plural Verbs

Like nouns, verbs have singular and plural forms. Problems involving number in verbs normally involve the third-person forms in the present tense (*she wants, they want*) and certain forms of the verb *be* (*I am, he is* or *was, we are* or *were*).

The chart shows all the basic forms of several different verbs in the present tense.

SINGULAR AND PLURAL VERBS IN THE PRESENT TENSE		
SINGULAR		**PLURAL**
First and Second Person	**Third Person**	**First, Second, and Third Person**
(I, you) send	(he, she, it) sends	(we, you, they) send
(I, you) go	(he, she, it) goes	(we, you, they) go
(I, you) look	(he, she, it) looks	(we, you, they) look
(I, you) dance	(he, she, it) dances	(we, you, they) dance
(I, you) visit	(he, she, it) visits	(we, you, they) visit
(I, you) work	(he, she, it) works	(we, you, they) work
(I, you) run	(he, she, it) runs	(we, you, they) run
(I, you) discuss	(he, she, it) discusses	(we, you, they) discuss
(I, you) vote	(he, she, it) votes	(we, you, they) vote
(I, you) choose	(he, she, it) chooses	(we, you, they) choose
(I, you) learn	(he, she, it) learns	(we, you, they) learn

Notice that the form of the verb changes only in the third-person singular, when an *-s* or *-es* is added to the verb. Unlike nouns, which usually become plural when *-s* or *-es* is added, verbs with *-s* or *-es* added to them are singular.

The helping verb *be* may also indicate whether a verb is singular or plural. The following chart shows only those forms of the verb *be* that are always singular.

FORMS OF THE HELPING VERB *BE* THAT ARE ALWAYS SINGULAR			
am	is	was	has been

Making Verbs Agree With Singular and Plural Subjects

To check subject–verb agreement, determine the number of the subject. Then, make sure the verb has the same number.

SINGULAR SUBJECT AND VERB

Jeff **enjoys** the beach.

She **was** here earlier today.

PLURAL SUBJECT AND VERB

Surfers **enjoy** the beach.

They **were** here earlier today.

RULE 11.1.2

A prepositional phrase that comes between a subject and its verb does not affect subject–verb agreement.

Often, a subject is separated from its verb by a prepositional phrase. In these cases, it is important to remember that the object of a preposition is never the subject of a sentence.

INCORRECT   The **arrival** of the firefighters **have caused** much excitement at the picnic.

CORRECT   The **arrival** of the firefighters **has caused** much excitement at the picnic.

INCORRECT   The **cheers** of the crowd **was heard** several blocks away.

CORRECT   The **cheers** of the crowd **were heard** several blocks away.

In the first example, the subject is *arrival*, not *firefighters*, which is the object of the preposition *of*. Because *arrival* is singular, the singular verb *has caused* must be used. In the second example, the subject is the plural *cheers*, not *crowd*; therefore, it takes the plural verb *were heard*.

See Practice 11.1A
See Practice 11.1B

PRACTICE 11.1A ▷ **Making Subjects and Verbs Agree**

Read the sentences. Write the verb in parentheses that agrees with the subject. Then, label the subject *singular* or *plural*. Be sure to think about prepositional phrases and their influence on subject-verb agreement.

EXAMPLE   They (is, are) on time.

ANSWER   *are* — plural

1. This tree (provides, provide) a home for birds and squirrels.

2. The girls (plays, play) basketball after school.

3. The progress of the group of students (was, were) slowed by the weather.

4. The boys (thinks, think) math is easy.

5. Derek (believe, believes) it is bad to litter.

6. Members of the band (is, are) raising money for new uniforms.

7. She (meets, meet) her friends every Friday for dinner.

8. The pecan, the almond, and the cashew (is, are) my favorite nuts.

9. Twila (wants, want) to study ballet.

10. We (sees, see) the clouds in the distance.

PRACTICE 11.1B ▷ **Revising for Subject-Verb Agreement**

Read the sentences. Then, if a sentence has an error in subject-verb agreement, rewrite the sentence correctly. If a sentence has no error, write *correct*.

EXAMPLE   We is excited about vacation.

ANSWER   We *are* excited about vacation.

11. They brings their lunches to school.

12. The girls in this group have decided on a project.

13. One of the police officers have a radio.

14. The flowers in the garden is starting to bloom.

15. My friends plans to go to college.

16. The players on that team practice every day.

17. The Smiths' dog barks at everyone.

18. I'll be happy when I gets home.

19. The cost of ten rides is fifteen dollars.

20. My sister often borrow my clothes.

SPEAKING APPLICATION

With a partner, take turns talking about teams or groups and individual members of those teams or groups. Your partner should listen for and identify at least one singular subject and one plural subject and the verbs that agree with them.

WRITING APPLICATION

Write three sentences about school activities. In one sentence, have a singular subject; in one, a plural subject; and in one, a subject with a prepositional phrase between the subject and the verb. Make sure subjects and verbs agree.

Making Verbs Agree With Collective Nouns

Collective nouns—such as *assembly, audience, class, club,* and *committee*—name groups of people or things. Collective nouns are challenging as subjects because they can take either singular or plural verbs. The number of the verb depends on the meaning of the collective noun in the sentence.

> **Use a singular verb with a collective noun acting as a single unit. Use a plural verb when the individual members of the group are acting individually.**

SINGULAR	The **committee votes** on issues.
PLURAL	The **committee have split** their votes.
SINGULAR	The chess **club plans** a tournament.
PLURAL	The chess **club were pleased** with their games.
SINGULAR	The **class plants** a vegetable garden.
PLURAL	The **class have divided** the responsibilities of planting among the members.
SINGULAR	The scout **troop marches** in the parade.
PLURAL	The scout **troop have earned** badges in many areas.
SINGULAR	The **audience applauds** after the show.
PLURAL	The **audience squirm** in their seats.

See Practice 11.1C
See Practice 11.1D

PRACTICE 11.1C> **Making Verbs Agree With Collective Nouns**

Read the sentences. Then, write the verb in parentheses that agrees with the subject.

EXAMPLE   After a game, the team (changes, change) their clothes before going home.

ANSWER   *change*

1. Once the assignment is given, the class (opens, open) their books.
2. I read that the army (trains, train) recruits very well.
3. The audience (doesn't, don't) enjoy the movie.
4. A group of students (plans, plan) the annual bake sale.
5. The jury (disagrees, disagree) among themselves.
6. The band (travels, travel) by bus.
7. The cleaning crew (begins, begin) their different tasks.
8. A swarm of bees (is, are) moving across the field.
9. The family (takes, take) their places around the table.
10. The company (relies, rely) on the honesty of its employees.

PRACTICE 11.1D> **Revising for Agreement Between Verbs and Collective Nouns**

Read the sentences. Then, if a sentence has an error in subject-verb agreement, rewrite the sentence correctly. If a sentence has no error, write *correct*.

EXAMPLE   The cast learns their lines for the play.

ANSWER   *The cast **learn** their lines for the play.*

11. Congress vote on a tax bill tomorrow.
12. The majority think their rights are protected.
13. The committee often argues among themselves.
14. The jury come to a verdict.
15. The team practice or read while they wait.
16. This bunch of bananas look good.
17. The class begins their research reports.
18. The Girl Scout troop says the Pledge of Allegiance.
19. The student council help set rules.
20. The whole herd waits at the gate.

SPEAKING APPLICATION

With a partner, take turns talking about groups you know about, such as school clubs or community groups. Your partner should listen for and name two collective nouns you used. Discuss why the noun is singular or plural.

WRITING APPLICATION

Write three sentences, in the present tense, using these collective nouns as subjects: *committee, team,* and *class.* Label the subjects *plural* or *singular.*

Making Verbs Agree With Compound Subjects

A **compound subject** refers to two or more subjects that share a verb. Compound subjects are connected by conjunctions such as *and, or,* or *nor.*

EXAMPLES   The **museums** and **historical sites** in
                      compound subject

Philadelphia **attract** many visitors.
                   plural verb

Either **Robert** or **Jennifer** **knows** the way to the
            compound subject   singular
                                        verb

bus stop.

Neither the **Liberty Bell** nor **Independence**
                    compound subject

Hall **disappoints** tourists.
     singular
      verb

A number of rules can help you choose the right verb to use with a compound subject.

Compound Subjects Joined by *And*

RULE 11.1.4

> When a compound subject is connected by *and*, the verb that follows is usually plural.

EXAMPLE   **Austin** and **Dallas** **are** my favorite Texas cities.
                 compound subject   plural verb

There is an exception to this rule: If the parts of a compound subject are thought of as one person or thing, the subject is singular and takes a singular verb.

EXAMPLES   **Spaghetti and meatballs** **is** my favorite meal.
                      compound subject   singular
                                                  verb

Salt and pepper **is** on the table.
      compound subject singular
                          verb

Compound Subjects Joined by *Or* or *Nor*

> When two singular subjects are joined by *or* or *nor*, use a singular verb. When two plural subjects are joined by *or* or *nor*, use a plural verb.

SINGULAR   A **car** or a **train** **provides** good transportation to
                  compound subject   singular
                                                verb
             the city.

PLURAL   Neither **children** nor **adults** **like** to wait in line.
                          compound subject   plural verb

In the first example, *or* joins two singular subjects. Although two vehicles make up the compound subject, the subject does not take a plural verb. Either a car or a train provides good transportation, not both of them.

> When a compound subject is made up of one singular and one plural subject joined by *or* or *nor*, the verb agrees with the subject closer to it.

EXAMPLES   Either the **monuments** or the **White House**
                          plural subject   singular subject
             is interesting to see.
             singular verb

             Either the **White House** or the **monuments**
                          singular subject   plural subject
             are interesting to see.
             plural verb

See Practice 11.1E

Agreement in Inverted Sentences

In most sentences, the subject comes before the verb. Sometimes, however, this order is turned around, or **inverted.** In other sentences, the helping verb comes before the subject even though the main verb follows the subject.

When a subject comes after the verb, the subject and verb still must agree with each other in number.

EXAMPLE **Do** the historical **attractions** in Boston sound
plural verb   plural subject

exciting to you?

Sentences Beginning With a Prepositional Phrase
In sentences that begin with a prepositional phrase, the object of the preposition may look like a subject, even though it is not.

EXAMPLE Along the shore **were** many nervous **soldiers**.
plural verb   plural subject

In this example, the plural verb *were* agrees with the plural subject *soldiers*. The singular noun *shore* is the object of the preposition *along*.

Sentences Beginning With *There* or *Here*
Sentences beginning with *there* or *here* are almost always in inverted word order.

EXAMPLES There **were** several **books** about holidays.
plural verb   plural subject

Here **is** the latest **book** about holidays.
singular verb   singular subject

The contractions *there's* and *here's* both contain the singular verb *is*: *there is* and *here is*. Do not use these contractions as plural subjects.

INCORRECT Here**'s** the **keys** to the house.

CORRECT Here **are** the **keys** to the house.

Questions With Inverted Word Order
Many questions are also written in inverted word order.

EXAMPLE Where **are** the **keys** to the house?
plural verb   plural subject

See Practice 11.1F

204   Making Words Agree

PRACTICE 11.1E > Making Verbs Agree With Compound Subjects

Read the sentences. Then, write the verb in parentheses that agrees with the subject.

EXAMPLE   Chloe and Emily (is, are) going to dance class.

ANSWER   *are*

1. Either Jason or Kevin (needs, need) to bring the basketball.
2. Weeding and watering (is, are) important parts of gardening.
3. Neither students nor teachers (enjoys, enjoy) fire drills.
4. Macaroni and cheese (is, are) easy to make.
5. My dog and the neighbor's cat (acts, act) like friends.
6. A bus or a taxi (leaves, leave) for the airport every few minutes.
7. Neither the coach nor the players (is, are) ready for this game.
8. The budding trees and the new grass (promises, promise) that spring is near.
9. Either the frills or the lace (needs, need) to be taken off the dress.
10. The canned vegetables and soup (goes, go) into the cupboard.

PRACTICE 11.1F > Revising for Agreement Between Verbs and Compound Subjects

Read the sentences. Then, if a sentence has an error in subject-verb agreement, rewrite the sentence correctly. If a sentence has no error, write *correct*.

EXAMPLE   A button or hook are needed for that skirt.

ANSWER   *A button or hook is needed for that skirt.*

11. Skiing and skating is winter sports.
12. Neither the parents nor the children wants that rule.
13. The gathering clouds and rising wind signal an approaching storm.
14. Either dirt or sand are needed for planting these seeds.
15. The eggs and milk goes into the refrigerator.
16. Neither the hippo nor the elephant seems to notice the zoo's visitors.
17. The maps and guidebook helps us find our way.
18. The museum or aquarium offer classes.
19. Peanut butter and jelly is my favorite sandwich.
20. Either the band or the chorus have a bake sale today.

SPEAKING APPLICATION

With a partner, talk about shopping for food. What sorts of things fill the shopping cart? Where are they found? Your partner should listen for and name three compound subjects and note whether the verbs agree.

WRITING APPLICATION

Write three sentences about your favorite season of the year. Use compound subjects in each sentence. Make sure the verbs agree with the subjects.

Verb Agreement With Indefinite Pronouns

Indefinite pronouns refer to people, places, or things in a general way.

> When an **indefinite pronoun** is the subject of a sentence, the verb must agree in number with the pronoun.

INDEFINITE PRONOUNS				
SINGULAR			PLURAL	SINGULAR OR PLURAL
anybody	everyone	nothing	both	all
anyone	everything	one	few	any
anything	much	other	many	more
each	neither	somebody	several	most
either	nobody	someone	others	none
everybody	no one	something		some

Indefinite Pronouns That Are Always Singular

Indefinite pronouns that are always singular take singular verbs. Do not be misled by a prepositional phrase that follows an indefinite pronoun. The singular verb agrees with the indefinite pronoun, not with the object of the preposition.

EXAMPLES **Each** of the basketball team banners **is** blue
singular subject   singular verb
and white.

Either of the hats in the closet **is** warm.
singular subject   singular verb

Everyone in the first five rows **was** delighted
singular subject   singular verb
by the play.

Each of the boys **plays** on a town team.
singular subject   singular verb

Indefinite Pronouns That Are Always Plural

Indefinite pronouns that are always plural are used with plural verbs.

EXAMPLE   **Both** of my suitcases **are** in the closet.
plural subject   plural verb

Many of the children **are waiting** until it gets
plural subject   plural verb
cooler to go out.

Several have not **started** their projects yet.
plural subject   plural verb

Few have chosen a gift yet.
plural subject   plural verb

Indefinite Pronouns That May Be Either Singular or Plural

Many indefinite pronouns can take either a singular or a plural verb.

> The number of the indefinite pronoun is the same as the number of its **referent,** or the noun to which it refers.

11.1.9 RULE

The indefinite pronoun is singular if the referent is singular. If the referent is plural, the indefinite pronoun is plural.

SINGULAR   **Some** of the **milk is** frozen.

PLURAL   **Some** of the **apples are** frozen, too.

In the examples above, *some* is singular when it refers to *milk,* but plural when it refers to *apples.*

SINGULAR   **All** of my **money is** gone.

PLURAL   **All** of these **presents are** for you.

See Practice 11.1G
See Practice 11.1H

In these examples, *all* is singular when it refers to *money,* but plural when it refers to *presents.*

> **PRACTICE 11.1G** **Making Verbs Agree With Indefinite Pronouns**

Read the sentences. Then, write the verb in parentheses that agrees with the subject.

EXAMPLE   Few (is, are) chosen for this honor.

ANSWER   *are*

1. Nothing (happens, happen) at school on Sundays.
2. Both (is, are) good choices.
3. Many of us (likes, like) Chinese food.
4. Each of the participants (gets, get) a certificate.
5. Everything (depends, depend) on teamwork.
6. All of the eggs (is, are) broken.
7. Most of the lake (freezes, freeze) in the winter.
8. Everyone (knows, know) what to do.
9. Several (is, are) going to appear at the event.
10. Anything (happens, happen) at these games.

> **PRACTICE 11.1H** **Revising for Agreement Between Verbs and Indefinite Pronouns**

Read the sentences. Then, if a sentence has an error in subject-verb agreement, rewrite the sentence correctly. If a sentence has no error, write *correct*.

EXAMPLE   Each of the balloons float.

ANSWER   *Each of the balloons* **floats.**

11. I don't think anybody come here now.
12. Both of the glasses broke when shipped.
13. Let me know if anything happen.
14. Others disagrees with the idea.
15. On a good team, everyone works together.
16. Most of the work end today.
17. Several has already volunteered.
18. Nothing is on the table.
19. Each of the shirts need ironing.
20. All of the students is early.

SPEAKING APPLICATION

With a partner, take turns talking about events that occur in your town or school. Your partner should listen for and name two indefinite pronouns and note whether the verbs agree.

WRITING APPLICATION

Write three sentences using at least three of the following indefinite pronouns: *some, most, all, both, others, many, each, everyone, nothing, anybody,* and *anything*. Make sure the verbs agree with the pronouns you choose.

11.2 Agreement Between Pronouns and Antecedents

An **antecedent** is the word or words for which a pronoun stands. A pronoun's antecedent may be a noun, a group of words acting as a noun, or even another pronoun. As with subjects and verbs, pronouns should agree with their antecedents.

Making Personal Pronouns and Antecedents Agree

Person tells whether a pronoun refers to the person speaking (first person), the person spoken to (second person), or the person, place, or thing spoken about (third person). **Number** tells whether the pronoun is singular or plural. **Gender** tells whether a third-person-singular antecedent is masculine or feminine.

> A personal pronoun must agree with its antecedent in person, number, and gender.

11.2.1 RULE

EXAMPLE   I told **David** to bring a bathing suit with **him**.

In this example, the pronoun *him* is third person and singular. It agrees with its masculine antecedent, *David*.

Avoiding Shifts in Person

A personal pronoun must have the same person as its antecedent. Otherwise, the meaning of the sentence is unclear.

INCORRECT   The **skydivers** know **we** must check the parachutes before takeoff.
(Who must check the parachutes? *We* must.)

CORRECT   The **skydivers** know **they** must check the parachutes before takeoff.
(Who must check the parachutes? *The skydivers* must.)

As you can see, a shift in the person of the personal pronoun can make it unclear who is going to check the parachutes.

Avoiding Problems With Number and Gender

Making pronouns and antecedents agree in number and gender can be difficult. Problems may arise when the antecedent is a collective noun, when the antecedent is a compound joined by *or* or *nor,* or when the gender of the antecedent is not known.

Making Pronouns Agree in Number With Collective Nouns
Collective nouns are challenging because they can take either singular or plural pronouns. The number of the pronoun depends on the meaning of the collective noun in the sentence.

> Use a singular pronoun to refer to a collective noun that names a group that is acting as a single unit. Use a plural pronoun to refer to a collective noun when the members or parts of a group are acting individually.

SINGULAR   The **class showed its** joy with a cheer.

PLURAL   The **class voted** for **their** favorite candidates.

In the first example above, the class is acting as a single unit when it shows its joy, so the singular pronoun, *its,* refers to *class.* In the second example, each member of the class is voting individually, so the plural pronoun, *their,* refers to *class.*

Making Pronouns Agree in Number With Compound Nouns

> Use a singular personal pronoun to refer to two or more singular antecedents joined by *or* or *nor.* Use a plural pronoun with two or more singular antecedents joined by *and.*

Two or more singular antecedents joined by *or* or *nor* must have a singular pronoun, just as they must have a singular verb.

INCORRECT   **Becca** or **Megan** will take **their** backpack.

CORRECT   **Becca** or **Megan** will take **her** backpack.

CORRECT   **Becca** and **Megan** will take **their** backpacks.

Avoiding Problems With Gender

When the gender of a third-person-singular antecedent is not known, you can make the pronoun agree with its antecedent in one of three ways:

(1) Use *he or she, him or her,* or *his or hers.*

(2) Rewrite the sentence so that the antecedent and pronoun are both plural.

(3) Rewrite the sentence to eliminate the pronoun.

Traditionally, the masculine pronouns *he* and *his* have been used to stand for both males and females. Today, using *he or she* and *him or her* is preferred. If any of these corrections seem awkward to you, rewrite the sentence.

Making Personal Pronouns and Indefinite Pronouns Agree

Indefinite pronouns are words such as *each, everybody, either,* and *one.* Pay special attention to the number of a personal pronoun when the antecedent is a singular indefinite pronoun.

> **Use a singular personal pronoun when its antecedent is a singular indefinite pronoun.**

RULE 11.2.4

Do not be misled by a prepositional phrase that follows an indefinite pronoun. The personal pronoun agrees with the indefinite pronoun, not with the object of the preposition.

INCORRECT	**One** of the cats has lost **their** collar.
CORRECT	**One** of the cats has lost **its** collar.
INCORRECT	**Everyone** in the two groups expressed **their** opinion.
CORRECT	**Everyone** in the two groups expressed **his or her** opinion.
CORRECT	**All** of the groups expressed **their** opinions.

See Practice 11.2A
See Practice 11.2B

PRACTICE 11.2A Making Pronouns and Antecedents Agree

Read the sentences. Then, write the pronoun in parentheses that agrees with its antecedent.

EXAMPLE   Marcia went to the store, and Carmine went with (him, her).

ANSWER   *her*

1. Each player took (his or her, their) place on the field.

2. This shirt is too small, so (it, they) must be returned.

3. I told my brother to bring the binoculars with (him, them).

4. Either Ramon or Danny will present (his, their) project next.

5. The firefighters worked hard, and (he, they) soon had the fire under control.

6. Marissa needed money and asked (her, his) father for ten dollars.

7. If most of the group want to go, (you, they) should go.

8. Both the builder and the designer gave (his, their) opinions.

9. Each of the dogs buried (its, their) bone.

10. Neither Sandra nor Letitia got (her, their) homework done.

PRACTICE 11.2B Revising for Pronoun-Antecedent Agreement

Read the sentences. If a sentence has an error in pronoun-antecedent agreement, rewrite the sentence correctly. Then, circle the pronoun and underline its antecedent. If a sentence has no error, write *correct*.

EXAMPLE   Each child wears a name tag they decorated.

ANSWER   *Each child wears a name tag he or she decorated.*

11. The boys must wear jackets at his school dance.

12. Juanita or Mary will get a prize for their project.

13. We asked the police officers if they could tell us how to get home.

14. Phillip and Pedro said he would help.

15. Everyone took their books home.

16. Jason and Steve will bring their baseball mitts.

17. My older sister likes their job.

18. Neither Gina nor Jessica wanted their project to be late.

19. Bella and I said we would happily share our ideas with the group.

20. Each student will read the essay they wrote.

SPEAKING APPLICATION

With a partner, take turns talking about places you or your family regularly goes to (for fun or errands). Your partner should listen for and name three pronouns and their antecedents and note if they agree.

WRITING APPLICATION

Choose three sentences from Practice 11.2B and rewrite each one so that a different pronoun is correct. You may change the number or gender of the antecedents or change conjunctions to accomplish this.

USING MODIFIERS

Knowing how to use different forms of adjectives and adverbs to make comparisons will enrich the descriptions in your writing.

WRITE GUY *Jeff Anderson, M.Ed.*

WHAT DO YOU NOTICE?

Look for modifiers as you zoom in on these sentences from the essay "Jackie Robinson: Justice at Last" by Geoffrey C. Ward and Ken Burns.

MENTOR TEXT

> Slowly his teammates accepted him, realizing that he was the spark that made them a winning team. No one was more daring on the base paths or better with the glove.

Now, ask yourself the following questions:

- In the second sentence, why do the authors use the word *more* instead of adding another ending to the adjective *daring*?
- Why do the authors use the adjective *better* instead of *best* in the second sentence?

For most one- and two-syllable modifiers, you add -*er* or -*est* to make a comparison. However, adding either ending to *daring* sounds awkward; *more* or *most* is used to make the comparison instead. *Better* is used to make a comparison between two people, while *best* is used to compare three or more people. The authors said that no *one* player on the team was more talented with the glove than Jackie Robinson, so they used *better*. If they had compared Robinson to *all* players, they would have used *best*.

Grammar for Writers Writers can create vivid images when they use adjectives and adverbs to make comparisons. Check how many you are comparing to make sure you use the right form.

I'm the best player on the team.

Do you think of yourself as superlative, too?

12.1 Comparisons Using Adjectives and Adverbs

You may recall that adjectives and adverbs are **modifiers.** Adjectives can modify nouns or pronouns. Adverbs can modify verbs, adjectives, or other adverbs. You can use modifiers to make comparisons.

Three Forms of Comparison

Modifiers change their form when they show comparison. These different forms are called **forms,** or **degrees, of comparison.**

RULE 12.1.1 Most adjectives and adverbs have three forms, or degrees, of comparison: **positive, comparative,** and **superlative.**

The **positive degree** is used when no comparison is being made. This is the form of a word that is listed in a dictionary. The **comparative degree** is used when two items are being compared. The **superlative degree** is used when three or more items are being compared. When the superlative degree is used, the article *the* is often added.

DEGREE	ADJECTIVE	ADVERB
Positive	The hermit crab moved into a **large** shell.	Sue ran **fast**.
Comparative	Soon, it will need a **larger** shell.	Sue ran **faster** than Mari.
Superlative	The crab is living in the **largest** shell it has ever had.	Of the three runners, Sue ran the **fastest**.

Like verbs, adjectives and adverbs change forms in different ways. Some adjectives and adverbs change in regular ways, or according to predictable patterns. As you can see in the chart above, *large* and *fast* form their comparative and superlative degrees regularly, by adding *-er* and *-est* to their positive form.

Regular Modifiers With One or Two Syllables

Most modifiers are **regular**—their degrees of comparison are formed in predictable ways.

> **Use *-er* or *more* to form the comparative degree and use *-est* or *most* to form the superlative degree of most one- and two-syllable modifiers.**

12.1.2 RULE

COMPARATIVE AND SUPERLATIVE DEGREES FORMED WITH *-ER* AND *-EST*		
POSITIVE	COMPARATIVE	SUPERLATIVE
deep	deeper	deepest
fast	faster	fastest
friendly	friendlier	friendliest
narrow	narrower	narrowest
sunny	sunnier	sunniest

Use *more* to form a modifier's comparative degree when adding *-er* sounds awkward. Use *most* to form a modifier's superlative degree when adding *-est* sounds awkward.

COMPARATIVE AND SUPERLATIVE DEGREES FORMED WITH *MORE* AND *MOST*		
POSITIVE	COMPARATIVE	SUPERLATIVE
careful	more careful	most careful
complete	more complete	most complete
handsome	more handsome	most handsome
often	more often	most often
quietly	more quietly	most quietly

See Practice 12.1A

More and *most* should not be used when the result sounds awkward, however. If you are not sure which form to use, check a dictionary. Most dictionaries list modifiers formed with *-er* and *-est*.

Regular Modifiers With Three or More Syllables

Modifiers for words with three or more syllables follow the same rules.

RULE 12.1.3

Use *more* and *most* to form the comparative and superlative degrees of all modifiers of three or more syllables. Do not use *-er* or *-est* with modifiers of more than two syllables.

DEGREES OF MODIFIERS WITH THREE OR MORE SYLLABLES		
POSTIVE	COMPARATIVE	SUPERLATIVE
expensive	more expensive	most expensive
flexible	more flexible	most flexible

Adverbs Ending in *-ly*

To modify most adverbs ending in *-ly*, use *more* or *most*.

RULE 12.1.4

Use *more* to form the comparative degree and *most* to form the superlative degree of most adverbs ending in *-ly*.

EXAMPLES   quickly, more quickly, most quickly

gracefully, more gracefully, most gracefully

Using *Less* and *Least*

Less and *least* can show decreasing comparisons.

RULE 12.1.5

Use *less* with a modifier to form the decreasing comparative degree and *least* to form the decreasing superlative degree.

EXAMPLES   flexible, less flexible, least flexible

quickly, less quickly, least quickly

See Practice 12.1B

PRACTICE 12.1A Forming Comparatives and Superlatives of One- and Two-Syllable Modifiers

Read the modifiers. Write the comparative and superlative forms of each modifier.

EXAMPLE   soft

ANSWER   *softer, softest*

1. cool
2. happy
3. willing
4. long
5. slowly
6. young
7. small
8. shiny
9. alert
10. straight

PRACTICE 12.1B Using Forms of Modifiers

Read the sentences. Then, write each sentence, using the form of the modifier specified in parentheses.

EXAMPLE   I am the _____ of the three children. (*old*, superlative)

ANSWER   I am the *oldest* of the three children.

11. Callie has the _____ shoe collection. (*fabulous*, superlative)
12. An apple would be a _____ choice. (*healthy*, comparative)
13. A computer is _____ than a typewriter. (*efficient*, comparative)
14. Coach was _____ than usual. (*angry*, comparative)
15. Johnny is the _____ of their children. (*young*, superlative)
16. Claire is my _____ friend. (*funny*, superlative)
17. Are there stars _____ than our sun? (*bright*, comparative)
18. The little boy ran _____ than his brother. (*slowly*, comparative)
19. I got there _____ than you. (*soon*, comparative)
20. What is the _____ way to the park? (*quick*, superlative)

SPEAKING APPLICATION

With a partner, talk about athletes you have seen or know about. Use modifiers to compare their performances or skills. Your partner should listen for and name at least two modifiers used in the comparative or superlative form.

WRITING APPLICATION

Write three or four sentences about animals you have seen or read about. Use modifiers to compare the animals' appearance, behavior, or other characteristics. Underline modifiers that are in the comparative or superlative form.

Irregular Adjectives and Adverbs

A few adjectives and adverbs are irregular.

RULE
12.1.6

Memorize the comparative and superlative forms of adjectives and adverbs that have irregular spellings.

The chart lists the most common irregular modifiers.

DEGREES OF IRREGULAR ADJECTIVES AND ADVERBS		
POSITIVE	COMPARATIVE	SUPERLATIVE
bad (adjective)	worse	worst
badly (adverb)	worse	worst
far (distance)	farther	farthest
far (extent)	further	furthest
good (adjective)	better	best
well (adverb)	better	best
many	more	most
much	more	most

When you are unsure about how a modifier forms its degrees of comparison, check a dictionary.

See Practice 12.1C

Using Comparative and Superlative Degrees

Keep these rules in mind when you use the comparative and superlative degrees.

RULE
12.1.7

Use the comparative degree to compare *two* people, places, or things. Use the superlative degree to compare *three or more* people, places, or things.

Usually, you do not need to mention specific numbers when you are making a comparison. Other words in the sentence should help make the meaning clear whether you are comparing two items or three or more items.

EXAMPLES   The captain felt **better** once all the crew was safely on shore.

The rescue team completed the practice session in their **best** time this week.

Pay particular attention to the modifiers you use when you are comparing just two items. Do not use the superlative degree with fewer than three items.

INCORRECT   Of their two practice runs, that one was **best**.

CORRECT   Of their two practice runs, that one was **better**.

INCORRECT   They were the **fastest** of the two teams competing.

CORRECT   They were the **faster** of the two teams competing.

> **Do not make double comparisons.** Do not use both -*er* and *more* to form the comparative degree or both -*est* and *most* to form the superlative degree. Also, be sure not to use -*er, more,* and *most* with an irregular modifier.

RULE 12.1.8

INCORRECT   That student ran the **most fastest**.

CORRECT   That student ran the **fastest**.

INCORRECT   The thunderstorm was **more worse** than the one last summer.

CORRECT   The thunderstorm was **worse** than the one last summer.

See Practice 12.1D

PRACTICE 12.1C **Forming Comparatives and Superlatives of Irregular Adjectives and Adverbs**

Read the modifiers. Write the comparative and superlative forms of each modifier.

EXAMPLE   good (adjective)

ANSWER   *better, best*

1. far (distance)

2. bad (adjective)

3. many

4. badly (adverb)

5. far (extent)

6. well (adverb)

7. much

PRACTICE 12.1D **Using Comparatives and Superlatives of Irregular Adjectives and Adverbs**

Read the sentences. Then, write each sentence, using the form of the modifier in parentheses.

EXAMPLE   He walked _____ than anyone else. (*far*, comparative)

ANSWER   He walked *farther* than anyone else.

8. This is the _____ cold he has ever had. (*bad*, superlative)

9. He looks _____ like his father. (*much*, comparative)

10. This is the _____ work you have done so far. (*good*, superlative)

11. He played _____ before he got a new coach. (*badly*, comparative)

12. She has the _____ books. (*many*, superlative)

13. He did _____ on the test than he expected. (*well*, comparative)

14. After the dog in the story died, I could not read _____. (*far*, comparative)

15. That is the _____ price. (*good*, comparative)

16. Do you have _____ envelopes? (*many*, comparative)

17. Of the two, that is the _____. (*bad*, comparative)

SPEAKING APPLICATION

With a partner, take turns talking about a competition (cooking, music, sports, or another) that you have seen on television. Whom did you like? Who should have won? Your partner should listen for and confirm the correct use of irregular modifiers.

WRITING APPLICATION

Write three sentences describing a place in nature you have visited or seen in pictures. Use at least two modifiers in either the comparative or superlative form. One modifier should be three or more syllables, and one should be irregular.

Making Logical Comparisons

In most situations, you will have no problem forming the degrees of modifiers and using them correctly in sentences. Sometimes, however, you may find that the way you have phrased a sentence makes your comparison unclear. You will then need to think about the words you have chosen and revise your sentence, making sure that your comparison is logical.

> **When you make a comparison, be sure you are comparing things that have clear similarities.**

Balanced Comparisons

Most comparisons make a statement or ask a question about the way in which similar things are either alike or different.

EXAMPLE   Is **Chesapeake Bay** **deeper** than **Puget Sound** ?
(Both bodies of water have depths that can be measured and compared.)

Because the sentence compares depth to depth, the comparison is balanced. Problems can occur, however, when a sentence compares dissimilar things. For example, it would be illogical to compare the depth of one bay to the shape of another bay. Depth and shape are not similar things and cannot be compared meaningfully.

ILLOGICAL   The plants in our garden are prettier than your garden.
(*Plants* and a *garden* cannot be logically compared.)

LOGICAL   The plants in our garden are prettier than the plants in your garden.
(Two sets of plants can be logically compared.)

> **Make sure that your sentences compare only similar items.**

An unbalanced comparison is usually the result of carelessness. The writer may have simply left something out. Read the following incorrect sentences carefully.

INCORRECT	**Building a ship** is **harder** than a **house**. The **number of shipwrecks** near the East Coast is **larger** than the **West Coast**.

In the first sentence, building a ship is mistakenly compared to a house. In the second sentence, events are compared to a place. Both sentences can easily be corrected to make the comparisons balanced.

CORRECT	**Building a ship** is **harder** than **building a house**. The **number of shipwrecks** near the East Coast is **larger** than the **number** near the West Coast.

See Practice 12.1E

Other and *Else* in Comparisons
Another common error in writing comparisons is to compare something to itself.

> **RULE 12.1.11**
>
> When comparing one of a group to the rest of the group, make sure your sentence contains the word *other* or *else.*

Adding *other* or *else* can make a comparison clear. For example, in the second sentence below, because the *United States* is itself a country, it cannot logically be compared to *all countries.* It must be compared to *all other countries.*

PROBLEM SENTENCES	CORRECTED SENTENCES
A salvor is someone who returns an abandoned or sunken ship to shore before anyone.	A salvor is someone who returns an abandoned or sunken ship to shore before anyone else.
U.S. laws may allow a salvor to collect a larger reward than any country's laws do.	U.S. laws may allow a salvor to collect a larger reward than any other country's laws do.

See Practice 12.1F

PRACTICE 12.1E **Making Balanced Comparisons**

Read the sentences. Rewrite each sentence, correcting the unbalanced comparison.

EXAMPLE   My dad's car is newer than your dad.

ANSWER   *My dad's car is newer than your dad's car.*

1. Our school library is bigger than their school.
2. The number of tigers in Asia is larger than zoos.
3. My brother's bicycle is faster than your brother.
4. The amount of money I owe is less than him.
5. The high school's playing field is nicer than the university.
6. There are fewer students in this classroom than that classroom.
7. Mariana's project is more complicated than Ciara.
8. The paint on this wall is drier than that wall.
9. This store's prices are lower than that store.
10. The distance this bus has traveled is longer than that bus.

PRACTICE 12.1F **Using *Other* and *Else* to Make Comparisons**

Read the sentences. Rewrite each sentence, adding *other* or *else* to make the comparisons more logical.

EXAMPLE   Russia is bigger than any country.

ANSWER   *Russia is bigger than any **other** country.*

11. My brother is better at math than anyone.
12. I think the rose is lovelier than any flower.
13. My grandfather is older than anyone in our family.
14. The Pacific Ocean is bigger than any ocean.
15. Rafael studied harder than anyone in class.
16. Our park is cleaner than any park in the state.
17. This chair is more comfortable than anything.
18. She practiced longer than anyone on the team.
19. I was earlier than anyone.
20. My sister draws better than anyone in my family.

SPEAKING APPLICATION

With a partner, take turns talking about sports. Compare the sports or athletes, making sure that your comparisons are balanced and correct. Your partner should listen for and name any comparisons you might need to fix.

WRITING APPLICATION

Write three sentences comparing current clothing styles with images you have seen of past styles. One sentence should have a balanced comparison, and one should have either *else* or *other* to complete the comparison.

12.2 Troublesome Adjectives and Adverbs

The common adjectives and adverbs listed below often cause problems in both speaking and writing.

(1) bad and badly *Bad* is an adjective. Use it after linking verbs, such as *are, appear, feel, look,* and *sound. Badly* is an adverb. Use it after action verbs, such as *act, behave, do,* and *perform.*

INCORRECT   Jan looked **badly** after the trip.

CORRECT   Jan looked **bad** after the trip.

INCORRECT   I did **bad** on the test.

CORRECT   I did **badly** on the test.

(2) good and well *Good* is an adjective. *Well* can be either an adjective or an adverb, depending on its meaning. A common mistake is the use of *good* after an action verb. Use the adverb *well* instead.

INCORRECT   The children behaved **good** all day.

The apple tastes **well** .

CORRECT   The children behaved **well** all day.

The apple tastes **good** .

As adjectives, *good* and *well* have slightly different meanings, which are often confused. *Well* usually refers simply to health.

EXAMPLES   Janet felt **good** after the hike.

The fresh bread smells **good** .

That puppy is not **well** .

(3) *fewer and less* Use the adjective *fewer* to answer the question, "How many?" Use the adjective *less* to answer the question, "How much?"

| HOW MANY | **fewer** calories | **fewer** chores |
| HOW MUCH | **less** food | **less** work |

EL7

(4) *just* When used as an adverb, *just* often means "no more than." When *just* has this meaning, place it right before the word it logically modifies.

INCORRECT   Do you **just** want **one baked potato**?

CORRECT   Do you want **just** **one baked potato**?

(5) *only* The position of *only* in a sentence sometimes affects the sentence's entire meaning. Consider the meaning of these sentences.

EXAMPLES   **Only** she answered that question.
(Nobody else answered that question.)

She **only** answered the question.
(She did nothing else with the question.)

She answered **only** that question.
(She answered that question and no other question.)

Mistakes involving *only* usually occur when its placement in a sentence makes the meaning unclear.

UNCLEAR   **Only** take advice from me.

BETTER   Take advice **only** from me.
(not from anyone else)

See Practice 12.2A
See Practice 12.2B

Take **only** advice from me.
(nothing but advice)

PRACTICE 12.2A **Using *Bad* and *Badly*, *Good* and *Well***

Read the sentences. Write the word in parentheses that correctly completes each sentence.

EXAMPLE   I did (good, well) on the test.

ANSWER   *well*

1. He performed (bad, badly) during the concert.

2. We expected a (good, well) outcome.

3. I felt (bad, badly) about the competition results.

4. The projection equipment worked (good, well).

5. The garbage is beginning to smell (bad, badly).

6. The sets for the play look really (good, well).

7. Dad's car is running (bad, badly).

8. Did your brother finish (good, well) in the race?

9. Our dog (bad, badly) needs to be bathed.

10. The warm sunshine feels (good, well).

PRACTICE 12.2B **Revising for Troublesome Modifiers**

Read the sentences. Rewrite the sentences that contain errors in the use of modifiers. If a sentence has no error, write *correct*.

EXAMPLE   The baking bread smells well.

ANSWER   *The baking bread smells good.*

11. The pollution is badly in this town.

12. A warm blanket feels good on a cold night.

13. These bruises still hurt bad.

14. I did good in yesterday's race.

15. Everyone felt bad about the coach leaving.

16. My brothers work good together.

17. This yellow dress looks badly on me.

18. I was sick for a while, but I'm well now.

19. The plumber did the work bad.

20. Everything the chef made was well.

SPEAKING APPLICATION

With a partner, take turns talking about a movie you enjoyed. Did the actors perform well or badly? Was the story good or bad? Your partner should listen for and confirm that you have used these troublesome modifiers correctly.

WRITING APPLICATION

Write three or four sentences about characters in a story you like. What do they do? How do they do it? Use at least three of the following: *well, good, bad,* and *badly*. Be sure to use them correctly in your sentences.

Cumulative Review \ Chapters 9–12

PRACTICE 1 > Identifying Verb Tenses

Read the sentences. For each sentence, write whether the verb is in the *present, past, future, present perfect, past perfect,* or *future perfect* tense. Also indicate if the verb is *progressive.*

1. Lureen sings in the choir.
2. The new restaurant opened on Friday.
3. Mrs. Macy has operated a crane at a construction site before.
4. The secretary of state will visit India.
5. By noon, Samantha will have been working on the project for six hours.
6. My father is stuffing the turkey for our Thanksgiving dinner.
7. Jeff Jackson had once starred in a musical version of *Old Yeller.*
8. The Lopez family will be leaving shortly on their vacation.
9. Elizabeth had been dancing for years.
10. Ten trumpeters were marching with the band.

PRACTICE 2 > Revising to Use Active Voice

Read the sentences. Then, rewrite each sentence in passive voice so that it is in active voice. If a sentence is already in active voice, write *active.*

1. The best music is played by that salsa band.
2. The poem was written by Emily Dickinson.
3. The Tremonts live in a large house by the lake.
4. This award is shared by all the people involved in our great film.
5. Todd is leaving for Denver tomorrow.

PRACTICE 3 > Using Verbs Correctly

Read the sentences. Then, rewrite the sentences to correct any incorrect verb tenses. If a sentence has no errors, write *correct.*

1. A week ago, Lawrence run his best time on the track.
2. Last Saturday the phone rung all afternoon.
3. The concert has finally begun.
4. Yesterday I accidentally lay my books at the bottom of the wrong locker.
5. I always sit a vase of flowers in the center of the table.
6. Bonnie finally done her homework.
7. At the grand opening last week, Cindy says to me, "Calm down."
8. Mrs. Menendez has spoke to me about the problem with the microphones.
9. I seen the Memorial Day parade for the first time last May.
10. All day the monkeys have swinged in the trees.

PRACTICE 4 > Identifying Pronoun Cases and Uses

Read the sentences. Write whether each underlined pronoun is in the *nominative, objective,* or *possessive* case. Then, write whether it is used as a *subject,* a *predicate pronoun,* a *direct object,* an *indirect object,* or the *object of a preposition.*

1. Polly talked to <u>him</u> for two hours.
2. The teacher gave <u>her</u> a high grade.
3. <u>Mine</u> is the jacket with the fake fur trim.
4. Pedro showed <u>us</u> around the computer room.
5. The winners were Robin and <u>I</u>.

Continued on next page ▶

Cumulative Review Chapters 9–12

 Using Pronouns Correctly

Read the sentences. Then, rewrite the sentences to correct any incorrect pronouns. If a sentence has no errors, write *correct*.

1. Us and Roberto went to the library.

2. The shopkeeper gave Yvonne and I a discount.

3. Whom did Anthony invite to the party?

4. The cat ate it's dinner.

5. The newest counselors were Sonya and me.

6. Ali is the one who the team appointed as leader.

7. There was an agreement between Lou and she.

8. The house at the end of the street is their's.

9. The problem worries Christine and he.

10. Young people do not know whom that actor is.

 Revising for Subject–Verb Agreement

Read the sentences. Then, rewrite the sentences to correct any errors in subject-verb agreement. If a sentence has no errors, write *correct*.

1. A book of poems sit on the shelf.

2. Each of the members belong to other clubs too.

3. Neither Miranda nor I like radio talk shows.

4. The family sometimes argues at dinner.

5. None of the triplets are in my class.

6. Cara and Leslie enjoy scuba diving.

7. The manager or her assistants greets shoppers.

8. Do Jane or Randy come here after school?

9. The committee have named her as treasurer.

10. Macaroni and cheese are my favorite dish.

PRACTICE 7 **Revising for Pronoun–Antecedent Agreement**

Read the sentences. Then, rewrite the sentences to correct any errors in pronoun-antecedent agreement. If a sentence has no errors, write *correct*.

1. Each of the girls spent their money on magazines.

2. Several of the runners had their blisters treated.

3. Nate takes a class where you learn yoga.

4. Neither the dog nor the cat ate their food.

5. Back then, everyone had their shoes polished.

6. Belle and Natalie finished their homework.

7. Both of the horses had scars on its legs.

8. Either Jane or Ann wore lip balm on her lips.

9. None of the workers did his or her own cooking.

10. Everybody remembered his or her manners.

PRACTICE 8 **Using Modifiers Correctly**

Read the sentences. Then, rewrite the sentences to correct any errors involving modifiers. If a sentence has no errors, write *correct*.

1. Less people visit the museum on weekdays.

2. Of the three papers, hers is the most good.

3. Stuart did good in his first attempt.

4. You can walk more far in comfortable shoes.

5. Of the two villains, who is badder?

6. Pearl is the prettiest cat we have ever owned.

7. Many office workers only work on weekdays.

8. The stale crackers taste really badly.

9. Most border collies are smarter than any dogs.

10. How bad did she perform in the play?

CHAPTER 13

PUNCTUATION

Each punctuation mark plays an important role in making your writing understandable and unified.

WRITE GUY *Jeff Anderson, M.Ed.*

WHAT DO YOU NOTICE?

Keep track of commas as you zoom in on these sentences from the story "Why the Tortoise's Shell Is Not Smooth" by Chinua Achebe.

MENTOR TEXT

> When all the birds had gathered together, they set off in a body. Tortoise was very happy as he flew among the birds, and he was soon chosen as the man to speak for the party because he was a great orator.

Now, ask yourself the following questions:

- Why does the author use a comma after *together*?
- Why is a comma needed before *and* in the second sentence?

The first sentence begins with the subordinate clause *when all the birds had gathered together*. Therefore, a comma is needed after *together* to separate the subordinate clause from the main or independent clause that follows. In the second sentence, a comma is needed before the conjunction *and* because there are complete thoughts on either side of it.

Grammar for Writers Well-placed commas can help readers follow your ideas. When in doubt about whether to use a comma, read the sentence aloud. If you come to a brief pause, that might be a place where the rules call for a comma.

Stop! I forgot a comma!

Commas are for pauses, not for stops.

13.1 End Marks

End marks signal the end or conclusion of a sentence, word, or phrase. There are three end marks: the **period (.)**, the **question mark (?)**, and the **exclamation mark (!)**.

Using Periods

A **period** indicates the end of a sentence or an abbreviation.

RULE 13.1.1 | Use a period to end a **declarative** sentence—a statement of fact or opinion.

DECLARATIVE SENTENCE   This is a beautiful park.

RULE 13.1.2 | Use a period to end most **imperative** sentences—sentences that give directions or commands.

IMPERATIVE SENTENCE   Finish reading the chapter.

RULE 13.1.3 | Use a period to end a sentence that contains an **indirect question.**

An **indirect question** restates a question in a declarative sentence. It does not give the speaker's exact words.

INDIRECT QUESTION   Mae asked me if I could stay.

RULE 13.1.4 | Use a period after most **abbreviations** and **initials.**

ABBREVIATIONS   Gov.   Mrs.   Rd.   in.   Jr.

INITIALS   E. B. White   Robin F. Brancato

Note: The abbreviation for *inch, in.,* is the only measurement abbreviation that uses a period after it.

When a sentence ends with an abbreviation that uses a period, do not put a second period at the end.

EXAMPLE   Be sure to include Jack Jenkins Jr.

> Do not use periods with **acronyms**, words formed with the first or first few letters of a series of words.

RULE 13.1.5

EXAMPLES   USA   United States of America

                UN   United Nations

Using Question Marks

A **question mark** follows a word, phrase, or sentence that asks a question.

> Use a question mark after an **interrogative sentence**—one that asks a direct question.

RULE 13.1.6

INTERROGATIVE   Do snakes hatch from eggs?
SENTENCES
                Would you like to come over?

Sometimes a single word or brief phrase is used to ask a direct question. This type of question is punctuated as though it were a complete sentence because the words that are left out are easily understood.

> Use a question mark after a word or phrase that asks a question.

RULE 13.1.7

EXAMPLES   Many small birds build false nests. Why?

See Practice 13.1A   Let's meet for lunch. Where?

Using Exclamation Marks

RULE
13.1.8

Use an **exclamation mark** to end a word, phrase, or sentence that shows strong emotion.

EXAMPLES

Look at that huge vulture!

Watch out!

RULE
13.1.9

Use an exclamation mark after an **imperative** sentence that gives a forceful or urgent command.

IMPERATIVE SENTENCE

Don't spill the water!

Let's go!

While imperative sentences containing forceful commands often end with an exclamation mark, mild imperatives should end with a period.

MILD IMPERATIVES

Please sit down.

Go to the store for me tomorrow.

RULE
13.1.10

Use an exclamation mark after an **interjection** that expresses strong emotion.

INTERJECTIONS

Wow! That was a great throw.

Oh! Look what I found.

Exclamation marks should not be used too often. Overusing them reduces their emotional effect and makes writing less effective.

See Practice 13.1B

PRACTICE 13.1A **Using Question Marks and Periods**

Read the sentences. Rewrite each sentence, adding missing question marks and periods.

EXAMPLE   Dr Smith checked my heart rate

ANSWER   *Dr. Smith checked my heart rate.*

1. Mrs Cohen lives at 14 Maple Rd
2. Have you read anything by C S Lewis
3. Molly asked if I had 18 in of string
4. Has Mr Martinez arrived yet
5. Mrs Jones lives across the street
6. He lives at 20 Elm St
7. I need to practice before the game
8. We read about Dr Martin Luther King Jr
9. Where are they going on vacation
10. Did Mr Nguyen receive his package

PRACTICE 13.1B **Using Exclamation Marks and Periods**

Read the sentences. Rewrite each sentence, adding missing exclamation marks and periods.

EXAMPLE   Clean your room

ANSWER   *Clean your room!*

11. Please turn to page five
12. Wow That was a good catch
13. Dr Amir's house is so large
14. J R R Tolkien wrote *The Hobbit*
15. That's terrible
16. Oh I didn't know you were here
17. Watch out
18. I walked from 12 Oak St to 12 Central Rd
19. Hey I'd like some privacy, please
20. They were amazing

SPEAKING APPLICATION

With a partner, read the following sentences aloud. Use your voices to show how the different punctuation changes meaning. *Close the door. Close the door! Bring it here. Bring it here!* Discuss what the exclamation mark adds to the sentences.

WRITING APPLICATION

Write three or four sentences about working in the kitchen. Use a question mark in one, a period in another, and an exclamation mark in another.

13.2 Commas

End marks signal a full stop. **Commas** signal a brief pause. A comma may be used to separate elements in a sentence or to set off part of a sentence. Include a comma in your writing when you want your reader to group information in your sentence.

Using Commas in Compound Sentences

A **compound sentence** consists of two or more main or independent clauses that are joined by a coordinating conjunction, such as *and, but, for, nor, or, so,* or *yet.*

RULE 13.2.1

> Use a comma before the conjunction to separate two main or independent clauses in a **compound sentence.**

COMPOUND SENTENCE	Chimpanzees are full grown at age five, but their mothers still take care of them.

Use a comma before a conjunction only when there are complete sentences on both sides of the conjunction. If the conjunction joins single words, phrases, or subordinate clauses, do not use a comma.

SINGLE WORDS	Heat and sand are common desert features.
PHRASES	Teri likes both green apples and red apples.
SUBORDINATE CLAUSES	They have decided that you should study more and that they will check on you.

In some compound sentences, the main or independent clauses are very brief, and the meaning is clear. When this occurs, the comma before the conjunction may be omitted.

EXAMPLE	Jon listened carefully but he heard nothing.	See Practice 13.2A

Avoiding Comma Splices

A **comma splice** occurs when two or more sentences have been joined with only a comma between them.

> Avoid **comma splices** by making sure all of your ideas are properly linked.

INCORRECT   The snow clumped on the trees**,** many branches snapped under its weight.

CORRECT   The snow clumped on the trees**.** Many branches snapped under its weight.

Using Commas in a Series

Sometimes, a sentence lists a number of single words or groups of words. When three or more of these items are listed, the list is called a **series.** Separate the items in a series with commas.

> Use commas to separate three or more words, phrases, or clauses in a **series.**

A comma follows each of the items except the last one in a series. The conjunction *and* or *or* is added after the last comma.

SERIES OF WORDS   The desert animals included camels**,** toads**,** gerbils**,** and insects.

SERIES OF PHRASES   The treasure map directed them over the dunes**,** into the oasis**,** and past the palm tree.

There are two exceptions to this rule. If each item except the last one in a series is followed by a conjunction, do not use commas. Also, do not use a comma to separate groups of words that are considered to be one item.

EXAMPLES   I visited castles and museums and forts.

Every table in the diner was set with a knife and fork**,** a cup and saucer**,** and salt and pepper.

See Practice 13.2B

Using Commas Between Adjectives

Sometimes, two or more adjectives are placed before the noun they describe.

Use commas to separate adjectives of equal rank.

There are two ways to tell whether adjectives in a sentence are of equal rank:

- If the word *and* can be placed between the adjectives without changing the meaning, the adjectives are of equal rank.

- If the order of the adjectives can be changed, they are of equal rank.

EXAMPLE A smooth, round stone was cupped in her hand.

(*A smooth and round stone* does not change the sentence's meaning. *A round, smooth stone* also does not change the meaning.)

Do not use commas to separate adjectives that must appear in a specific order.

Do not use a comma if adding *and* or changing the order of the adjectives would result in a sentence that makes no sense.

INCORRECT It will take three and brief hours to reach the park.

INCORRECT It will take brief three hours to reach the park.

CORRECT It will take three brief hours to reach the park.

Do not use a comma to separate the last adjective in a series from the noun it modifies.

INCORRECT A large, gentle, camel stood by the road.

CORRECT A large, gentle camel stood by the road.

See Practice 13.2C
See Practice 13.2D

PRACTICE 13.2A > Using Commas in Compound Sentences

Read the sentences. Rewrite each sentence, adding commas where they are needed.

EXAMPLE   Julie will meet us at the field and she will bring the soccer ball.

ANSWER   *Julie will meet us at the field, and she will bring the soccer ball.*

1. I don't know how to skate but I can learn.

2. Angela wants to go to the store but she has to stay home.

3. Mom and Dad fixed dinner and my sister and I washed the dishes.

4. We will have to get up at dawn for we must start early.

5. Joseph won't be here Monday nor will he be here Tuesday.

6. Tony and Chen went to a movie but Michelle went to a concert.

7. You could paint the fence now or you could wait until later.

8. I wanted to go yet something held me back.

9. I have to do my work so I'll see you later.

10. We need to fix this bike or I won't be in the race.

PRACTICE 13.2B > Using Commas in a Series

Read the sentences. Rewrite each sentence, adding commas as needed.

EXAMPLE   She looked under the desk behind the dresser and in the closet.

ANSWER   *She looked under the desk, behind the dresser, and in the closet.*

11. I had a sandwich milk and an apple for lunch.

12. Florence Rome and Venice are cities in Italy.

13. At the museum I like the mummies dinosaurs fossils and old jewelry.

14. I wrote the letter folded it and mailed it.

15. Mom could not decide whether she wanted pears peaches or grapes.

16. Justin prepared the soil planted the seeds and watered the garden.

17. The menu offered macaroni and cheese salad and spaghetti with meatballs.

18. Our dog ran across the lawn through the gate and into the street.

19. My sister used flowers grasses and ferns in the arrangement.

20. This year I'm taking math Spanish English science and history.

SPEAKING APPLICATION

With a partner, take turns reading the sentences in Practice 13.2A and 13.2B. Use a pause in your speaking to show where the commas belong. Discuss whether natural pauses in speaking might help you remember where commas are needed in compound sentences and in series.

WRITING APPLICATION

Write three sentences about preparing for a party. Include series of tasks, supplies, and food you would want. Use commas correctly in each series. Then, use a comma in a compound sentence that tells what you hope the party will be like.

| PRACTICE 13.2C | Using Commas Between Adjectives |

Read the sentences. Rewrite the sentences, adding commas where necessary. If no comma is needed, write *correct*.

EXAMPLE   That large heavy book is an atlas

ANSWER   *That large, heavy book is an atlas.*

1. Rows of healthy tall sunflowers filled the field.

2. The little Boston terrier ran up to the fence.

3. Australia's wild rugged scenery is fascinating.

4. I need a small gift box.

5. This wet rich land is good for growing rice.

6. The new music teacher seems very young.

7. Arizona's hot dry climate appeals to many people.

8. The sunset offered bright beautiful colors.

9. There are just four short blocks until we reach home.

10. The deep cold lake looked refreshing.

| PRACTICE 13.2D | Proofreading Sentences for Commas |

Read the sentences. Rewrite each sentence, adding commas where they are needed.

EXAMPLE   We need flour milk lettuce, and fruit.

ANSWER   *We need flour, milk, lettuce, and fruit.*

11. The days are getting longer but the air is still cold.

12. This bright hard stone is a diamond.

13. The gardener mowed the grass watered the flowers and pulled the weeds.

14. Mom and Dad went out to dinner and we stayed home.

15. Do you like spicy hot food?

16. The menu listed sandwiches salads and soups.

17. We can go to the library or we can study here.

18. The rich heavy fabric hung in loose folds.

19. The excited fans jumped up cheered and clapped.

20. The team won this game so they can go to the finals.

SPEAKING APPLICATION

With a partner, pick two sentences from Practice 13.2C that needed to be fixed and two that were correct. Read the sentences aloud, reversing the order of the adjectives. Talk about how you can tell when a group of adjectives doesn't need commas.

WRITING APPLICATION

Write a brief description of someplace you have visited. Include at least two different instances in which commas are needed, such as in a compound sentence and between adjectives.

Using Commas After Introductory Words, Phrases, and Clauses

When a sentence begins with an introductory word, phrase, or other structures, that word or phrase is usually separated from the rest of the sentence by a comma.

> **Use a comma after most introductory words, phrases, or dependent clauses.**

13.2.7 RULE

KINDS OF INTRODUCTORY MATERIAL	
Introductory Word	Hey, give me your camera quickly before the kangaroo moves.
	Pete, please bring me my shoes and socks.
	Well, I certainly didn't expect that to happen.
	Tomi, where are you?
Introductory Phrase	To conserve water, some plants drop their leaves.
	With Mark gone, Jake didn't know how he would get home.
	In the center of the city, you will see many skyscrapers.
	To visit Japan, you need a passport.
Introductory Adverbial Clause	Although the alarm had gone off, the police arrived too late.
	When the mice got into the garage, they ate the birdseed.
	When the home team entered the stadium, the crowd loudly cheered every player.

When a prepositional phrase of only two words begins a sentence, a comma is not absolutely necessary.

EXAMPLES   At night we heard the crickets.

                 In July we go to the lake.

See Practice 13.2E   For hours she patiently waited for the plane.

Using Commas With Parenthetical Expressions

A **parenthetical expression** is a word or phrase that is not essential to the meaning of the sentence. These words or phrases generally add extra information to the basic sentence.

RULE 13.2.8

> Use commas to set off **parenthetical expressions** from the rest of the sentence.

A parenthetical expression in the middle of a sentence needs two commas. A parenthetical expression at the end of a sentence needs only one.

KINDS OF PARENTHETICAL EXPRESSIONS	
Names of People Being Addressed	Listen carefully, Lucinda, while I explain. Don't be late, Randy.
Certain Adverbs	The sand dune, therefore, is several meters higher. Your answer is incorrect, however.
Common Expressions	They believe in her ability, of course. She was not given enough credit, in my opinion.
Contrasting Expressions	The decision should be mine, not yours. These flowers, not those, are ready to be picked.

See Practice 13.2F
See Practice 13.2G

Using Commas With Nonessential Expressions

To determine when a phrase or clause should be set off with commas, decide whether the phrase or clause is **essential** or **nonessential** to the meaning of the sentence. Nonessential expressions can be left out without changing the meaning of the sentence.

Use commas to set off **nonessential** expressions from the main clause. Do not set off **essential** material with commas.

13.2.9 RULE

Appositives and Appositive Phrases
Appositives are often set off with commas, but only when their meaning is not essential to the sentence. In the first example below, the appositive *the 1943 movie* is not set off with commas because it clarifies which movie is being discussed.

ESSENTIAL   The 1943 movie *Sahara* takes place in North Africa.

NONESSENTIAL   *Sahara*, a 1943 movie, takes place in North Africa.

Participial Phrases
Like appositives, participial phrases are set off with commas when their meaning is nonessential. In the first example below, *waiting in the van* is essential because it tells which man is the guide.

ESSENTIAL   The man waiting in the van is our guide.

NONESSENTIAL   Pat, waiting in the van, asked us to hurry.

Adjectival Clauses
Adjectival clauses, too, are set off with commas only if they are nonessential. In the second example below, *who could lead us to the playing field* is nonessential because it adds information about Darius. The main clause in the sentence is about people cheering, not about what Darius can do.

ESSENTIAL   We need someone who can lead us to the playing field.

NONESSENTIAL   We cheered enthusiastically for Darius, who could lead us to the playing field.

See Practice 13.2H

Using Commas After Introductory Words, Phrases, or Clauses

Read the sentences. Rewrite each sentence, adding the comma needed after the introductory word, phrase, or clause.

EXAMPLE   If you are done with the book put it back.

ANSWER   *If you are done with the book, put it back.*

1. No I do not think we have any left.

2. After you finish eating you may go outside.

3. Jerome are you going to the library?

4. With just two days left we had to work faster on our project.

5. My that was a big yawn.

6. Whether or not he is here we are leaving.

7. Well I'm not sure that's why he's going.

8. In the sequel to the movie there were even more special effects.

9. Sherry tell us about your voice lessons.

10. Even though we were late we still got in.

Proofreading a Passage for Commas

Read the paragraph. Rewrite the paragraph, adding commas where they are needed.

EXAMPLE   To earn some money during the summer I decided to make and sell necklaces. Well sometimes events surprise you.

ANSWER   *To earn some money during the summer, I decided to make and sell necklaces. Well, sometimes events surprise you.*

When I first started this project I thought it would last one summer. I wanted to buy beads make necklaces and sell them at craft fairs. Well it was a lot of work. I bought hundreds of beads and I began stringing them. The beads were red blue gold silver and green. Some were metal but others were glass or stone. Although I liked all the different kinds of beads the blue glass beads were among my favorites. I made forty necklaces that first summer but I could have sold more. Once I started I could not stop. It has now been three years and I am still making and selling necklaces.

SPEAKING APPLICATION

With a partner, read this sentence aloud: *In the new book I found a story about spiders.* Discuss where the comma should go and why a comma would help someone reading the sentence.

WRITING APPLICATION

Write three sentences about activities you do in school or at home. Start each sentence with an introductory word, phrase, or clause that requires a comma.

PRACTICE 13.2G Using Commas With
Parenthetical Expressions

Read the sentences. Rewrite each sentence,
adding commas as needed to set off parenthetical
expressions.

EXAMPLE   That play will be I think a success.

ANSWER   *That play will be, I think, a
success.*

1. Do you think Tyler that you would like to go?

2. The information however is out of date.

3. I wanted red not purple.

4. When you arrive Manny let me know.

5. She thinks she is right of course.

6. That is a blue jay not a robin.

7. The outcome therefore can be predicted.

8. Well Anita what do you think?

9. I wanted fruit not yogurt.

10. You will need to clean up the mess however.

PRACTICE 13.2H Using Commas With
Nonessential Expressions

Read the sentences. Rewrite the sentences,
adding commas where necessary. If a sentence
is punctuated correctly, write *correct*.

EXAMPLE   My brother staring at his feet
mumbled an apology.

ANSWER   *My brother, staring at his feet,
mumbled an apology.*

11. George Washington our first president took
his oath of office on April 30, 1789.

12. The wallaby and the kangaroo carry their
young in pouches.

13. Our guide standing on the hilltop waved to
us to follow.

14. The phone a wonderful invention really
changed communication.

15. The 1893 World's Fair was held in Chicago.

16. The Komodo dragon the world's largest lizard
is found in Indonesia.

17. The man handing out papers is our teacher.

18. That table a real antique was made by my
great-grandfather.

19. My sister standing on tiptoe could just reach
the bottom shelf.

20. Seeing a dentist regularly is important.

SPEAKING APPLICATION

With a partner, act as if you are trying out for
a play and the sentences in Practice 13.2G are
your lines. Take turns reading the lines aloud.
Talk about how hard it would be to read a
script with no punctuation.

WRITING APPLICATION

Rewrite three of the correct sentences in
Practice 13.2H so that they need commas.
You may rearrange words or add words of
your own so that the sentences now require
commas.

Using Commas With Dates and Geographical Names

Dates usually have several parts, including months, days, and years. Commas prevent dates from being unclear.

RULE 13.2.10

> When a date is made up of three parts, use a comma after each item, except in the case of a month followed by a day.

Notice in the examples that commas are not used to set off a month followed by a numeral standing for a day. Commas are used when both the month and the date are used as an appositive to rename a day of the week.

EXAMPLES   On July 12, 1979, Aunt Mei arrived in this country with just a few possessions.

Tuesday, March 18, was carefully circled on his calendar.

When a date contains only a month and a year, commas are unnecessary.

EXAMPLES   I will graduate in June 2010.

Most of the storms we experienced in March 2011 dropped a lot of snow.

RULE 13.2.11

> When a geographical name is made up of a city and a state, use a comma after each item.

EXAMPLES   They lived in Marietta, Georgia, for several years and then moved to Sarasota, Florida.

Mari went to Santa Fe, New Mexico, to visit the many art galleries in the area.

See Practice 13.2l

Using Commas in Numbers

Numbers of one hundred or less and numbers made up of two words (for example, *three thousand*) are generally spelled out in words. Other large numbers (for example, 8,463) are written in numerals. Commas make large numbers easier to read.

> **With large numbers of more than three digits, count from the right and add a comma to the left of every third digit to separate it from every fourth digit.**

EXAMPLES

2,532 bricks

749,000 birds

a population of 1,806,421

> **Use commas with three or more numbers written in a series.**

EXAMPLES

Read pages 123, 124, and 125 carefully.

The groups originally had 12, 14, and 25 members.

> **Do not use a comma with ZIP Codes, telephone numbers, page numbers, years, serial numbers, or house numbers.**

ZIP CODE	14878
TELEPHONE NUMBER	(607) 555-1328
PAGE NUMBER	on page 1817
YEAR	the year 2010
SERIAL NUMBER	402 36 4113
HOUSE NUMBER	1801 Houston Street

See Practice 13.2J

PRACTICE 13.2I > Using Commas in Dates and Geographical Names

Read the sentences. Rewrite each sentence, adding commas where they are needed.

EXAMPLE   On June 21 1788 the United States Constitution went into effect.

ANSWER   *On June 21, 1788, the United States Constitution went into effect.*

1. Friday March 12 is the date of our meeting.

2. St. Augustine Florida is the oldest city in the United States.

3. Mr. and Mrs. Sanchez were married on November 12 1988.

4. We visited Philadelphia Pennsylvania.

5. On July 20 1969 American astronauts first set foot on the moon.

6. We met on Tuesday November 5 in Boston Massachusetts.

7. The Wright brothers made their historic flight on December 17 1903.

8. Austin Texas was named for Stephen Austin.

9. On Wednesday February 24 we will be moving to Denver Colorado.

10. It is almost two thousand miles from Atlanta Georgia to Los Angeles California.

PRACTICE 13.2J > Using Commas in Numbers

Read the items. Rewrite each item, adding commas where needed. If no commas are needed, write *correct*.

EXAMPLE   1874 miles

ANSWER   *1,874 miles*

11. 2142 hours

12. a population of 4709875

13. 1629 West Street

14. 1945580 seconds

15. ZIP Code 07960

16. 295943 minutes

17. 24321 days

18. page 1024

19. 397000 trees

20. the year 1993

WRITING APPLICATION

Write three sentences with dates and place names. You may use places or dates that have meaning for you or any dates or places. Be sure to use commas correctly.

WRITING APPLICATION

Write one sentence that contains a number that requires a comma. Then, write one sentence with a number that does not require a comma.

Using Commas With Addresses and in Letters

Commas are also used in addresses, salutations of friendly letters, and closings of friendly or business letters.

> **Use a comma after each item in an address made up of two or more parts.**

13.2.15 RULE

In the following example, commas are placed after the name, street, and city. There is no comma between the state and the ZIP Code.

EXAMPLE   She is writing to Helen Till, 1402 Cray Street, Carey, Ohio 43316.

Fewer commas are needed when an address is written in a letter or on an envelope.

EXAMPLE   Maxwell Hunnicutt
54 Monmouth Avenue
Dallas, Texas 75243

> **Use a comma after the salutation in a personal letter and after the closing in all letters.**

13.2.16 RULE

See Practice 13.2K
See Practice 13.2L

SALUTATION   Dear Shawn,   CLOSING   Sincerely,

Using Commas With Direct Quotations

Commas are also used to separate **direct quotations** from other phrases in a sentence.

> **Use commas to set off a direct quotation from the rest of a sentence.**

13.2.17 RULE

EXAMPLES   Bret said, "Hold the door open."

"I can't, " Lorna replied, "because my arms are full."

PRACTICE 13.2K ▸ Using Commas in Addresses and Letters

Read the items. Rewrite each item, adding commas where needed. If no commas are needed, write *correct*.

EXAMPLE   Dear Grandmother

ANSWER   *Dear Grandmother,*

1. 52 Hampton Road

2. With love

3. Dear Janice

4. Santa Barbara, California 93103

5. Yours truly

6. He is writing to Ellen Green 1219 Main Street Wheeling Illinois 60090.

7. Dearest Daddy

8. Sincerely

9. 846 Howland Drive

10. James Paige
    479 Ashton Court
    Richmond VA 23173

PRACTICE 13.2L ▸ Revising a Letter by Adding Commas

Read the letter. Rewrite the letter, adding commas where necessary.

EXAMPLE   I like to use pencils pens and markers when I draw.

ANSWER   *I like to use pencils, pens, and markers when I draw.*

Mr. Xavier Martinez Jr.
48 Felton Way
Houston Texas 77020

October 16 2010

Dear Mr. Martinez

Thank you for the pens markers ribbons and glue. They were exactly what I needed and now I can start my project. Mr. Smith my art teacher loves my ideas for the project. Thanks to you I shall be able to do it right.

Your friend

Carlos

SPEAKING APPLICATION

With a partner, talk about the people to whom you might write a personal letter. Look at the examples in Practice 13.2K, and come up with some salutations of your own—ones that would be followed by a comma.

WRITING APPLICATION

Write a sentence that includes your full address, using proper punctuation. Then, write your address as if you were addressing an envelope.

13.3 Semicolons and Colons

The **semicolon (;)** joins related **independent clauses** and signals a longer pause than a comma. The **colon (:)** is used to introduce lists of items and in other special situations.

Using Semicolons to Join Independent Clauses

Sometimes two **independent clauses** are so closely connected in meaning that they make up a single sentence, rather than two separate sentences.

> Use a **semicolon** to join related **independent clauses** that are not joined by the conjunctions *and, or, nor, for, but, so,* or *yet.*

13.3.1 RULE

INDEPENDENT CLAUSES	The fire began with a tossed match. Jamestown was burned in 1676.
CLAUSES JOINED BY SEMICOLONS	The fire began with a tossed match; all of Jamestown began to burn.

A semicolon should be used only when there is a close relationship between the two independent clauses. If the clauses are not very closely related, they should be written as separate sentences with a period or another end mark to separate them or joined with a coordinating conjunction.

Note that when a sentence contains three or more related independent clauses, they may still be separated with semicolons.

EXAMPLES	The birds vanished; the sky grew dark; the little pond was still. Marie won the backstroke events; Tamara won the freestyle events; Jana won the butterfly.

Using Semicolons to Join Clauses Separated by Conjunctive
Adverbs or Transitional Expressions

Semicolons help writers show how their ideas connect.

Use a semicolon to join independent clauses separated by
either a **conjunctive adverb** or a **transitional expression.**

CONJUNCTIVE
ADVERBS
*also, besides, consequently, first, furthermore, however,
indeed, instead, moreover, nevertheless, otherwise,
second, then, therefore, thus*

TRANSITIONAL
EXPRESSIONS
*as a result, at this time, for instance, in fact, on the other
hand, that is*

EXAMPLE
We were impressed with Martin's knowledge of
history ; **indeed** , he was very well informed about
colonization.

Remember to place a comma after the conjunctive adverb or
transitional expression. The comma sets off the conjunctive
adverb or transitional expression, which acts as an introductory
expression to the second clause.

Using Semicolons to Avoid Confusion

Sometimes, to avoid confusion, semicolons are used to separate
items in a series.

Consider the use of semicolons to avoid confusion when items
in a series already contain commas.

Place a semicolon after all but the last complete item in a series.

EXAMPLES
The fans , cheering ; the band , playing loudly ; and
the cheerleaders , yelling , helped inspire the team to
play well.

Three important dates in this year are April 30 , 2011 ;
May 10 , 2011 ; and June 7 , 2011.

See Practice 13.3A

Using Colons

The **colon (:)** is used to introduce lists of items and in certain special situations.

Use a colon after an independent clause to introduce a list of items.

RULE 13.3.4

The independent clause that comes before the colon often includes the words *the following, as follows, these,* or *those.*

EXAMPLE Some orchids grow only in the following countries: Costa Rica, Peru, and Brazil.

Remember to use commas to separate three or more items in a series.

Do not use a colon after a verb or a preposition.

RULE 13.3.5

INCORRECT Veronica always orders: soup, salad, and dessert.

CORRECT Veronica always orders soup, salad, and dessert.

Use a colon to introduce a long or formal quotation.

RULE 13.3.6

EXAMPLE The sign clearly states the law: "Dogs within the park boundaries must be leashed at all times."

SOME ADDITIONAL USES OF THE COLON	
To Separate Hours and Minutes	3:15 P.M. 9:45 A.M.
After the Salutation in a Business Letter	Gentlemen: Dear Miss Robinson:
On Warnings and Labels	Warning: The ice is thin. Note: Shake before using. Caution: Children Playing

See Practice 13.3B

PRACTICE 13.3A ▸ Using Semicolons

Read the sentences. Rewrite each sentence, adding any necessary semicolons.

EXAMPLE   We won the game everyone celebrated the victory.

ANSWER   *We won the game; everyone celebrated the victory.*

1. I watched television last night consequently, I did not do very well on today's test.

2. My dad is a great cook I really like his food.

3. I was really tired the bed was soft I fell asleep quickly.

4. We were sorry to lose the tree on the other hand, the garden gets more sun.

5. The book was good I liked the characters the plot was exciting.

6. There were total lunar eclipses on March 3, 2007 September 11, 2007 and February 21, 2008.

7. Dad wants to watch a movie Mom wants to watch a travel program.

8. We have one dog, a mutt one cat, a stray and two birds, a canary and a parakeet.

9. There is really nothing on television besides, I need to do some work on my project.

10. The swimming race started the swimmers dove into the pool.

PRACTICE 13.3B ▸ Using Colons

Read the items. Rewrite each item, adding any necessary colons. If no colon is needed, write *correct*.

EXAMPLE   I need the following for school, pencils, notebooks, paper, and a ruler.

ANSWER   *I need the following for school: pencils, notebooks, paper, and a ruler.*

11. Can you bring me some bread, peanut butter, and milk?

12. Here's what goes in the fruit basket, peaches, apples, and grapes.

13. I wrote a note to Grandmother, thanking her for my birthday present.

14. The judge made the rules clear "You must not discuss this case with anyone."

15. We ordered soup, salad, chicken, and potatoes.

16. Warning Keep away from heat.

17. Mom and Dad want to get started by 900 A.M.

18. I want a bike; my brother wants a scooter.

19. Dear Sir

20. Put this on the shopping list, milk, carrots, lettuce, bread.

WRITING APPLICATION

Write three sentences about a big event you saw or heard about. Use semicolons in at least two different ways in your description of the event.

WRITING APPLICATION

Write two sentences that require colons. One sentence should include a list, and one should include a time of day.

13.4 Quotation Marks, Underlining, and Italics

Quotation marks (" ") set off direct quotations, dialogue, and certain types of titles. Other types of titles may be **underlined** or set in *italics,* a slanted type style.

Using Quotation Marks With Quotations

Quotation marks identify the spoken or written words of others. A **direct quotation** represents a person's exact speech or thoughts. An **indirect quotation** reports the general meaning of what a person said or thought.

Both types of quotations are acceptable when you write. Direct quotations, however, generally result in a livelier writing style.

> Direct quotations should be enclosed in quotation marks.

13.4.1 RULE

EXAMPLES   Kate said, "Williamsburg had the first theater."

             "Where is the key?" asked Caroline.

> Indirect quotations do not require quotation marks.

13.4.2 RULE

EXAMPLES   Margo said that she would take the dog out.

             Don wondered why the president hadn't called him with the results of the election.

Using Direct Quotations With Introductory, Concluding, and Interrupting Expressions

Commas help you set off introductory information so that your reader understands who is speaking. Writers usually identify a speaker by using words such as *he asked* or *she said* with a quotation. These expressions can introduce, conclude, or interrupt a quotation.

Direct Quotations With Introductory Expressions

Commas are also used to indicate where **introductory expressions** end.

> When an **introductory expression** precedes a direct quotation, place a comma after the introductory expression, and write the quotation as a full sentence.

EXAMPLES
> The guide explained **,** **"**All historical buildings should be treated with respect.**"**
>
> The coach warned **,** **"**If you don't show up for every practice, you won't play in the game.**"**

If an introductory expression is very long, set it off with a colon instead of a comma.

EXAMPLE
> At the end of the practice, Sarah spoke of her dreams **:** **"**I hope to be able to run the final leg in the relay by my senior year.**"**

Direct Quotations With Concluding Expressions

Direct quotations may sometimes end with **concluding expressions.**

> When a **concluding expression** follows a direct quotation, write the quotation as a full sentence ending with a comma, question mark, or exclamation mark inside the quotation mark. Then, write the concluding expression. Be sure to use end punctuation to close the sentence.

Concluding expressions are not complete sentences; therefore, they do not begin with capital letters. Notice also that the closing quotation marks are always placed outside the punctuation at the end of direct quotations.

EXAMPLE
> **"**Could you show us one of the houses **?** **"** interrupted Barney.

Direct Quotations With Interrupting Expressions

You may use an interrupting expression in a direct quotation, which is also called a **divided quotation.** Interrupting expressions help writers clarify who is speaking and can also break up a long quotation.

> When the direct quotation of one sentence is interrupted, end the first part of the direct quotation with a comma and a quotation mark. Place a comma after the **interrupting expression,** and then use a new set of quotation marks to enclose the rest of the quotation.

RULE
13.4.5

EXAMPLES   "What would we have done," asked Corrina, "if we had lived in the path of the tornado?"

"If you get a new bicycle," my mother warned, "you'll have to remember to lock it up."

Do not capitalize the first word of the second part of the sentence.

> When two sentences in a direct quotation are separated by an **interrupting expression,** end the first quoted sentence with a comma, question mark, or exclamation mark and a quotation mark. Place a period after the interrupter, and then write the second quoted sentence as a full quotation.

RULE
13.4.6

EXAMPLES   "Did you see those rooms?" asked Mark. "Can you imagine having such a large house?"

"I know I had my keys when I left," Jane said. "They are probably in my pocket."

See Practice 13.4A
See Practice 13.4B

PRACTICE 13.4A > **Using Quotation Marks With Direct Quotations**

Read the sentences. If the sentence contains a direct quotation, write *D*. If it contains an indirect quotation, write *I*. Then, rewrite each sentence that contains a direct quotation, adding the quotation marks where needed.

EXAMPLE   Marlene said, I do not know anything about fishing.

ANSWER   *D — Marlene said, "I do not know anything about fishing."*

1. Jason asked me if I knew the answer.

2. We went to the movies last night, Brianna said.

3. Rafael told us he knew a shortcut.

4. We heard from Mr. Smith that there would be no more watermelon at the fruit stand.

5. Just wait, Gail said, and I will get it for you.

6. I need help with math, my brother said.

7. Justine shared with everyone her hope that she would get a new bike.

8. Mrs. Johnson yelled, Look out for that car!

9. There is room for one more, Mr. Chen said.

10. I was told that the Taylor twins were going to compete in the race.

PRACTICE 13.4B > **Punctuating With Expressions**

Read the sentences. Rewrite each sentence, adding commas and quotation marks where needed.

EXAMPLE   We will have a visit from a firefighter the teacher announced.

ANSWER   *"We will have a visit from a firefighter," the teacher announced.*

11. Coach said We will get in an extra practice this week.

12. A tadpole grows into a frog Miss Jenner explained.

13. When will my car be ready? Dad asked.

14. Hold still Mom said or your haircut will not be right.

15. The old fisherman said There are no trout in these waters now.

16. I prefer country music said Melanie.

17. The principal announced There will be a fire drill today.

18. Let me go with you my brother begged.

19. Why Anna asked would you not tell me about the party?

20. Dad shouted Turn that music down.

SPEAKING APPLICATION

With a partner, read aloud two or three of the direct quotations in Practice 13.4A and 13.4B. Only read the part that should be within quotations. Talk about why using quotation marks makes sense.

WRITING APPLICATION

Write a four-sentence conversation between two friends who are planning to go to lunch together. Vary the location of the expressions within the sentences. Make sure to use proper punctuation for quotations and expressions.

Using Quotation Marks With Other Punctuation Marks

You have seen that a comma or period used with a direct quotation goes inside the final quotation mark. In some cases, however, end marks should be placed outside of quotation marks.

> Always place a comma or a period inside the final quotation mark.

RULE 13.4.7

EXAMPLES "This area needs work," Mrs. Finch said.

She added, "It looks like you're living in a junkyard, not a room."

> Place a **question mark** or an **exclamation mark** inside the final quotation mark if the end mark is part of the quotation. Do not use an additional end mark outside the quotation marks.

RULE 13.4.8

EXAMPLES Joe asked, "Didn't I already clean that room?"

Salvatore, his brother, protested loudly, "I helped rebuild three buildings last summer!"

> Place a **question mark** or **exclamation mark** outside the final quotation mark if the end mark is part of the entire sentence, not part of the quotation.

RULE 13.4.9

See Practice 13.4C

EXAMPLES Did he say, "You have wasted your entire day"?

I can't believe he said, "I like taking tests."!

Using Single Quotation Marks for Quotations Within Quotations

Double quotation marks are used to enclose the main quotation. The rules for using commas and end marks with **single quotation marks (' ')** are the same as they are with double quotation marks.

Single quotation marks are used to separate a quote that appears inside of another quotation.

Use **single quotation marks** to set off a quotation within a quotation.

EXAMPLES "Did you mean to say, 'That's my cat,' or 'That's my hat'?" Lori asked.

Steve said, "I thought I heard him yell, 'Fire!' That's why I ran out the door."

Punctuating Explanatory Material Within Quotes

Sometimes it is necessary to add information to a quotation that explains the quote more fully. In that case, brackets tell your reader which information came from the original speaker and which came from someone else. (See Section 13.7 for more information on brackets.)

Use brackets to enclose an explanation located within a quotation to show that the explanation is not part of the original quotation.

EXAMPLE The mayor said, "This bridge is more than a link between two communities [Oceanville and Riverton]."

"We [the students of Center High School] wish to express our support of the student council." See Practice 13.4D

258 **Punctuation**

PRACTICE 13.4C Using Quotation Marks With Other Punctuation Marks

Read the sentences. Decide whether the missing punctuation goes inside or outside the quotation marks. Then, rewrite the sentences, adding the proper punctuation for quotations.

EXAMPLE   "When will he arrive" she asked.

ANSWER   *"When will he arrive?" she asked.*

1. "Come right home afterwards" Dad instructed.
2. Our teacher asked, "Who knows where the equator is"
3. Didn't Mom say, "No television tonight"
4. I heard Lacie scream, "Look out"
5. "Do you like this bowl" the potter asked.
6. I can't believe you said, "No"
7. "Bread is easy to make" Wally stated.
8. Coach said, "We have a good chance of getting to the finals"
9. What did you mean by, "It's all over now"
10. "Ouch" cried Jill. "Did you have to pull the bandage off so fast"

PRACTICE 13.4D Punctuating Quotations Within Quotations and Explanatory Material

Read the sentences. Rewrite each sentence, adding single quotation marks or brackets where needed.

EXAMPLE   Marcia asked, "Do you remember when he said, I'll take care of it?"

ANSWER   *Marcia asked, "Do you remember when he said, 'I'll take care of it'?"*

11. The teacher said, "Please say to the museum guide, Thank you for the tour."
12. "Did she say, I can help you?" Mom asked.
13. Coach shouted, "Next person who says, We can't win, does twenty push-ups"
14. "Did he say, I'm too busy?" Maria asked.
15. "He declared, It's so good to see you, when he saw me at the concert," Betsy said.
16. "Did he say, I found my keys?" Carlos asked.
17. Denise related, "Nikki asked, What am I doing here?"
18. "Which subject biology or math do you like better?" the teacher wondered.
19. Ravi reported, "My father said, You should have known better."
20. Stella demanded, "Why did she say, I wouldn't go anywhere with you?"

WRITING APPLICATION

Write three sentences of a conversation you might have with someone at school. Be sure to use quotation marks and other punctuation marks correctly.

WRITING APPLICATION

Write an imagined conversation of three or four lines between two people discussing a book or movie. Each "speaker" should quote something or someone within his or her own statement.

Using Quotation Marks for Dialogue

A conversation between two or more people is called a **dialogue.**
Adding dialogue makes your writing lively because it brings
different points of view into your work. It makes your work sound
like speech, so dialogue makes your reader feel involved in the
scene you describe.

> When you are writing a **dialogue,** indent to begin a new
> paragraph with each change of speaker. Also be sure to add
> quotation marks around a speaker's words. When a new
> speaker is quoted, be sure to indicate the change to your reader
> by adding information that identifies the new speaker.

EXAMPLE

"Will you be going with us on the family trip
again this summer?" Noreen asked her cousin.

Gwen hesitated before answering. "I'm afraid
so. My parents think I enjoy the experience of
traveling with our whole family."

"You fooled me, too," Noreen replied.
"Maybe the trip will be better this year. I think
we're going to places that have large parks. If
we're lucky, we might even be able to go on a
few rides."

"Well, at least it can't be any worse," sighed
Gwen. "On the last trip, we waited in line for one
hour at three different historic homes in one day!"

"I remember those lines," said Noreen.
"Didn't you get sunburned while we were
waiting?"

Notice that each sentence is punctuated according to the rules
discussed earlier in this section.

See Practice 13.4E
See Practice 13.4F

> **PRACTICE 13.4E** **Using Quotation Marks in Dialogue**

Read the dialogue. Then, rewrite the dialogue. Use proper spacing for quotations and create additional paragraphs where needed. Be sure to use quotation marks and other punctuation correctly.

EXAMPLE   What do you know about the United States Constitution the teacher asked. Keisha answered, I think the U.S. Constitution explains how our government works.

ANSWER   *"What do you know about the U.S. Constitution?" the teacher asked.*

Keisha answered, "I think the U.S. Constitution explains how our government works."

Attention please the teacher said. We will be starting a new project today. Will this be something we do at home Melanie asked. No the teacher responded we will be able to work on it during class time. Is it a history project asked Francisco. Yes it will be about the U.S. Constitution the teacher said. Sarah blurted out I know the opening We the people of the United States . . . Very good, Sarah the teacher said. Now turn to page 498 in your books, and let's read about the writing of the Constitution. Those writers must have been really smart Noah added.

> **PRACTICE 13.4F** **Revising Dialogue for Punctuation and Paragraphs**

Read the dialogue. Then, rewrite the dialogue. Add quotation marks and other punctuation, and begin new paragraphs where needed.

EXAMPLE   I asked my mom Is there a new museum exhibit? My mom answered Yes, there's one that just opened last week.

ANSWER   *I asked my mom, "Is there a new museum exhibit?"*

My mom answered, "Yes, there's one that just opened last week."

The museum has a new exhibit the guide told us. It's on the third floor, if you'd like to see it. What is in the exhibit my brother asked. It has Egyptian mummies the guide said and wooden carvings from their tombs. There are also photographs of where the mummies were found. Great! I love anything from Egypt said my dad. So do I added my mom. I chimed in That makes three of us, so let's go. There is an elevator on the left the guide advised. Thank you for telling us about this my dad said, heading for the elevator.

SPEAKING APPLICATION

With a partner, take turns reading a few lines of your corrected dialogues. Talk about why you think there is a new paragraph each time the speaker changes.

WRITING APPLICATION

Write a brief dialogue between two friends planning their weekend. Write enough dialogue so that you have to start a new paragraph at least twice. Be sure you punctuate the dialogue correctly.

Using Quotation Marks in Titles

Quotation marks are generally used to set off the titles of shorter works.

> Use **quotation marks** to enclose the titles of short written works and around the title of a work that is mentioned as part of a collection.

WRITTEN WORKS THAT USE QUOTATION MARKS	
Title of a Short Story	"The Gift of the Magi"
Chapter From a Book	"The Test Is in the Tasting" from *No-Work Garden Book*
Title of a Short Poem	"Lucy"
Title of an Article	"How to Build a Birdhouse"
Title Mentioned as Part of a Collection	"Uncle Vanya" in *Eight Great Comedies*

> Use **quotation marks** around the titles of episodes in a television or radio series, songs, and parts of a long musical composition.

ARTISTIC WORKS THAT USE QUOTATION MARKS	
Title of an Episode	"The Nile" from *Cousteau Odyssey*
Title of a Song	"The Best Things in Life Are Free"
Title of a Part of a Long Musical Work	"The Storm" from the *William Tell Overture*

Using Underlining and Italics in Titles

Underlining and **italics** help make titles and other special words and names stand out in your writing. Underlining is used only in handwritten or typewritten material. In printed material, italic (slanted) print is used instead of underlining.

UNDERLINING   <u>The Hobbit</u>   ITALICS   *The Hobbit*

Underline or *italicize* the titles of long written works and publications that are published as a single work.

RULE 13.4.15

WRITTEN WORKS THAT ARE UNDERLINED OR ITALICIZED	
Title of a Book or Play	*War and Peace, Guys and Dolls*
Title of a Long Poem	*Paradise Lost*
Title of a Magazine or Newspaper	*People, The New York Times*

Underline or *italicize* the titles of movies, television and radio series, long works of music, and art.

RULE 13.4.16

ARTISTIC WORKS THAT ARE UNDERLINED OR ITALICIZED	
Title of a Movie	*Notting Hill*
Title of a Television Series	*Friends*
Title of a Long Work of Music	*Surprise Symphony*
Title of a Music Album	*TJ's Greatest Hits*
Title of a Painting	*Mona Lisa*
Title of a Sculpture	*The Thinker*

Underline or *italicize* the names of individual air, sea, and spacecraft.

RULE 13.4.17

EXAMPLES   *Gemini 5*   the *Titanic*

Underline or *italicize* words and letters used as names for themselves and foreign words.

RULE 13.4.18

EXAMPLES   How do you spell *alligator*?

A Japanese *obento* is a homemade, boxed lunch.

See Practice 13.4G
See Practice 13.4H

PRACTICE 13.4G **Underlining Titles, Names, and Words**

Read the sentences. Rewrite each sentence, underlining titles, names, and words where needed. You can use italics if you are typing your answers.

EXAMPLE   I read Charlotte's Web in fifth grade.

ANSWER   *I read <u>Charlotte's Web</u> in fifth grade.*

1. Have you seen the movie Beauty and the Beast?

2. I just read all seven books of The Chronicles of Narnia.

3. My dad reads The New York Times.

4. What does duplex mean?

5. I enjoy watching Best Westerns on television.

6. The play Romeo and Juliet always makes me cry.

7. Write noun and pronoun at the top of the page.

8. I learned that merci is French for "thank you."

9. Did you like the book Waltzing Australia?

10. The aircraft carrier Intrepid is now a floating museum.

PRACTICE 13.4H **Using Underlining and Quotation Marks**

Read the sentences. Rewrite each sentence, enclosing the titles in quotation marks or underlining them. You can use italics if you are typing your answers.

EXAMPLE   I read the article The Titanic.

ANSWER   *I read the article "The <u>Titanic</u>."*

11. Robert Frost's short poem Out, Out is in this collection.

12. I read the article The Spice Is Right in North Shore Magazine.

13. My brother loves the short story The Tell-Tale Heart.

14. Isn't the song Ol' Man River from the musical Showboat?

15. Did you see the Live and Learn episode of the television show Happy Days?

16. The encyclopedia has a biographical article titled Stephen F. Austin.

17. I love the song Yesterday.

18. Aquarium is my favorite part of the musical work The Carnival of the Animals.

19. Did you ever hear the song What a Wonderful World by Louis Armstrong?

20. I think Just You Wait is the funniest song in the musical My Fair Lady.

SPEAKING APPLICATION

With a partner, say a few sentences that need underlining or quotation marks. Discuss which seems to draw more attention to a word or title, the underlining or the quotation marks.

WRITING APPLICATION

Write three sentences recommending things a friend should read or see. Use proper mechanics, including underlining, or italics if typing, and quotation marks.

13.5 Hyphens

Hyphens (-) are used to combine words and to show a connection between the syllables of words that are broken at the ends of lines.

Using Hyphens in Numbers

Hyphens are used to join compound numbers and fractions.

> **Use a hyphen when you write two-word numbers from twenty-one through ninety-nine.**

EXAMPLES seventy - eight   thirty - five

> **Use a hyphen when you use a fraction as an adjective but not when you use a fraction as a noun.**

ADJECTIVE This glass is two - thirds full.

NOUN Two thirds of the members were present.

Using Hyphens for Prefixes and Suffixes

Many words with common prefixes are no longer hyphenated. The following prefixes are often used before proper nouns: *ante-, anti-, post-, pre-, pro-,* and *un-.* Check a dictionary when you are unsure about using a hyphen.

> **Use a hyphen after a prefix that is followed by a proper noun or adjective.**

EXAMPLES pre - Columbian   mid - August

> **Use a hyphen in words with the prefixes *all-, ex-,* and *self-* and the suffix *-elect.***

EXAMPLES all - American   mayor - elect

Using Hyphens in Compound Words

Compound words are two or more words that must be read together to create a single idea.

> Use a **hyphen** to connect two or more nouns that are used as one compound word, unless the dictionary gives a different spelling.

EXAMPLES   great-grandfather   secretary-treasurer

Using Hyphens With Compound Modifiers

Hyphens help your reader group information properly.

> Use a hyphen to connect a **compound modifier** that comes before a noun. Do not use a hyphen with a compound modifier that includes a word ending in *-ly* or in a compound proper adjective.

EXAMPLE   Cass was a big-hearted dog-lover.

INCORRECT   clearly-written text   West-Indian music

CORRECT   clearly written text   West Indian music

A hyphen is not necessary when a compound modifier follows the noun it describes.

MODIFIER
BEFORE NOUN   They traveled in well-equipped wagons.

MODIFIER
AFTER NOUN   They traveled in wagons that were well equipped.

However, if a dictionary spells a word with a hyphen, the word must always be hyphenated, even when it follows a noun.

EXAMPLE   The design is up-to-date.

See Practice 13.5A
See Practice 13.5B

PRACTICE 13.5A Using Hyphens in Numbers and Words

Read the following phrases. Then, write each phrase, adding hyphens where needed.

EXAMPLE   thirty five days

ANSWER   *thirty-five days*

1. the country's president elect
2. forty three pages
3. Mom's father in law
4. mid December party
5. three fourths full
6. seventy four miles
7. half price sale
8. self appointed leader
9. twenty one years ago
10. hard earned reward

PRACTICE 13.5B Proofreading for Hyphens

Read the sentences. Rewrite each sentence, adding hyphens where needed.

EXAMPLE   We are the all district champions.

ANSWER   *We are the all-district champions.*

11. There were thirty two sets of clearly written instructions.
12. The project is three fourths done.
13. My dad's brother in law is an ex Marine.
14. The pro freedom rally was attended by the governor elect.
15. He bought twenty eight high definition DVDs.
16. Prices are one third off at the mid June sale.
17. It was the top selling movie of the summer.
18. I inherited my great grandmother's well worn cookbook.
19. It's another forty seven miles to the highway exit.
20. Please complete the self evaluation form.

SPEAKING APPLICATION

Go through the lesson and create your own example for each rule of hyphen usage.

WRITING APPLICATION

Write three or four sentences about a trip to a store or shopping mall. Use three different applications of hyphens (numbers, compound words, compound modifiers, and so on) in your sentences.

Practice   267

Using Hyphens at the Ends of Lines

Hyphens serve a useful purpose when they are used to divide words at the ends of lines. They should not, however, be used more often than is necessary because they can make reading feel choppy.

Avoid dividing words at the end of a line whenever possible. If a word must be divided, always divide it between syllables.

EXAMPLE   The soccer coach's pep talks are usually quite unin-
spiring and short.

Check a dictionary if you are unsure how a word is divided into syllables. Looking up the word *seriously*, for example, you would find that its syllables are *se-ri-ous-ly*.

A hyphen used to divide a word should never be placed at the beginning of the second line. It must be placed at the end of the first line.

INCORRECT   Knock down this par
-tition.

CORRECT   Knock down this par-
tition.

Using Hyphens Correctly to Divide Words

One-syllable words cannot be divided.

Do *not* divide one-syllable words even if they seem long or sound like words with two syllables.

INCORRECT   sch-ool   bru-ised   thro-ugh

CORRECT   school   bruised   through

13.5.10 RULE

Do *not* divide a word so that a single letter stands alone.

INCORRECT	a-mid	ver-y	o-kay
CORRECT	amid	very	okay

Also avoid placing *-ed* at the beginning of a new line.

INCORRECT   The school awards ceremony was halted by the blackout.

CORRECT   The school awards ceremony was
halted by the blackout.

13.5.11 RULE

Avoid dividing proper nouns or proper adjectives.

INCORRECT	Eliza-beth	Ger-man
CORRECT	Elizabeth	German

13.5.12 RULE

Divide a hyphenated word only immediately following the existing hyphen.

INCORRECT   It was a post-sea-
son soccer game.

See Practice 13.5C
See Practice 13.5D

CORRECT   It was a post-
season soccer game.

PRACTICE 13.5C **Using Hyphens to Divide Words**

Read the following words. Rewrite each word, and draw vertical lines between syllables that can be divided at the end of a line. Do nothing to words that cannot be divided.

EXAMPLE   responsible

ANSWER   *re | spon | si | ble*

1. insurance
2. wary
3. tasteless
4. forward
5. English
6. uninteresting
7. parted
8. Audrey
9. stunned
10. undoubtedly

PRACTICE 13.5D **Using Hyphens in Words in Sentences**

Read the sentences. If a word has been divided correctly, write *correct*. If not, rewrite the sentence, dividing the word correctly or writing it as one word if it cannot be divided.

EXAMPLE   I was absent from today's Fre-nch class.

ANSWER   *I was absent from today's French class.*

11. The animal in that story is imag-inary.
12. The news showed the pro-Amer-ican forces winning.
13. I thought you would be bringing Kar-en with you.
14. It had rained for days, but it stopped even-tually.
15. Losing the game to a rival school end-ed our hopes of a district championship.
16. All the musicians were on hand for the pre-concert rehearsal.
17. Everyone gasped when I fell, but I was o-kay.
18. For the potluck, Christina had bro-ught a casserole.
19. The math book said we should multi-ply first, and then divide.
20. On the map, we located the Rus-sian city of Moscow.

WRITING APPLICATION

Think of long words you know, and write them down. Then, divide them into syllables. Check a dictionary if necessary.

WRITING APPLICATION

Choose three of the rules for dividing words with hyphens. For each of the rules, write a sentence that puts the rule into practice.

13.6 Apostrophes

The **apostrophe (')** is used to show possession or ownership. It is also used in shortened forms of words called contractions. In a contraction, the apostrophe marks the place where letters have been omitted.

Using Apostrophes With Possessive Nouns

Apostrophes are used with nouns to show ownership or possession.

> **Add an apostrophe and -s to show the possessive case of most singular nouns and plural nouns that do not end in -s or -es.**

13.6.1 RULE

EXAMPLES   My dog's favorite toy is a ball.

The men's trek up Mt. Everest was strenuous.

Even when a singular noun already ends in -s, you can usually add an apostrophe and -s to show possession.

EXAMPLE   An iris's colors are often purple and white.

In classical or ancient names that end in -s, it is common to omit the final -s to make pronunciation easier.

EXAMPLE   Odysseus' voyages were dangerous.

> **Add an apostrophe to show the possessive case of plural nouns ending in -s or -es. Do not add an -s.**

13.6.2 RULE

EXAMPLE   The bears' den is hidden in the mountains.

Add an apostrophe and *-s* (or just an apostrophe if the word is a plural ending in *-s*) to the last word of a compound noun to form the possessive.

EXAMPLES   the Girl Scouts **'** cookie sale

my sister-in-law **'**s car

See Practice 13.6A

Using Apostrophes With Pronouns

Both indefinite and personal pronouns can show possession.

Use an apostrophe and *-s* with indefinite pronouns to show possession.

EXAMPLES   another **'**s preference   nobody else **'**s business

Do not use an apostrophe with possessive personal pronouns.

POSSESSIVE PERSONAL PRONOUNS		
	SINGULAR	PLURAL
First Person	I, me, my, mine	we, us, our, ours
Second Person	you, your, yours	you, your, yours
Third Person	he, him, his; she, her, hers; it, its	they, them; their, theirs

Some of these pronouns act as adjectives.

EXAMPLES   The spider caught a fly in its web.

Our house is for sale.

Others act as subjects, objects, and subject complements.

EXAMPLES   Mine is the yellow crayon.

Someone broke yours.

See Practice 13.6B

Using Apostrophes With Contractions

Contractions are used in informal speech and writing, especially in dialogue because they create the sound of speech.

> Use an **apostrophe** in a **contraction** to show where one or more letters have been omitted.

COMMON CONTRACTIONS		
Verb + *not*	is not = isn't	cannot = can't
Noun or Pronoun + *will*	I will = I'll	we will = we'll
Noun or Pronoun + *be*	you are = you're	Andy is = Andy's
Noun or Pronoun + *would*	she would = she'd	who would = who'd

> Avoid using contractions in formal speech and writing.

Contractions may be used in dialogue and in informal speech and writing, but they should be avoided in formal usage.

INFORMAL WRITING   What's the solution?

FORMAL WRITING   What is the solution?

Using Apostrophes to Create Plurals

Do not use an apostrophe to form plurals, except in specific instances.

> Use an **apostrophe** and -*s* to create the plural form of a letter, numeral, or a word used as a name for itself.

See Practice 13.6C
See Practice 13.6D

EXAMPLES   Mind your *p*'s and *q*'s.

Remember your *please*'s, please.

Using Apostrophes to Show Ownership

Read each phrase. Write the possessive form of each item.

EXAMPLE   the book of Charles

ANSWER   *Charles's book*

1. the collar of the shirt
2. the project of the student
3. the songs of the children
4. the decision of the judges
5. the mooing of the cow
6. the suggestion of my mom
7. the bicycle of Marcus
8. the efforts of the women
9. the chirping of the sparrows
10. the pocket watch of my great-grandfather

Using Apostrophes With Pronouns

Read the sentences. If all pronouns in a sentence are used correctly, write *correct*. If one or more pronouns are used incorrectly, rewrite the sentence correctly.

EXAMPLE   We found everyone else's name tag, but not her's.

ANSWER   *We found everyone else's name tag, but not* **hers.**

11. We respected one anothers privacy.
12. Celeste wanted her books, not his.
13. We have ours, but where are their's?
14. This must be someone's ruler.
15. If it is not hers, whose is it?
16. Is this anybodys lunch?
17. One must be careful where one puts one's glasses.
18. It is your turn now, but soon it will be our's.
19. Josh asked if his' bicycle had been found.
20. Everyone was asked if the watch was his or hers.

SPEAKING APPLICATION

With a partner, take turns reading aloud the possessive forms you wrote in Practice 13.6A. Compare the ending sound of *judges/judges'* and *Marcus/Marcus's*. Talk about how what you hear matches what you wrote.

WRITING APPLICATION

Write three or four sentences about things you and your friends or family own. Use possessive forms of a singular noun, a plural noun, and at least one pronoun.

PRACTICE 13.6C **Using Apostrophes in Contractions**

Read the sentences. Each sentence contains a word group that can be written as a contraction. Write the contractions.

EXAMPLE   I cannot find my hat.

ANSWER   *can't*

1. Who is coming to dinner?
2. I will get the front door.
3. More homework is not what I wanted.
4. She would like to see you.
5. You are welcome to come in.
6. Stella is planning on coming to the play.
7. The twins are not able to do that.
8. He would make a good catcher.
9. That will be enough.
10. Do not slam the door.

PRACTICE 13.6D **Proofreading for Apostrophes**

Read the sentences. Rewrite each sentence, adding apostrophes where needed.

EXAMPLE   I cant be responsible for my youngest brothers behavior.

ANSWER   *I can't be responsible for my youngest brother's behavior.*

11. Everyones supposed to bring his or her own lunch.
12. Well try to come, but its not easy to get away from work.
13. Id like to introduce you to Cindy, Bonnies cousin.
14. Theyll bring sandwiches if youll bring salad.
15. Is this someones jacket?
16. My moms new sweater isnt the right size.
17. The paint in the doctors office wasnt dry.
18. If youre in this area, stop by.
19. Hed fix Tylers bike if he could, but its too badly damaged.
20. They wont let us open Seans mail.

SPEAKING APPLICATION

With a partner, read aloud the original form of two or three sentences in Practice 13.6C. Then, say the sentence aloud, using contractions. Talk about which form sounds more like regular speech.

WRITING APPLICATION

Write two sentences about interesting people you know or have read about. Use both possessives (nouns or pronouns) and contractions in your sentences.

13.7 Parentheses and Brackets

Parentheses and **brackets** enclose explanations or other information that may be omitted from the rest of the sentence without changing its basic meaning or construction.

Parentheses

Parentheses are used to separate information from the rest of a sentence or paragraph.

Use a parenthesis to set off explanations or other information that is loosely related to the rest of the sentence.

EXAMPLE   During the Civil War **(**1861–1865**)** he helped soldiers stay in touch with their families.

A parenthetical sentence within another sentence should not begin with a capital letter unless the parenthetical sentence begins with a word that should be capitalized.

EXAMPLE   Tickets for the play **(**click here to see the schedule**)** go on sale Thursday.

A parenthetical sentence within another sentence may end with a question mark or exclamation mark if applicable, but it should not end with a period.

INCORRECT   Tickets for the play **(**click here to see the schedule**.)** go on sale Thursday**.**

CORRECT   Tickets for the play **(**they haven't posted the schedule yet**!)** go on sale Thursday**.**

Parenthetical Sentences That Stand on Their Own
Parenthetical sentences add information to another sentence or
a paragraph.

> **A parenthetical sentence** that stands on its own should
> begin with a capital letter and end with an end mark before the
> closing parenthesis.

RULE 13.7.4

EXAMPLE   Tickets for the play go on sale Thursday.
(Click here to see the schedule.)

Brackets

Brackets have one major use: to enclose a word or words into a
quotation that were not spoken by the person or source that is
quoted.

> Use **brackets** to enclose an explanation located within a quote
> to show that the explanation is not part of the original quote.

RULE 13.7.5

EXAMPLE   An eyewitness to the inaugural celebration said,
"I have not seen such excitement since the last
landslide victory [in 2008]."

> Use **brackets** to enclose an explanation that is located within
> parenthetical text.

RULE 13.7.6

See Practice 13.7A
See Practice 13.7B

EXAMPLE   George Washington (the first president of the
United States [1789–1797]) was known for his
leadership and honesty.

PRACTICE 13.7A Using Parentheses and Brackets

Read the sentences. Rewrite each sentence, adding parentheses or brackets where appropriate.

EXAMPLE Alaska was once called Seward's Folly. It was bought by William Seward.

ANSWER *Alaska was once called Seward's Folly. (It was bought by William Seward.)*

1. The United States entered the war World War II in 1941.

2. Georgia O'Keeffe 1887–1986 was an American artist.

3. My mom said, "I remember my last year of school 1989 as if it were yesterday."

4. Clara Barton's organization the American Red Cross was started in 1881.

5. Franklin Roosevelt was president of the United States for longer than anyone else four terms 1933–1945.

6. Our teacher said, "By that time two o'clock you should all be finished."

PRACTICE 13.7B Proofreading for Parentheses and Brackets

Read the sentences. Rewrite each sentence, adding parentheses or brackets where appropriate.

EXAMPLE We picked fourteen baskets of apples count them! at the orchard.

ANSWER *We picked fourteen baskets of apples (count them!) at the orchard.*

7. Two presidents, John Quincy Adams 1825–1829 and George W. Bush 2001–2009, were sons of earlier presidents.

8. Emily Dickinson 1830–1886 wrote, "Tell all the Truth but tell it slant."

9. Wolfgang Amadeus Mozart wrote more than 40 symphonies in his short life 36 years.

10. "The actor's Lee Upshaw portrayal of a loner will both move and upset you," wrote the movie reviewer.

11. Benjamin Franklin 1706–1790 offered this tip for a good life: "Early to bed and early to rise, makes a man healthy, wealthy, and wise still good advice today."

12. During World War II 1941–1945, many American women Rosie the riveter, for example took the place of men in factories.

SPEAKING APPLICATION

With a partner, take turns reading sentences in Practice 13.7B, leaving out the parts in parentheses or brackets. Discuss what taking out the information does to the sentence.

WRITING APPLICATION

Write three sentences about a period of history or a historical event that interests you. Use parentheses or brackets to add information to your sentences.

13.8 Ellipses and Dashes

An **ellipsis** (. . .) shows where words have been omitted from a quoted passage. It can also mark a pause in dialogue. A **dash** (—) shows a strong, sudden break in thought or speech.

Using the Ellipsis

An **ellipsis** consists of three evenly spaced periods, or ellipsis points, in a row. There is a space before the first ellipsis point, between ellipsis points, and after the last ellipsis point. The plural form of the word *ellipsis* is *ellipses*.

> Use an **ellipsis** to show where words have been omitted from a quoted passage. Including an ellipsis shows the reader that the writer has chosen to omit some information.

13.8.1 RULE

QUOTED PASSAGE	"Four score and seven years ago our fathers brought forth on this continent a new nation conceived in liberty and dedicated to the proposition that all men are created equal." –Abraham Lincoln, *The Gettysburg Address,* November 19, 1863

QUOTED PASSAGE WITH WORDS OMITTED	"Fourscore and seven years ago our fathers brought forth . . . a new nation . . . dedicated to the proposition that all men are created equal."

Ellipses in Advertising

Ellipses are commonly used in ads for movies and other media. When you see an ellipsis in an ad, think about what might have been omitted. You might want to find the original review because the ad might be giving a different impression from what the reviewer intended.

ORIGINAL REVIEW	"It is amazing that anyone would think this was a love story."

AD WORDING	" . . . amazing . . . love story"

RULE 13.8.2 Use an **ellipsis** to mark a pause in a dialogue or speech.

EXAMPLE "But, in a larger sense, we can not dedicate ... we can not consecrate ... we can not hallow ... this ground."

RULE 13.8.3 It is not necessary to use an **ellipsis** to show an omission at the beginning of material you are quoting. However, if you choose to omit any words *within* material you quote, you must use an ellipsis to show where information has been omitted.

UNNECESSARY " ... Now we are engaged in a great civil war, testing whether that nation, or any nation, so conceived and so dedicated, can long endure."

CORRECT "Now we are engaged in a great civil war, testing whether that nation, or any nation so conceived and so dedicated, can long endure."

RULE 13.8.4 Use an **ellipsis** to show an omission, pause, or interruption in the middle of a sentence.

EXAMPLE "But, in a larger sense, we cannot dedicate ... this ground."

RULE 13.8.5 Use an **ellipsis** and an end mark to show an omission or a pause at the end of a sentence.

EXAMPLE "I wonder how we are ever going to finish this project. Maybe we could ... ."

If you omit words from a source you are quoting, omit the punctuation that accompanies the words unless it is correct in your sentence.

See Practice 13.8A

Dashes

Like commas and parentheses, **dashes** separate certain words, phrases, or clauses from the rest of the sentence or paragraph. Dashes, however, signal a stronger, more sudden interruption in thought or speech than commas or parentheses. A dash may also take the place of certain words before an explanation.

> **Use a dash to show a strong, sudden break in thought or speech.**

RULE 13.8.6

EXAMPLE   I can't believe how many free throws my brother missed — I don't even want to think about it!

If the interrupting expression is in the middle of the sentence, use a dash on either side of it to set it off from the rest of the sentence.

EXAMPLE   I read an article — I forget who wrote it — about renewable energy sources.

> **Use a dash in place of *in other words, namely,* or *that is* before an explanation.**

RULE 13.8.7

EXAMPLES   Ruth plays ball for one purpose — to win.

To see his jersey hanging from the rafters — this was his greatest dream.

Dashes can also be used to set off nonessential appositives or modifiers.

EXAMPLE   The selfish player — a "star" who is more concerned with his own glory — will not pass the ball.

See Practice 13.8B

PRACTICE 13.8A **Using Ellipses**

Read the sentences. For each sentence, tell whether ellipses (or ellipsis points) are used to indicate a *pause,* an *interruption,* or an *omission.*

EXAMPLE   Mom said, "Don't go . . . ," but I didn't hear the rest.

ANSWER   *omission*

1. I'm not sure . . . perhaps we should wait.

2. "We hold these truths to be self-evident . . . endowed . . . with certain . . . rights . . . ."

3. "I pledge allegiance to the flag . . . and to the republic . . . ."

4. Gosh . . . I . . . uh . . . I'm not sure.

5. This is important . . . really important . . . maybe the most important thing I've ever done.

6. I love the song that begins, "O beautiful for spacious skies . . . ."

7. Wait . . . please . . . I can't do this alone.

8. I heard, "Read page 280 through . . . ," but I didn't catch the final page number.

9. "We the people of the United States . . . do ordain and establish this Constitution . . . ."

10. I was slowing down . . . and I wasn't sure . . . I would make it.

PRACTICE 13.8B **Using Dashes**

Read the sentences. Rewrite each sentence, adding dashes where they are needed.

EXAMPLE   It was important so important, in fact, I couldn't let anything stop me.

ANSWER   *It was important—so important, in fact, I couldn't let anything stop me.*

11. The United States had a mission to be the first to the moon.

12. I would like to show you my collection of hey, what was that?

13. We went to a store I don't remember which one to look for a dress.

14. I have one purpose in life to become a scientist.

15. See you tomorrow oh, don't forget to take the handouts.

16. He needed a job even a part-time one for the money.

17. We saw a movie I don't remember the title on Saturday.

18. We'll talk after class you do have time, don't you? about our plans.

19. She came for a reason to clean up this place.

20. When we go and we will go you can come with us.

WRITING APPLICATION

Write two sentences in which you either pause or have an omission. Use ellipses to show the pauses or omissions.

WRITING APPLICATION

Write two sentences about your weekend. In each sentence, use a dash to show a sudden break in thought or speech or to replace *in other words, namely,* or *that is* before an explanation.

CAPITALIZATION

Knowing which words to capitalize will make the content of your writing clearer and easier to read.

CHAPTER 14

WRITE GUY *Jeff Anderson, M.Ed.*

WHAT DO YOU NOTICE?

Search for examples of capitalization as you zoom in on sentences from the story "Stray" by Cynthia Rylant.

MENTOR TEXT

> In January, a puppy wandered onto the property of Mr. Amos Laccy and his wife, Mamie, and their daughter, Doris.

Now, ask yourself the following questions:

- Why is the word *January* capitalized?
- Why does the abbreviation *Mr.* begin with a capital letter?

The word *January* is capitalized because it names a specific period of time. The abbreviation *Mr.* begins with a capital letter because it stands for *Mister,* which is part of Amos Lacey's name. *Mamie* and *Doris* are capitalized because they are also proper nouns that name specific people.

Grammar for Writers Knowing the rules of capitalization helps a writer signal the start of a new sentence and present specific people, places, things, and events accurately. Be sure to check your writing for words that need to be capitalized.

What is the capital of Texas?

I'm sure it's the letter *T.*

14.1 Using Capitalization

Capital letters are used for the first words in all sentences and in many quotations. They are also used for the word *I*, whatever its position in a sentence.

The Word *I*

RULE 14.1.1

> The pronoun *I* is always capitalized.

EXAMPLE **I** worked for two years as a clerk before **I** received a promotion.

Sentences

One of the most common uses of a capital letter is to signal the beginning of a sentence. The first word in a sentence must begin with a capital letter.

RULE 14.1.2

> Capitalize the first word in **declarative, interrogative, imperative,** and **exclamatory** sentences.

DECLARATIVE **S**trong gusts of wind made it dangerous to drive on the bridge.

INTERROGATIVE **W**ho found the clue leading to the suspect's arrest?

IMPERATIVE **T**hink carefully before you decide.

EXCLAMATORY **W**hat an amazing coincidence this is!

Sometimes only part of a sentence is written. The rest of the sentence is understood. In these cases, a capital is still needed for the first word.

EXAMPLES **W**hen? **W**hy not? **C**ertainly!

Quotations

A capital letter also signals the first word in a **direct quotation,** a person's exact words.

> **Capitalize the first word in a quotation if the quotation is a complete sentence.**

RULE 14.1.3

EXAMPLES   Several people shouted, "**S**top the bus!"

"**S**he really wants to see that movie," Arlene confided.

My father asked, "**W**hen will you be home?"

> **When a quotation consists of one complete sentence in two parts, only capitalize the first part of the quotation.**

RULE 14.1.4

EXAMPLES   "**H**ow much longer," asked Brian, "**i**s this speech going to last?"

"**T**he Hawaiian islands, " she said, "**h**ave so many birds and flowers that are not found anywhere else."

> **If a quotation contains more than one sentence, the first word of each sentence begins with a capital.**

RULE 14.1.5

EXAMPLES   "**P**lease distribute these maps to everyone," said the director. "**T**hey show the location of each exhibit."

"**R**emember to bring your calculator," said the teacher. "**Y**ou will need it for class tomorrow."

See Practice 14.1A
See Practice 14.1B

PRACTICE 14.1A > **Supplying Capitalization**

Read the sentences. Rewrite each sentence, adding the missing capitals.

EXAMPLE   he and i went to the movies.

ANSWER   *He* and *I* went to the movies.

1. Mom said, "you need to finish that."

2. are we going to get there soon?

3. Jason asked, "when will we arrive?"

4. the container read, "do not shake. do not place near heat."

5. who? what? when was this decided?

6. the Schmidts said i could use their pool.

7. when i was younger, i wanted to be a doctor.

8. the teacher announced, "there will be no test next week."

9. Dad said, "we might go, but it depends on the weather."

10. my sister warned, "if i were you, i would keep quiet."

PRACTICE 14.1B > **Proofreading for Capitalization**

Read the sentences. Rewrite each sentence, adding the missing capitals.

EXAMPLE   "is it true?" i asked.

ANSWER   *"Is* it true?" *I* asked.

11. when was your father born?

12. the coach said, "this is a new season. everything is different."

13. Sarah and i went to the park.

14. the health reporter wrote, "avoid sugar."

15. mom asked, "could you bring me two eggs?"

16. "when i was young," my grandma said, "we didn't have a television."

17. steel made it possible to build skyscrapers.

18. Greg said, "when i'm older, i want to go to college."

19. the librarian said, "please keep your voices down."

20. "what is that?" he wondered.

WRITING APPLICATION

Write three sentences: one declarative, one interrogative, and one exclamatory. Use capitalization correctly in each sentence.

WRITING APPLICATION

Write three sentences about your family or friends. Include a quotation in each sentence. Use capitalization correctly.

Using Capitalization for Proper Nouns

An important use of capital letters is to show that a word is a **proper noun.** Proper nouns name specific people, places, or things.

> Capitalize all **proper nouns**.

14.1.6 RULE

EXAMPLES   **J**oe **S**mith

           Joshua **T**ree **N**ational **M**onument

           Tappan **Z**ee **B**ridge

           Eiffel **T**ower

Names of People

> Capitalize each part of a person's full name, including initials.

14.1.7 RULE

EXAMPLES   **M**argaret **R**ose **W**indsor

           Brian **J**. **T**. **J**ameson

           L. **T**. **C**ornwall

When a last name has two parts and the first part is *Mac, Mc, O',* or *St.,* the second part of the last name must also be capitalized.

EXAMPLES   **M**ac**I**ntosh

           Mc**M**urphy

           O'**C**onnor

           St. **J**ohn

See Practice 14.1C

For two-part last names that do not begin with *Mac, Mc, O',* or *St.,* the capitalization varies. Check a reliable source, such as a biographical dictionary, for the correct spelling.

Geographical Places

Any specific geographical location listed on a map should be capitalized.

RULE
14.1.8

Capitalize geographical names.

GEOGRAPHICAL NAMES	
Streets	Warren Street, Carlton Avenue, Interstate 10
Cities	Baltimore, London, Memphis, Tokyo
States	Arizona, Florida, Hawaii, Idaho
Nations	Italy, Canada, Kenya, France, Peru, South Korea
Continents	North America, Asia, Africa, Antarctica
Deserts	Sahara, Negev, Mojave
Mountains	Mount Everest, Rocky Mountains
Regions	Great Plains, Appalachian Highlands, Northwest
Islands	Canary Islands, Fiji Islands
Rivers	Mississippi River, Amazon River
Lakes	Lake Michigan, Great Salt Lake, Lake Erie
Bays	Hudson Bay, Baffin Bay, Biscayne Bay
Seas	Black Sea, Mediterranean Sea, North Sea
Oceans	Atlantic Ocean, Arctic Ocean

Regions and Map Directions

Names of regions, such as the South and the Northeast, are capitalized because they refer to a specific geographical location. Map directions that do not refer to a specific geographical location are not capitalized.

RULE
14.1.9

Do not capitalize compass points, such as north, southwest, or east, when they simply refer to direction.

REGION   We spent our vacation in the Southeast.

DIRECTION   Our boat headed north on the river.

Capitalize the names of specific events, periods of time, and documents.

14.1.10 RULE

The following chart contains examples of events, periods of time, and documents that require capitalization.

SPECIFIC EVENTS AND TIMES	
Historical Periods	Age of Enlightenment, Middle Ages, the Renaissance
Historical Events	World War II, Boston Tea Party, Battle of Lexington
Documents	Bill of Rights, Treaty of Paris, Declaration of Independence
Days	Wednesday, Saturday
Months	December, October
Holidays	Thanksgiving, Labor Day
Religious Days	Christmas, Passover, Ramadan
Special Events	Fiddlers' Convention, Boston Marathon, Super Bowl

Names of Seasons
The names of the seasons are an exception to this rule. Even though they name a specific period of time, the seasons of the year are not capitalized unless they are part of a title or an event name.

SEASONS   The most popular color this **f**all is rust.

The students traveled in the **s**ummer.

TITLE   During a hot **s**ummer, I read *The Long Winter.*

EVENT   It was so cold at the **S**pring Festival it felt like **w**inter.

See Practice 14.1D

PRACTICE 14.1C ▷ Using Capitalization for Names of People

Read the sentences. Write each name, adding the missing capitals.

EXAMPLE   Our third president was thomas jefferson.

ANSWER   *Thomas Jefferson*

1. ulysses s. grant was a general during the Civil War.

2. The inventor who perfected a machine to cut wheat was cyrus mccormick.

3. Do you like the writing of j.r.r. tolkien?

4. orville and wilbur wright built and flew the first successful airplane.

5. sandra day o'connor was the first woman appointed to the Supreme Court.

6. The first African American secretary of state was colin powell.

7. President ronald reagan helped bring the Cold War to an end.

8. harriet beecher stowe wrote a book that helped Americans realize the cruelty of slavery.

9. *Winnie the Pooh* was written by a. a. milne.

10. When pocahontas married john rolfe, it helped create peace in Jamestown.

PRACTICE 14.1D ▷ Using Capitalization for Geographical Places, Specific Events, and Time Periods

Read the sentences. Write the name of each geographical place, specific event, and time period, adding the missing capitals.

EXAMPLE   The mississippi river is the longest river in the united states.

ANSWER   *Mississippi River, United States*

11. My aunt visited london, england, in June.

12. We are studying about south america.

13. Have you ever visited the blue ridge mountains?

14. The nile river flows through egypt.

15. The weather in the northeast can be cold.

16. I enjoyed studying renaissance paintings at the museum.

17. The pacific ocean is the largest ocean.

18. We drove across pennsylvania, ohio, and indiana.

19. The gobi desert covers the southern part of mongolia.

20. Last year, my favorite baseball team won the world series.

WRITING APPLICATION

Write three sentences about people who played a part in the history of the United States. Be sure to capitalize the names correctly.

WRITING APPLICATION

Write three sentences about places you have studied or would like to visit. Be sure to capitalize geographical names correctly.

Specific Groups

Proper nouns that name specific groups also require capitalization.

> **Capitalize the names of various organizations, government bodies, political parties, and nationalities, as well as the languages spoken by different groups.**

14.1.11
RULE

EXAMPLES   The ambassadors attended the first session of the **A**ustrian **P**arliament.

She delivered a brief address in **J**apanese and received warm applause.

Three **E**agle **S**couts demonstrated search and rescue techniques.

The proper nouns shown in the chart are groups with which many people are familiar. All specific groups, however, must be capitalized, even if they are not well known.

SPECIFIC GROUPS	
Clubs	**K**iwanis **C**lub **R**otary **C**lub
Organizations	**N**ational **G**overnors **A**ssociation **N**ational **O**rganization for **W**omen
Institutions	**M**assachusetts **I**nstitute of **T**echnology **S**mithsonian **I**nstitution
Businesses	**S**imon **C**hemical **C**orporation **F**ido's **F**avorite **P**et **F**oods
Government Bodies	**U**nited **S**tates **C**ongress **S**upreme **C**ourt
Political Parties	**D**emocrats **R**epublican **P**arty
Nationalities	**C**hinese, **G**erman **N**igerian, **I**ranian
Languages	**E**nglish, **S**panish **K**orean, **S**wahili

See Practice 14.1E

Religious References

Use capitals for the names of the religions of the world and certain other words related to religion.

> **Capitalize references to religions, deities, and religious scriptures.**

The following chart presents words related to five of the world's major religions. Next to each religion are examples of some of the related religious words that must be capitalized. Note that the name of each religion is also capitalized.

RELIGIOUS REFERENCES	
Christianity	God, Lord, Father, Holy Spirit, Bible, books of the Bible (Genesis, Deuteronomy, Psalms, and so on)
Judaism	Lord, Father, Prophets, Torah, Talmud, Midrash
Islam	Allah, Prophet, Mohammed, Qur'an
Hinduism	Brahma, Bhagavad Gita, Vedas
Buddhism	Buddha, Mahayana, Hinayana

Note in the following examples, however, that the words *god* and *goddess* in references to mythology are not capitalized. A god's or goddess's name, however, is capitalized.

EXAMPLES   In Roman mythology, the supreme god was Jupiter.

The goddess Juno was the wife of Jupiter and was the goddess of women.

Specific Places and Items

Monuments, memorials, buildings, celestial bodies, awards, the names of specific vehicles, and trademarked products should be capitalized.

> Capitalize the names of specific places and items.

14.1.13 RULE

OTHER SPECIAL PLACES AND ITEMS	
Monuments	Statue of Liberty Washington Monument
Memorials	Winston Churchill Memorial Vietnam Veterans Memorial
Buildings	Houston Museum of Fine Arts Empire State Building the Capitol Building (in Washington, D.C.)
Celestial Bodies (except the moon and sun)	Earth, Milky Way Jupiter, Aries
Awards	Newbery Medal Nobel Peace Prize
Air, Sea, and Space Craft	Spirit of St. Louis Monitor Voyager 2 Metroliner
Trademarked Brands	Krazy Korn Eco-Friendly Cleanser
Names	Zenox Kermit the Frog the Great Houdini

> Capitalize the names of awards.

14.1.14 RULE

Notice that *the* is not capitalized in these examples.

EXAMPLES   the Academy Awards

the Fulbright Scholarship

the Pulitzer Prize

See Practice 14.1F   the Medal of Honor

PRACTICE 14.1E> **Using Capitalization for Groups and Organizations**

Read the sentences. Write each group or organization, adding the missing capitals.

EXAMPLE   My brother joined the boy scouts.

ANSWER   *Boy Scouts*

1. My dad is a member of the american medical association.

2. Do you know who represents you in congress?

3. We flew on capital airlines to California.

4. Our state is divided between democrats and republicans.

5. The north central high school basketball team is one of the best teams in the state.

6. The midwest writers association held a meeting on Tuesday.

7. Both girl scouts and boy scouts were in the parade.

8. He has cuban, russian, and indian neighbors.

9. Instead of a house of representatives, England has a house of commons.

10. Mariano speaks both english and spanish.

PRACTICE 14.1F> **Using Capitalization for Religious References and Specific Items and Places**

Read the sentences. Write each term that should be capitalized, adding the missing capitals.

EXAMPLE   A planet close to earth is mars.

ANSWER   *Earth, Mars*

11. I wanted to visit the washington monument.

12. genesis is the first book in the bible.

13. The museum of science and industry has wonderful displays.

14. In islam, people read the qur'an.

15. The largest of the planets is jupiter.

16. The pulitzer prize is awarded for great writing.

17. The jewish torah makes up part of the christian bible.

18. The holocaust memorial attracts many visitors.

19. The apollo 11 spacecraft landed on the moon on July 20, 1969.

20. In India, there are more hindu temples than buddhist temples.

WRITING APPLICATION

Write two sentences about groups to which you, friends, or family members belong, including clubs, businesses, or schools. Be careful to capitalize correctly.

WRITING APPLICATION

Choose the category that interests you more: religious references or specific places and items. Write three sentences that reflect your knowledge of or interest in any aspect of these categories. Be careful to capitalize correctly.

Using Capitalization for Proper Adjectives

When a proper noun or a form of a proper noun is used to describe another noun, it is called a **proper adjective.** Proper adjectives usually need a capital letter.

> **Capitalize most proper adjectives.**

In the following examples, notice that both proper nouns and proper adjectives are capitalized. Common nouns that are modified by proper adjectives, however, are not capitalized.

PROPER NOUNS	**W**orld **W**ar I
	Canada
PROPER ADJECTIVES	a **W**orld **W**ar I **b**attle
	a **C**anadian **f**lag

The names of some countries and states must be modified to be used as proper adjectives. For example, something from Kenya is Kenyan, someone from Texas is Texan, a chair from Spain is a Spanish chair, and a building in France is a French building.

Brand Names as Adjectives

Trademarked brand names are considered to be proper nouns. If you use a brand name to describe a common noun, the brand name becomes a proper adjective. In this case, capitalize only the proper adjective and not the common noun.

> **Capitalize brand names used as adjectives.**

14.1.16 RULE

PROPER NOUN	**H**ealthy **G**rains
PROPER ADJECTIVE	**H**ealthy **G**rains **c**ereal

See Practice 14.1G

Notice that only the proper adjective *Healthy Grains* is capitalized. The word *cereal* is not capitalized because it is a common noun; it is not part of the trademarked name.

Using Capitalization for Titles of People

A person's title shows his or her or relationship to other people. Whether a title is capitalized often depends on how it is used in a sentence.

Social and Professional Titles
Social and professional titles may be written before a person's name or used alone in place of a person's name.

RULE 14.1.17

> Capitalize the title of a person when the title is followed by the person's name or when it is used in place of a person's name in direct address.

BEFORE A NAME   **D**etective O'Toole and **D**octor Perkins have arrived.

IN DIRECT ADDRESS   Look, **S**ergeant, the fingerprints match!

TITLES OF PEOPLE	
Social	**M**ister, **M**adam or **M**adame, **M**iss, **M**s., **S**ir
Business	**D**octor, **P**rofessor, **S**uperintendent
Religious	**R**everend, **F**ather, **R**abbi, **B**ishop, **S**ister
Military	**P**rivate, **E**nsign, **C**aptain, **G**eneral, **A**dmiral
Government	**P**resident, **S**enator, **R**epresentative, **G**overnor, **M**ayor, **P**rince, **Q**ueen, **K**ing

In most cases, do not capitalize titles that are used alone or that follow a person's name—especially if the title is preceded by the articles *a, an,* or *the*.

EXAMPLES   Samantha Rodgers, the **d**octor on call, will be able to see you.

Tell your **s**enator how you feel about the issue.

My cousin Ralph, who is a **p**rivate in the army, will be home on leave soon.

Government Officials

> Capitalize the titles of government officials when they immediately precede the name of specific officials. If no person is named, these titles should be written in lower case.

14.1.18 RULE

EXAMPLES

President **O**bama will answer questions from reporters after the speech.

The club **p**resident will answer questions after the speech.

Mayor **W**alker will speak to the people about conserving energy.

The **m**ayor of a large city is responsible for energy conservation and planning.

Note: Certain honorary titles are always capitalized, even if the title is not used with a proper name or direct address. These titles include the First Lady of the United States, Speaker of the House of Representatives, Queen Mother of England, and the Prince of Wales.

Titles for Family Relationships

> Capitalize titles showing family relationships when the title is used with the person's name or as the person's name—except when the title comes after a possessive noun or pronoun.

14.1.19 RULE

BEFORE A NAME

We respect **U**ncle Frank's opinion.

IN PLACE OF A NAME

Is **G**randmother going?

AFTER POSSESSIVES

Alan's **f**ather is the team captain.

See Practice 14.1H

Notice that the family title *father* used in the last example is not capitalized because it is used after the possessive word *Alan's*.

PRACTICE 14.1G Using Capitalization for Proper Adjectives

Read the sentences. Write the proper adjectives, adding the correct capitalization.

EXAMPLE   Have you ever been to a french restaurant?

ANSWER   *French*

1. Each morning, they raise the american flag.

2. The soldier talked about a vietnam war battle he fought in.

3. We watched a spanish-language film.

4. I prefer the krazy corn brand of chips.

5. The conference was in the russian capital.

6. He was a world war II hero.

7. The japanese-influenced architecture was lovely.

8. I like chinese food.

9. That book won the newbery medal.

10. Were you on time for your german class?

PRACTICE 14.1H Using Capitalization for Titles of People

Read the sentences. If the title in each sentence is correctly capitalized, write *correct*. If it is not, rewrite the title correctly.

EXAMPLE   I met representative Dan Rutherford at the rally.

ANSWER   *Representative*

11. In England, queen Elizabeth has reigned for more than fifty years.

12. There is a sergeant on duty now.

13. He was talking with miss Jenner and mister Chen.

14. When she fell, we had to rush Juanita to doctor Pradesh's office.

15. We wondered what it was like to be a professor at that college.

16. Both general Patton and admiral Nimitz won important battles during World War II.

17. Look, Senator, they have begun the session.

18. The reverend Joel Sarnoff officiated at the wedding ceremony.

19. The sign on the door said Governor David Johnson.

20. Straighten up, private; no slouching on duty.

WRITING APPLICATION

Write two sentences about places or events in your social studies book. Include in each sentence something that can be modified by a proper adjective.

WRITING APPLICATION

Think of everyone you know, at school, at home, and anywhere else. Write people's names with their titles. Be careful to capitalize titles correctly.

Using Capitalization for Titles of Works

Capital letters are used for the titles of things such as written works, pieces of art, and school courses.

> **Capitalize the first word and all other key words in the titles of books, newspapers, magazines, short stories, poems, plays, movies, songs, and artworks.**

◁ 14.1.20 RULE

Do not capitalize articles (*a, an, the*), prepositions (*of, to*), and conjunctions (*and, but*) that are fewer than four letters long unless they begin a title. Verbs and personal pronouns, no matter how short, are always capitalized in titles.

EXAMPLE   "**O**verdoing **I**t" by Anton Chekhov

> **Capitalize the title of a school course when it is followed by a course number or when it refers to a language. Otherwise, do not capitalize school subjects.**

◁ 14.1.21 RULE

EXAMPLES   **F**rench   **H**istory 420   **A**lgebra II

I have **a**lgebra this morning.

Using Capitalization in Letters

Several parts of friendly and business letters are capitalized.

> **In the heading, capitalize the street, city, state, and the month.**

◁ 14.1.22 RULE

EXAMPLES   **M**ain **S**treet   **N**ewton   **O**hio   **M**ay

> **In the salutation, capitalize the first word, any title, and the name of the person or group mentioned. In the closing, capitalize the first word.**

◁ 14.1.23 RULE

See Practice 14.1I
See Practice 14.1J

SALUTATIONS   **M**y **d**ear **S**usan,   **D**ear **U**ncle **S**teve,

CLOSINGS   **Y**our **f**riend,   **Y**ours **t**ruly,   **L**ove,

PRACTICE 14.1I > **Using Capitalization for Titles of Things**

Read the sentences. Write the titles, adding the correct capitalization.

EXAMPLE   We subscribe to *national geographic* magazine.

ANSWER   *National Geographic*

1. I looked it up in the *encyclopedia international*.
2. Have you read the story "the tortoise and the hare"?
3. We watched the movie *the lion king*.
4. Pearl S. Buck wrote *the good earth*.
5. She performed "the star-spangled banner."
6. Da Vinci's painting *the last supper* is in Italy.
7. My dad reads *the daily express*.
8. I signed up for history 101.
9. My parents saw the play *the merchant of venice*.
10. I like the poem "the man from snowy river."

PRACTICE 14.1J > **Using Capitalization for Titles of Things**

Read the sentences. Rewrite each sentence, adding the missing capitals.

EXAMPLE   After lunch, I will take a quiz in spanish.

ANSWER   *After lunch, I will take a quiz in Spanish.*

11. I signed up for an english class.
12. *The phantom of the opera* is a popular musical.
13. He sang "pennies from heaven."
14. Did you see the movie *cinderella story*?
15. Mark Twain is the author of *the adventures of tom sawyer*.
16. She will be taking german.
17. Rudyard Kipling wrote "the sing-song of old man kangaroo."
18. The *daily herald* is our local paper.
19. Have you ever seen the painting *the potato eaters*?
20. My dad read me the poem "the charge of the light brigade."

WRITING APPLICATION

Write three sentences about the things you like to read. Be careful to capitalize titles correctly.

WRITING APPLICATION

Write a brief paragraph about the types of entertainment available in your area. Think of museums, movies, plays, and concerts, and then name the things you might see in these places or at these events. Be sure to check for correct capitalization.

Using Capitalization in Abbreviations, Acronyms, and Initials

An **abbreviation** is a shortened form of a word or phrase. An **acronym** is an abbreviation of a phrase that takes one or more letters from each word in the phrase being abbreviated.

> In general, capitalize **abbreviations, acronyms,** and **initials** if the words or names they stand for are capitalized.

RULE 14.1.24

INITIALS	**E** . **B** . White
TITLES	**R** ev. Martin Luther King **J** r.
ACADEMIC DEGREES	Mei Yan, **M.D.** , Ben King, **Ph.D.**
ACRONYMS	**NASA** , **UNICEF**

Abbreviations for most units of measurement are not capitalized.

EXAMPLES   **f** t (feet)   **t** sp (teaspoon)

> Capitalize **abbreviations** that appear in addresses.

RULE 14.1.25

Use a two-letter state abbreviation without periods only when the abbreviation is followed by a ZIP Code. Capitalize both letters of the state abbreviation.

EXAMPLE   Austin, **TX** 78701

> Capitalize **acronyms** that stand for proper nouns, such as businesses, government bodies, and organizations.

RULE 14.1.26

Spell out the name of an organization and include its acronym in parentheses the first time you use it. Use only the acronym in later references.

See Practice 14.1K
See Practice 14.1L

EXAMPLE   You may have heard of the Internal Revenue Service (**IRS**). The **IRS** collects federal taxes.

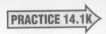 **PRACTICE 14.1K** Using Capitalization for Abbreviations

Read the sentences. Write each abbreviation, adding the missing capitals.

EXAMPLE   Have you seen mt. Rushmore?

ANSWER   *Mt.*

1. I addressed the letter to mr. William Park.

2. Did dr. Hill examine Mark's leg for any broken bones?

3. Benjamin O. Davis jr. organized the Tuskegee Airmen.

4. We visited st. Augustine, Florida.

5. Ben Carson, m.d., is one of the country's leading surgeons.

6. Her address is Cambridge, Ma 01773.

7. According to a Gallup poll, rev. Billy Graham is one of the country's most admired people.

8. The flag that inspired "The Star-Spangled Banner" flew over ft. McHenry.

9. His new address is Los Angeles, ca 90001.

10. Karen Phillips, ph.d., is the new professor in the economics department.

PRACTICE 14.1L Using Capitalization for Initials and Acronyms

Read the sentences. Write the initials and acronyms, adding the missing capitals.

EXAMPLE   The central intelligence agency (cia) gathers and analyzes information.

ANSWER   *Central Intelligence Agency (CIA)*

11. Some great science fiction stories were written by h. g. Wells.

12. I need a map of the usa.

13. He's a member of the cap (civil air patrol).

14. nasa (national aeronautics and space administration) is the government agency for space exploration.

15. The Chicago transit authority (cta) is a city government department.

16. The women's army corps (wac) was active during World War II.

17. The spca (society for the prevention of cruelty to animals) has an important job protecting animals.

18. Many drivers are members of the American automobile association (aaa).

19. Madame c. j. Walker was the first African American woman to become a millionaire.

20. The environmental protection agency (epa) monitors pollution levels.

WRITING APPLICATION

Write a complete address, real or imagined. Include at least three abbreviations in the address. Make sure abbreviations are capitalized correctly.

WRITING APPLICATION

Look up the following acronyms: HUD, VFW, USMC. Write the full names of the organizations.

Cumulative Review Chapters 13–14

PRACTICE 1 ▷ **Using Periods, Question Marks, and Exclamation Marks**

Read the sentences. Then, rewrite the sentences, adding periods, question marks, and exclamation marks where needed.

1. Are you going to the dog show
2. Please help me with the dishes
3. What a wonderful teacher she is
4. Mr Wu lives in Richmond
5. He asked if he could borrow the lawn mower
6. Many people visit the UN each year
7. Keep your hands away from the hot stove
8. Sabrina hopes to make the team Can she
9. Wow How magnificent the eagle looked
10. Will you be joining the book club

PRACTICE 2 ▷ **Using Commas Correctly**

Read the sentences. Then, rewrite the sentences, adding commas where needed. If a sentence is correct as is, write *correct*.

1. Those pants cost a lot but this shirt costs more.
2. Dirt got on my face in my shoe and on the floor.
3. The thick jagged object was a piece of glass.
4. To prevent snoring breathe through your nose.
5. Jack said "Tell me sir what is the problem?"
6. Exactly 3421 people visited on May 3 2009.
7. The manatee a sea mammal swam nearby.
8. Two white pillars held up the porch roof.
9. I first visited Austin Texas in March 2007.
10. "It must be finished soon of course" said Amy.

PRACTICE 3 ▷ **Using Colons, Semicolons, and Quotation Marks**

Read the sentences. Rewrite the sentences, using colons, semicolons, and quotation marks where needed. If a sentence is correct as is, write *correct*.

1. We moved last year, we love our new home.
2. Who said, Give me liberty, or give me death?
3. Bring these items a comb, a brush, and tissues.
4. I'm sorry, said Rose, but I must leave by 430.
5. He won a trophy, however, he soon broke it.
6. How I love the poem Birches!
7. Warning Keep out of the hands of children.
8. Luis likes chicken, rice, and corn.
9. Mia asked, When will this difficult day be over?
10. Native to the Americas are the turkey, a bird, the chipmunk, a rodent, and the tomato, a plant.

PRACTICE 4 ▷ **Using Apostrophes Correctly**

Read the sentences. Then, rewrite the sentences, adding or removing apostrophes as needed. If a sentence is correct as is, write *correct*.

1. Mom is deaf and cant hear Mels voice.
2. The horse stays in it's stall when its raining.
3. Silas's bags got mixed up with someone elses.
4. The five top students grades were all As.
5. The myth described the god Zeus' thunderbolts.
6. Donalds prized possession is an 08 yearbook.
7. I'm amazed that you dont tell him hes too loud.
8. Theirs is the best restaurant in town.
9. She couldn't make other plans on Tuesdays.
10. Its hard to tell whats hers and whats yours.

Continued on next page ▶

Cumulative Review   Chapters 13–14

PRACTICE 5 ▷ **Using Underlining (or Italics), Hyphens, Dashes, Parentheses, Brackets, and Ellipses**

Read the sentences. Then, rewrite the sentences, adding underlining (or italics if you type your answers on a computer), hyphens, dashes, brackets, parentheses, or ellipses. If a sentence is correct as is, write *correct*.

1. Who wrote the novel The Yearling?

2. My sister in law is a happy go lucky person.

3. I asked Bridget she is our new neighbor to be sure to join us at our block party.

4. The film is set during World War II 1939–1945.

5. This is a nicely written essay.

6. Today in court, one person shouted, "She meaning Mrs. Gibbs is guilty!"

7. Americans "pledge allegiance to the flag . . . with liberty and justice for all."

8. The Supreme Court ruled on the case. See page 4 for the actual ruling column 2.

9. The team's goal to win the championship finally seemed within reach.

10. The Pilgrims sailed here on the Mayflower.

PRACTICE 6 ▷ **Using Correct Capitalization**

Read the sentences. Then, rewrite each sentence, using capital letters where they are needed.

1. touring the southwest, we saw the grand canyon.

2. on sunday, reverend sykes gave a fine sermon.

3. the treaty of versailles ended world war I.

4. lewis carroll, a british author, wrote "the walrus and the carpenter."

5. every morning, grandma eats tasty choice cereal.

6. former vice president al gore jr. was awarded the nobel prize.

7. the planet jupiter is named for a roman god.

8. "i met mr. kim," said jo, "when i visited ohio."

9. the norton museum of art is on south olive avenue in west palm beach, florida.

10. the republican party met just north of houston.

11. my sister takes history 101 at yale university.

12. our family visited the lincoln memorial in washington, D.C.

13. "i believe doctor patel is from india," greta said. "he came to the united states in march of 2003."

14. the bible is sacred to christians.

15. was aunt meg in the girl scouts of america?

PRACTICE 7 ▷ **Writing Sentences With Correct Capitalization**

Write a sentence about each of the following people, places, or things. Be sure to use correct capitalization.

1. the governor of your state

2. a local museum or tourist attraction

3. your favorite vacation spot

4. your favorite television show

5. a book that you have enjoyed

Modes
of Writing

Writing is a process that begins with the exploration of ideas and ends with the presentation of a final piece of writing. Often, the types of writing we do are grouped into modes according to their form and purpose.

Narration

Whenever writers tell any type of story, they are using narration. Most narratives share certain elements, such as characters, a setting, a sequence of events, and, often, a theme. The following are some types of narration.

● **Autobiographical Writing** Autobiographical writing tells a true story about an important period, experience, or relationship in the writer's life.

Effective autobiographical writing includes:

- *A series of events that involve the writer as the main character*
- *Details, thoughts, feelings, and insights from the writer's perspective*
- *A conflict or an event that affects the writer*
- *A logical organization that tells the story clearly*

Types of autobiographical writing include personal narratives, autobiographical sketches, reflective essays, eyewitness accounts, and memoirs.

● **Short Story** A short story is a brief, creative narrative.

Most short stories contain:

- *Details that establish the setting in time and place*
- *A main character who undergoes a change or learns something during the course of the story*
- *A conflict or a problem to be introduced, developed, and resolved*
- *A plot—the series of events that make up the action of the story*
- *A theme or message about life*

Types of short stories include realistic stories, fantasies, historical narratives, mysteries, thrillers, science fiction, and adventure stories.

Description

Descriptive writing is writing that creates a vivid picture of a person, place, thing, or event.

Most descriptive writing includes:

- *Sensory details—sights, sounds, smells, tastes, and physical sensations*
- *Vivid, precise language*
- *Figurative language or comparisons*
- *Adjectives and adverbs that help to paint a word picture*
- *An organization suited to the subject*

Types of descriptive writing include description of ideas, observations, travel brochures, physical descriptions, functional descriptions, remembrances, and character sketches.

Persuasion

Persuasion is writing or speaking that attempts to convince people to accept a position or take a desired action. The following are some types of persuasion:

- **Persuasive Essay**
  A persuasive essay presents a position on an issue, urges readers to accept that position, and may encourage a specific action.

An effective persuasive essay:

- *Explores an issue of importance to the writer*
- *Addresses an arguable issue*
- *Is supported by facts, examples, statistics, or personal experiences*
- *Tries to influence the audience through appeals to the readers' knowledge, experiences, or emotions*
- *Uses clear organization to present a logical argument*

Forms of persuasion include editorials, position papers, persuasive speeches, grant proposals, advertisements, and debates.

- **Advertisements**
  An advertisement is a planned communication that is meant to be seen, heard, or read. It attempts to persuade an audience to buy or use a product or service. Advertisements may appear in print or broadcast form.

An effective advertisement includes:

- *A concept, or central theme*
- *A devise, such as a memorable slogan, that catches people's attention*
- *Language that conveys a certain view of a product or issue*

Common types of advertisements include public service announcements, billboards, merchandise ads, service ads, and public campaign literature.

Exposition

Exposition is writing that relies on facts to inform or explain. Effective expository writing reflects an organization that is well planned—one that includes a clear introduction, body, and conclusion. The following are some types of exposition:

● **Comparison-and-Contrast Essay**
A comparison-and-contrast essay analyzes similarities and differences between or among two or more things.

An effective comparison-and-contrast essay:
- *Identifies a purpose for comparing and contrasting*
- *Identifies similarities and differences between or among two or more things, people, places, or ideas*
- *Gives factual details about the subjects*
- *Uses an organizational plan suited to the topic and purpose*

● **Cause-and-Effect Essay** A cause-and-effect essay examines the relationship between events, explaining how one event or situation causes another.

A successful cause-and-effect essay includes:
- *A discussion of a cause, event, or condition that produces a specific result*
- *An explanation of an effect or result*
- *Evidence and examples to support the relationship between cause and effect*
- *A logical organization that makes the relationship between events clear*

● **Problem-and-Solution Essay** A problem-and-solution essay describes a problem and offers one or more solutions. It describes a clear set of steps to achieve a result.

An effective problem-and-solution essay includes:
- *A clear statement of the problem, with its causes and effects summarized*
- *A proposal of at least one realistic solution*
- *Facts, statistics, data, or expert testimony to support the solution*
- *A clear organization that makes the relationship between problem and solution obvious*

Research Writing

Research writing is based on information gathered from outside sources.

An effective research paper:

- *Focuses on a specific, narrow topic*
- *Presents relevant information from a variety of sources*
- *Is clearly organized and includes an introduction, body, and conclusion*
- *Includes a bibliography or works-cited list*

In addition to traditional research reports, types of research writing include statistical reports and experiment journals.

Response to Literature

When you write a response to literature, you can discover how a piece of writing affected you.

An effective response:

- *Reacts to a work of literature*
- *Analyzes the content of a literary work*
- *Focuses on a single aspect or gives a general overview*
- *Supports opinion with evidence from the text*

You might respond to a literary work in reader's response journals, literary letters, and literary analyses.

Writing for Assessment

Essays are commonly part of school tests.

An effective essay includes:

- *A clearly stated and well-supported thesis*
- *Specific information about the topic derived from your reading or from class discussion*
- *A clear organization with an introduction, body, and conclusion*

In addition to writing essays for tests, you might write essays to apply to schools or special programs, or to enter a contest.

Workplace Writing

Workplace writing communicates information in a structured format.

Effective workplace writing:

- *Communicates information concisely*
- *Includes details that provide necessary information and anticipate potential questions*

Common types of workplace writing include business letters, memorandums, résumés, forms, and applications.

Writing Effective
Paragraphs

A paragraph is a group of sentences that share a common topic or purpose. Most paragraphs have a main idea or thought.

Stating the Main Idea in a Topic Sentence

The main idea of a paragraph is directly stated in a single sentence called the topic sentence. The rest of the sentences in the paragraph support or explain the topic sentence, providing support through facts and details.

Sometimes the main idea of a paragraph is implied rather than stated. The sentences work together to present the details and facts that allow the reader to infer the main idea.

WRITING MODELS

from *The Secret Language of Snow*
Terry Tempest Williams and Ted Major

Many types of animal behavior are designed to reduce heat loss. Birds fluff their feathers, enlarging the "dead air" space around their bodies. Quails roost in compact circles, in the same manner as musk oxen, to keep warmth in and cold out. Grouse and ptarmigan dive into the snow, using it as an insulating blanket.

> In this passage, the stated topic sentence is highlighted.

from "The Old Demon"
Pearl S. Buck

The baker's shop, like everything else, was in ruins. No one was there. At first she saw nothing but the mass of crumpled earthen walls. But then she remembered that the oven was just inside the door, and the door frame still stood erect, supporting one end of the roof. She stood in this frame, and, running her hands in underneath the fallen roof inside, she felt the wooden cover of the iron cauldron. Under this there might be steamed bread. She worked her arm delicately and carefully in. It took quite a long time, but even so, clouds of lime and dust almost choked her. Nevertheless she was right. She squeezed her hand under the cover and felt the first smooth skin of the big steamed bread rolls, and one by one she drew out four.

> In this passage, all the sentences work together to illustrate the implied main idea of the paragraph: The woman searches persistently until she finds food.

Writing a Topic Sentence

When you outline a topic or plan an essay, you identify the main points you want to address. Each of these points can be written as a topic sentence—a statement of the main idea of a topical paragraph. You can organize your paragraph around the topic sentence.

A good topic sentence tells readers what the paragraph is about and the point the writer wants to make about the subject matter. Here are some tips for writing a strong topic sentence.

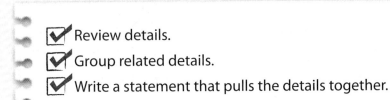

☑ Review details.

☑ Group related details.

☑ Write a statement that pulls the details together.

Writing Supporting Sentences

Whether your topic sentence is stated or implied, it guides the rest of the paragraph. The rest of the sentences in the paragraph will either develop, explain, or support that topic sentence.

You can support or develop the idea by using one or more of the following strategies:

Use Facts

Facts are statements that can be proved. They support your key idea by providing proof.

- **Topic Sentence:** Our football team is tough to beat.
- **Supporting Fact:** It wins almost all of its games.

Use Statistics

A statistic is a fact, usually stated using numbers.

- **Topic Sentence:** Our football team is tough to beat.
- **Supporting Statistic:** The football team's record is 10–1.

Use Examples, Illustrations, or Instances

An example, illustration, or instance is a specific thing, person, or event that demonstrates a point.

- **Topic Sentence:** Our football team is tough to beat.
- **Illustration:** Last week, the team beat the previously undefeated Tigers in an exciting upset game.

Use Details

Details are the specifics—the parts of the whole. They make your point or main idea clear by showing how all the pieces fit together.

- **Topic Sentence:** Our footbal team is tough to beat.
- **Detail:** There were only seconds left in last week's game, when the quarterback threw the winning pass.

Placing Your Topic Sentence

Frequently, the topic sentence appears at the beginning of a paragraph. Topic sentences can, however, be placed at the beginning, middle, or end of the paragraph. Place your topic sentence at the beginning of a paragraph to focus readers' attention. Place your topic sentence in the middle of a paragraph when you must lead into your main idea. Place your topic sentence at the end of a paragraph to emphasize your main idea.

Paragraph Patterns

Sentences in a paragraph can be arranged in several different patterns, depending on where you place your topic sentence. One common pattern is the TRI pattern (Topic, Restatement, Illustration).

- **T**opic sentence (State your main idea.)
- **R**estatement (Interpret your main idea; use different wording.)
- **I**llustration (Support your main idea with facts and examples.)

T	Participating in after-school clubs is one of the ways you can meet new people. Getting involved in extracurricular activities brings you in contact with a wide range of individuals. The drama club, for example, brings together students from several different grades.
R	
I	

Variations on the TRI pattern include sentence arrangements such as TIR, TII, IIT, or ITR.

I	This month alone the service club at our high school delivered meals to thirty shut-ins. In addition, members beautified the neighborhood with new plantings. If any school-sponsored club deserves increased support, the service club does.
I	
T	

Paragraphs
in Essays
and other Compositions

To compose means "to put the parts together, to create." Most often, composing refers to the creation of a musical or literary work—a composition. You may not think of the reports, essays, and test answers you write as literary works, but they are compositions. To write an effective composition, you must understand the parts.

The Introduction

The introduction does what its name suggests. It introduces the topic of the composition. An effective introduction begins with a strong lead, a first sentence that captures readers' interest. The lead is followed by the thesis statement, the key point of the composition. Usually, the thesis statement is followed by a few sentences that outline how the writer will make the key point.

The Body

The body of a composition consists of several paragraphs that develop, explain, and support the key idea expressed in the thesis statement. The body of a composition should be unified and coherent. The paragraphs in a composition should work together to support the thesis statement. The topic of each paragraph should relate directly to the thesis statement and be arranged in a logical organization.

The Conclusion

The conclusion is the final paragraph of the composition. The conclusion restates the thesis and sums up the support. Often, the conclusion includes the writer's reflection or observation on the topic. An effective conclusion ends on a memorable note, for example, with a quotation or call to action.

Recognizing Types of Paragraphs

There are several types of paragraphs you can use in your writing.

Topical Paragraphs

A topical paragraph is a group of sentences that contain one key sentence or idea and several sentences that support or develop that key idea or topic sentence.

Functional Paragraphs

Functional paragraphs serve a specific purpose. They may not have a topic sentence, but they are unified and coherent because the sentences (if there is more than one) are clearly connected and follow a logical order. Functional paragraphs can be used for the following purposes:

- **To create emphasis** A very short paragraph of one or two sentences focuses the reader on what is being said because it breaks the reader's rhythm.

- **To indicate dialogue** One of the conventions of written dialogue is that a new paragraph begins each time the speaker changes.

- **To make a transition** A short paragraph can help readers move between the main ideas in two topical paragraphs.

WRITING MODEL

from **"The Hatchling Turtles"**

by Jean Craighead George

One morning each small turtle fought for freedom within its shell.

They hatched two feet down in the sand, all of them on the same day. As they broke out, their shells collapsed, leaving a small room of air for them to breathe. It wasn't much of a room, just big enough for them to wiggle in and move toward the sky. As they wiggled they pulled the sand down from the ceiling and crawled up on it. In this manner the buried room began to rise, slowly, inch by inch.

> The highlighted functional paragraph emphasizes the struggle of the turtles to emerge from their shells.

Paragraph Blocks

Sometimes, you may have so much information to support or develop a main idea that it "outgrows" a single paragraph. When a topic sentence or main idea requires an extensive explanation or support, you can develop the idea in a paragraph block—several paragraphs that work together and function as a unit. Each paragraph in the block supports the key idea or topic sentence. By breaking the development of the idea into separate paragraphs, you make your ideas clearer.

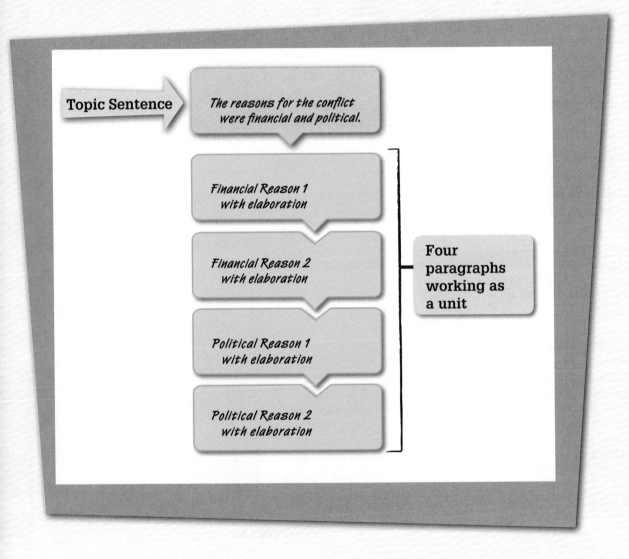

Topic Sentence → The reasons for the conflict were financial and political.

Financial Reason 1 with elaboration

Financial Reason 2 with elaboration

Political Reason 1 with elaboration

Political Reason 2 with elaboration

Four paragraphs working as a unit

Qualities
of Good Writing

The quality of your writing depends on how well you develop six important traits: ideas, organization, voice, word choice, sentence fluency, and conventions.

Ideas

Good writing begins with interesting ideas. Explore topics that you find interesting and that you think will interest others. Focus on presenting information that will be new and fresh to readers.

Organization

Organization refers to the way in which the ideas and details are arranged in a piece of writing. To enable readers to follow your ideas, choose an organization that makes sense for your topic, and stick with that organization throughout the piece of writing.

Voice

Just as you have a distinctive way of expressing yourself when you speak, you can develop a distinctive voice as a writer. Your voice consists of the topics you choose, the attitude you express toward those topics, the words you use, and the rhythm of your sentences. By developing your own voice, you let your personality come through in your writing.

Conventions

Conventions refer to the grammatical correctness of a piece of writing. Don't let errors in grammar, usage, mechanics, and spelling interfere with your message.

Word Choice

Words are the building blocks of a piece of writing. By choosing precise and vivid words, you will add strength to your writing and enable readers to follow your ideas and picture the things that you describe.

Sentence Fluency

In a piece of writing, it is important that sentences flow well from one to another. By using a variety of sentences—different lengths and different structures—and using transitions to connect them, you will create smooth rhythm in your writing.

Stages of the
Writing Process

Writing is called a process because it goes through a series
of changes or stages. These five stages are:

- In **prewriting**, you explore an idea by using various prewriting techniques, such as brainstorming and questioning.

- In **drafting**, you get your ideas down on paper or on the computer in roughly the format you intend.

- Once you finish your first draft, you decide on the changes, or **revisions**, you want to make.

- Finally, when you are happy with your work, you **edit** it, checking the accuracy of facts and for errors in spelling, grammar, usage, and mechanics.

- You then make a final copy and **publish** it, or share it with an audience.

You will not always progress through these stages in a straight line. You can backtrack to a previous stage, repeat a stage many times, or put the stages in a different sequence to fit your needs. To get an idea of what the writing process is like, study the following diagram. Notice that the arrows in the drafting and revising sections can lead you back to prewriting.

Prewriting
- Using prewriting techniques to gather ideas
- Choosing a purpose and an audience
- Ordering ideas

Drafting
- Putting ideas down on paper
- Exploring new ideas as you write

Publishing
- Producing a final polished copy of your writing
- Sharing your writing

Revising
- Consulting with peer readers
- Evaluating suggested changes
- Making revisions

Editing
- Checking the accuracy of facts
- Correcting errors in spelling, grammar, usage, and mechanics

Prewriting
• Using prewriting techniques to gather ideas
• Choosing a purpose and an audience
• Ordering ideas

Prewriting

No matter what kind of writing assignment you are given, you can use prewriting techniques to find and develop a topic. Some prewriting techniques will work better than others for certain kinds of assignments.

Choosing a Topic

Try some of the following ways to find topics that fit your assignment.

● **Look Through Newspapers and Magazines** In the library or at home, flip through recent magazines or newspapers. Jot down each interesting person, place, event, or topic you come across. Review your notes and choose a topic that you find especially interesting and would like to learn more about.

● **Keep an Events Log** Every day you probably encounter many situations about which you have opinions. One way to remember these irksome issues is to keep an events log. For a set period of time—a day or a week—take a small notebook with you wherever you go. Whenever you come across something you feel strongly about, write it down. After the specified time period, review your journal and select a topic.

● **Create a Personal Experience Timeline** Choose a memorable period in your life and map out the events that occurred during that period. Create a timeline in which you enter events in the order they occurred. Then, review your timeline and choose the event or events that would make the most interesting topic.

Narrowing Your Topic

Note that narrowing a topic is not an exact science. It is part of the creative process of writing, which involves experimentation and leads to discovery. Here are some specific techniques you can use.

● **Questioning** Asking questions often helps narrow your topic to fit the time and space you have available. Try asking some of the six questions that journalists use when writing news stories: *Who? What? When? Why? Where?* and *How?* Then, based on your answers, refocus on a narrow aspect of your topic.

● **Using Reference Materials** The reference materials you use to find information can also help you narrow a broad topic. Look up your subject in an encyclopedia, or find a book on it at the library. Scan the resource, looking for specific, narrow topics. Sometimes a resource will be divided into sections or chapters that each deal with a specific topic.

● **Using Graphic Devices** Another way to narrow a topic is to combine questioning with a graphic device, such as a cluster or inverted pyramid. Draw one in your notebook or journal, and write your broad topics across the top of the upside-down pyramid. Then, as the pyramid narrows to a point, break down your broad topic into narrower and narrower subcategories. The following graphic shows how questions can be used to do this.

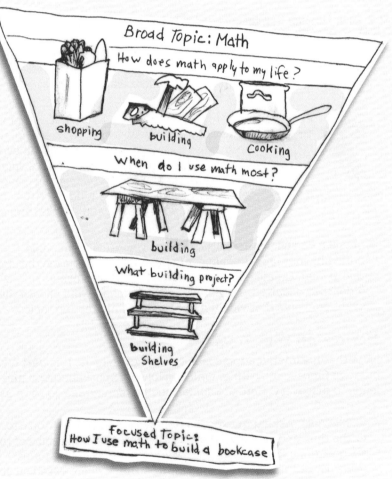

Broad Topic: Math

How does math apply to my life?

shopping   building   cooking

When do I use math most?

building

What building project?

building shelves

Focused Topic:
How I use math to build a bookcase

Purpose and Audience

Every piece of writing is written for an audience. Even when you write a secret in your journal, you are writing for an audience of one—yourself. To succeed in any writing task, you have to understand what your audience wants and needs to know.

Pinpointing your purpose is also essential when you write. Sometimes you write to fulfill an assignment; at other times you decide to whom you will write and why. For example, you might decide to write a letter to your sister about your bunkmates at camp. Your purpose might be to describe your bunkmates' looks and personalities. Another time you might write a letter to your principal about cell phones. Your purpose might be to convince her to ban cell phones inside your school.

● **Defining Your Purpose and Audience** Answering certain questions can help you define your purpose for writing and identify your audience.

- *What is my topic?*
- *What is my purpose for writing?*
- *Who is my audience?*
- *What does my audience already know about this topic?*
- *What does my audience need or want to know?*
- *What type of language will suit my audience and purpose?*

Gathering Details

After finding a topic to write about, you will want to explore and develop your ideas. You can do this on your own or with classmates. The following techniques may help you.

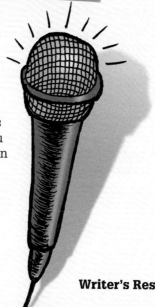

● **Interview a Classmate** Questioning a classmate can help both of you develop your topics. You can interview a friend who has a special skill. Find out how she or he developed that skill. You could also find an interview partner and question each other on an acceptable topic.

- **Fill In an Observation Chart** To come up with details to develop a piece of descriptive writing or to help you create the setting and characters for a narrative, you can fill in an observation chart. A writer created the chart that follows while wondering how to describe the school cafeteria at lunch time.

Once you have completed your own observation chart, circle the details you want to include in your piece of writing.

SUBJECT: CAFETERIA AT LUNCHTIME

See	Hear	Touch	Smell	Taste
swirl of motion	kids' voices	hot melted cheese	stuff they wash the floors with	tart juice
fluorescent lights	thuds and clunks of chairs and trays	wet plastic trays	delicious aroma of pizza	pepperoni
colors of plastic trays	scraping of chairs	cold, wet milk cartons	apple crisp baking	mild cheese

- **Do a Focused Freewriting** Freewriting can be used to either find or develop a topic. When it is used to develop a topic, it is called focused freewriting. Follow these four steps as you use focused freewriting to develop a topic:

1 Set a time limit. (Until you get used to freewriting, write for no more than five minutes at a time.)

2 Repeat to yourself the key words of your topic, and then write whatever comes to mind about them. Do not stop; do not read or correct what you write.

3 If you get stuck, repeat a word (even the word *stuck*), or write the last word you wrote until new ideas come. You can be sure they will.

4 When the time is up, read what you wrote. Underline parts that you like best. Decide which of these parts you will use in your piece of writing.

Drafting

Drafting
- Putting ideas down on paper
- Exploring new ideas as you write

In writing, an **organizational plan** is an outline or map that shows the key ideas and details that you want to include in the order that you want to include them. Following such a plan can help you structure your writing so that it makes a clearer and stronger impression on your audience.

Organizing Your Ideas

Often, a piece of writing lends itself to a particular order. For instance, if you are describing a scene so that readers can visualize it, spatial order may be your best option. However, if you are describing a person, you might compare and contrast the person with someone else you and your readers know, or you might reveal the person's character by describing a series of past incidents in chronological order.

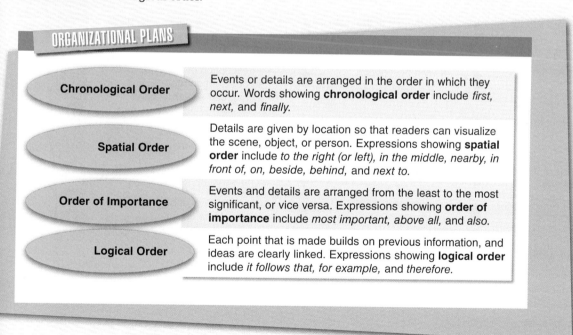

ORGANIZATIONAL PLANS

Chronological Order	Events or details are arranged in the order in which they occur. Words showing **chronological order** include *first, next,* and *finally.*
Spatial Order	Details are given by location so that readers can visualize the scene, object, or person. Expressions showing **spatial order** include *to the right (or left), in the middle, nearby, in front of, on, beside, behind,* and *next to.*
Order of Importance	Events and details are arranged from the least to the most significant, or vice versa. Expressions showing **order of importance** include *most important, above all,* and *also.*
Logical Order	Each point that is made builds on previous information, and ideas are clearly linked. Expressions showing **logical order** include *it follows that, for example,* and *therefore.*

Introductions

The introduction to your paper should include a **thesis statement**, a sentence about your central purpose or what you plan to "show" in your paper. Here is a thesis statement for a paper on the ancient Kingdom of Ghana:

> Ghana was one of the strongest, richest kingdoms of its time.

An effective written introduction draws your readers into your paper and interests them in the subject. The way you introduce your paper depends on the goal you want to achieve and the type of writing you are doing. The following are some possibilities.

GOAL	TYPE OF INTRODUCTION	COULD BE USED FOR
Be clear and direct	a statement of the main point	• an informative paper • a research report • an editorial
Appeal to readers' senses	a vivid description	• a description of a scene • an observation report • a character sketch
Get readers' attention	a startling fact or statistic	• an informative paper • a persuasive essay • a research report
Lure readers into the story quickly	dialogue	• a story • a personal narrative
Make readers wonder	a question	• an informative paper • a persuasive essay • a research report
Give your writing authority	a quotation	• a persuasive essay • an informative paper • a research report • a book review or report

Elaboration

Sometimes what you write seems to be only the bare bones of a composition. In order to flesh out your work, you must add the right details. This process is called **elaboration**.

Certain types of elaboration are more effective for certain forms of writing, but there are no hard-and-fast rules about which type of elaboration to use. You can use facts and statistics in a poem if you want to! Some types of elaboration include the following:

Facts and Statistics	Facts are statements that can be proved true. Statistics are facts that you express as numbers.
Sensory Details	Sensory details are details that appeal to the five senses—sight, hearing, touch, smell, and taste.
Anecdotes	An anecdote is a short account of an interesting or funny incident.
Examples	An example is an instance of something.
Quotations	A quotation is someone's words—often those of an expert or public figure.
Personal Feelings	Personal feelings are thoughts and emotions that are yours alone.
Memories	Memories are recollections from the past.
Observations	Observations are things you have seen or noticed firsthand.
Reasons	Reasons are explanations of why something is true.

● **Uses of Elaboration** Here is a chart showing the types of elaboration you can use and what each is used for.

TYPE OF ELABORATION		USED FOR
facts and statistics	➤	essays news stories feature articles business letters	advertisements reviews research reports
sensory details	➤	observations poems personal essays advertisements	stories plays descriptions
anecdotes	➤	journal entries personal letters news stories	personal essays feature articles
examples	➤	essays news stories business letters editorials advertisements poems	responses to literature book reports research reports feature articles reviews
quotations	➤	news stories feature articles essays	responses to literature book reports
personal feelings	➤	journal entries personal letters personal essays poems	editorials observations responses to literature persuasive essays
memories	➤	journal entries personal letters personal essays poems	descriptions observations stories
observations	➤	journal entries personal letters personal essays poems	reviews feature articles stories plays
reasons	➤	essays business letters reviews book reports news stories feature articles	editorials advertisements research reports responses to literature personal essays

● **Uses of Elaboration** Here is a chart showing the types of elaboration you can use and what each is used for.

TYPE OF ELABORATION	USED FOR	
facts and statistics	essays news stories feature articles business letters	advertisements reviews research reports
sensory details	observations poems personal essays advertisements	stories plays descriptions
anecdotes	journal entries personal letters news stories	personal essays feature articles
examples	essays news stories business letters editorials advertisements poems	responses to literature book reports research reports feature articles reviews
quotations	news stories feature articles essays	responses to literature book reports
personal feelings	journal entries personal letters personal essays poems	editorials observations responses to literature persuasive essays
memories	journal entries personal letters personal essays poems	descriptions observations stories
observations	journal entries personal letters personal essays poems	reviews feature articles stories plays
reasons	essays business letters reviews book reports news stories feature articles	editorials advertisements research reports responses to literature personal essays

Revising

Revising
- Consulting with peer readers
- Evaluating suggested changes
- Making revisions

When you have included all your ideas and finished your first draft, you are ready to revise it. Few writers produce perfect drafts the first time around. You can almost always improve your paper by reworking it. Here are some hints to help you revise your work.

● **Take a Break** Do not begin to revise right after you finish a draft. In a few hours or days you will be better able to see the strengths and weaknesses of your work.

● **Look It Over** When you reread your draft, look for ways to improve it. Use a pencil to mark places where an idea is unclear or the writing is jumpy or disjointed. Also, remember to let yourself know when you have written an effective image or provided a wonderful example. Write Good! next to the parts that work well.

● **Read Aloud** Your ear is a wonderful editor. Read your work aloud and listen for dull, unnecessary, or awkward parts that you did not notice when you read your work silently. Are there any passages that you stumble over as you read aloud? Try different wordings and then read them aloud with expression, emphasizing certain words. Listen and identify which wording sounds best.

● **Share Your Work** Your friends or family members can help you by telling you how your work affects them. Ask them whether your ideas are clear. What is interesting? What is boring?

When it is time to revise a draft, many writers are tempted to just correct a few spelling mistakes and combine a sentence or two. Eliminating surface errors, however, is only a small part of revising. After all, what good is a neat and perfectly spelled paper if it does not make sense or prove a point? The word *revise* means "to see again" or "to see from a new perspective." In order to revise your work, you need to rethink your basic ideas.

Revising by Rethinking

Taking a close look at the ideas in your draft is the most important part of revising. Usually, you will spot some "idea" problems. When you do, it is time to get to work. Here are some strategies to help you rethink your draft.

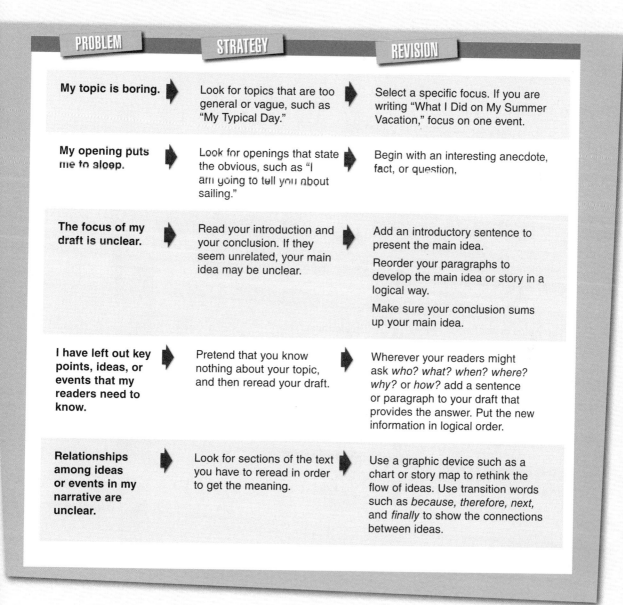

PROBLEM	STRATEGY	REVISION
My topic is boring.	Look for topics that are too general or vague, such as "My Typical Day."	Select a specific focus. If you are writing "What I Did on My Summer Vacation," focus on one event.
My opening puts me to sleep.	Look for openings that state the obvious, such as "I am going to tell you about sailing."	Begin with an interesting anecdote, fact, or question.
The focus of my draft is unclear.	Read your introduction and your conclusion. If they seem unrelated, your main idea may be unclear.	Add an introductory sentence to present the main idea. Reorder your paragraphs to develop the main idea or story in a logical way. Make sure your conclusion sums up your main idea.
I have left out key points, ideas, or events that my readers need to know.	Pretend that you know nothing about your topic, and then reread your draft.	Wherever your readers might ask *who? what? when? where? why?* or *how?* add a sentence or paragraph to your draft that provides the answer. Put the new information in logical order.
Relationships among ideas or events in my narrative are unclear.	Look for sections of the text you have to reread in order to get the meaning.	Use a graphic device such as a chart or story map to rethink the flow of ideas. Use transition words such as *because, therefore, next,* and *finally* to show the connections between ideas.

Revising by Elaborating

When you are sure your ideas are clear and in order, it is time to judge whether you have provided enough appropriate details. Remember, elaborating means developing and expanding on ideas by adding the right details. These details will help develop your ideas in clear and interesting ways.

You might choose any of the following types of details explained on page **TK**:

- *facts and statistics*
- *sensory details*
- *anecdotes*
- *examples*
- *quotations*
- *personal feelings*
- *memories*
- *observations*
- *reasons*

Revising by Reducing

Just as you need to add specific details when you revise your draft, you sometimes need to get rid of material that is unnecessary. Following are some ways you can solve revision problems by removing unneeded words.

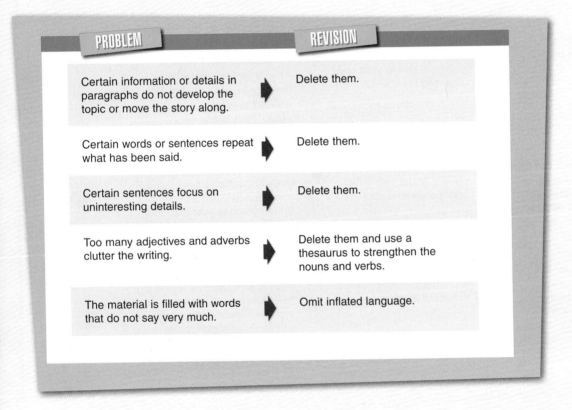

PROBLEM	REVISION
Certain information or details in paragraphs do not develop the topic or move the story along.	Delete them.
Certain words or sentences repeat what has been said.	Delete them.
Certain sentences focus on uninteresting details.	Delete them.
Too many adjectives and adverbs clutter the writing.	Delete them and use a thesaurus to strengthen the nouns and verbs.
The material is filled with words that do not say very much.	Omit inflated language.

Revising by Rewording

Choosing the right words is essential to good writing. As a final step in revising, improve your choice of words. At times, a better word will spring to mind. At other times, use a thesaurus to find words. As you rework your draft, you will reveal your own style.

The following chart can help you find the right word.

PROBLEM

Have I used the most effective word possible?

REVISION ACTIVITIES:

Choose specific nouns.
General: I wish I had some food.
Specific: I wish I had some pizza.

Choose active, colorful verbs.
General: The sick man walked to his bed.
Specific: The sick man hobbled to his bed.

Avoid the word *be*.
General: My horse is a good jumper.
Specific: My horse easily jumps four feet.

Choose the active voice.
General: Chocolate should never be fed to dogs.
Specific: Never feed dogs chocolate.

Editing

Editing is the process of finding and correcting errors in grammar, usage, and mechanics. When you have finished drafting and revising your paper, here is how to edit your work.

General Tips
- Look first for mistakes that you typically make.
- Proofread your paper for one type of error at a time.
- Read your work aloud word for word.
- When in doubt, use reference sources to help you.

Here are some specific editing strategies that may help you.

SPECIFIC TASKS	STRATEGY
Check Your Grammar	
Have you written any run-on sentences or fragments?	Check that each sentence has a subject and verb. Use a comma and conjunction to connect main clauses.
Do your subjects and verbs agree?	Make sure that singular subjects have singular verbs and plural subjects have plural verbs.
Check Your Usage	
Have you used the past forms of irregular verbs correctly?	Watch out for irregular verb forms such as *seen, done, gone,* and *taken.*
Have you used subject and object pronouns correctly?	Check that the pronouns *me, him, her, us,* and *them* are used only after verbs or prepositions.
Check Your Punctuation	
Does each sentence have the correct end mark?	Look for inverted word order that may signal a question.
Have you used apostrophes in nouns, but not in pronouns, to show possession?	Use a phrase with *of* to check for possession.
Have you used quotation marks around words from another source?	Avoid plagiarism by checking your notecards to be sure.
Check Your Capitalization	
Did you begin each sentence or direct quotation with a capital letter?	Look for an end mark and then check the next letter.
Have you capitalized proper nouns?	Look for the name of specific people and places.
Check Your Spelling	
Did you correctly spell all words?	Use a dictionary. Look for your common errors.

Publishing

Publishing
- Producing a final polished copy of your writing
- Sharing your writing

Once you have made a final, clean copy of a piece of writing that pleases you, you may want to share it with others. What you have to say might be important or meaningful to someone else. Here are some ways you can publish your writing—that is, bring it to the public eye.

- Submit your work to a school newspaper or magazine.

- Have a public reading of your work. Perform it in one of the following ways:
  - Over the school P.A. or radio system
  - In a school assembly or talent show
  - In a group in which members take turns reading their work
  - At your local library or community center

- If your work is a play or skit, have a group of classmates or the drama club present it.

- Work with classmates to put together a class collection of written work. You can have it copied and bound at a copy shop.

- Submit your piece to a local or national writing contest.

- Send your writing to a local newspaper or area magazine.

- Publish your own work and the writings of classmates by using a computer with a desktop publishing program.

Reflecting

Your writing can help you learn about your subject or the writing process—or even yourself. Once you have completed a writing assignment, sit back and think about the experience for a few minutes.

Ask yourself questions such as the following:

- What did I learn about my subject through my writing?

- Did I experiment with writing techniques and forms? If so, were my experiments successful? If not, what held me back?

- Am I pleased with what I wrote? Why or why not?

- Did I have difficulty with any part of the writing process? If so, which part gave me trouble? What strategies did I use to overcome my difficulties?

This resource section contains tips on writing in English and information on grammar topics that are sometimes challenging for English learners.

The numbered arrows in the side margins also appear on other pages of the Grammar Handbook that provide information on writing or instruction in these same grammar topics.

EL1

Understand the Demands of Writing in a Second Language

Talk with other writers.

When you write in an unfamiliar situation, it may be helpful to find a few examples of the type of writing you are trying to produce. For example, if you are writing a letter to the editor of a magazine, look at letters from readers that the magazine has published. Notice the various ways that readers presented their views in writing.

Use your native language as a resource.

You can also use your native language to develop your texts. Many people, when they cannot find an appropriate word in English, write down a word, a phrase, or even a sentence in their native language and consult a dictionary later. Incorporating key terms from your native language is also a possible strategy.

A Japanese term adds perspective to this sentence.

"Some political leaders need to have *wakimae*—a realistic idea of one's own place in the world."

Use dictionaries.

Bilingual dictionaries are especially useful when you want to check your understanding of an English word or find equivalent words for culture-specific concepts and technical terms. Some bilingual dictionaries also provide sample sentences.

Learner's dictionaries, such as the *Longman Dictionary of American English,* include information about count/non-count nouns and transitive/intransitive verbs. Many of them also provide sample sentences.

Understand English idioms.

Some English idioms function like proverbs. In the United States, for example, if someone has to "eat crow," that person has been forced to admit he or she was wrong about something. *Simpler* examples of idiomatic usage—word order, word choice, and combinations that don't follow any obvious set of rules—are common in even the plainest English. If you are unsure about idioms, use Google or another search engine to find out how to use them.

INCORRECT IDIOM	Here is the answer **of** your question.
ACCEPTED IDIOM	Here is the answer **to** your question.
INCORRECT IDIOM	I had jet **legs** after flying across the Pacific.
ACCEPTED IDIOM	I had jet **lag** after flying across the Pacific.

Understand Nouns in English

Perhaps the most troublesome conventions for nonnative speakers are those that guide usage of the common articles *the, a,* and *an.* To understand how articles work in English, you must first understand how the language uses **nouns.**

Proper nouns and common nouns

There are two basic kinds of nouns. A **proper noun** begins with a capital letter and names a unique person, place, or thing: *Elvis Presley, Russia, Eiffel Tower.*

The other basic kind of noun is called a **common noun.** Common nouns such as *man, country* and *tower,* do not name a unique person, place, or thing. Common nouns are not names and are not capitalized unless they are the first word in a sentence.

EL2

PROPER NOUNS
Beethoven   Michael Jordan   Honda
South Korea   Africa
Empire State Building

COMMON NOUNS
composer   athlete   vehicle   country
continent   building

Count and non-count nouns

Common nouns can be classified as either **count** or **non-count.** Count nouns can be made plural, usually by adding the letter *s* (*finger, fingers*) or by using their plural forms (*person, people; datum, data*).

Non-count nouns cannot be counted directly and cannot take the plural form (*information,* but not *informations; garbage,* but not *garbages*). Some nouns can be either count or non-count, depending on how they are used. *Hair* can refer to either a strand of hair, when it serves as a count noun, or a mass of hair, when it becomes a non-count noun.

Count nouns usually take both singular and plural forms, while non-count nouns usually do not take plural forms and are not counted directly. A count noun can have a number before it (as in *two books, three oranges*) and can be qualified with adjectives such as *many* (as in *many books*), *some* (as in *some schools*), and *few* (as in *few people volunteered*).

Non-count nouns can be counted or quantified in only two ways: either by general adjectives that treat the noun as a mass (*much* information, *some* news) or by placing another noun between the quantifying word and the non-count noun (two *kinds* of information, a *piece* of news).

EL3

CORRECT USE OF HAIR *AS A COUNT NOUN*
Three blonde hairs were in the sink.

CORRECT USE OF HAIR *AS A NON-COUNT NOUN*
My roommate spent an hour combing his hair.

INCORRECT	five horse many accident
CORRECT	five horses
	many accidents
INCORRECT	three breads
	I would like a mustard on my hot dog.
CORRECT	three loaves of bread
	I would like some mustard on my hot dog.

Understand Articles in English

EL4

Articles indicate that a noun is about to appear, and they clarify what the noun refers to. There are only two kinds of articles in English, definite and indefinite.

1. **the:** *The* is a **definite article,** meaning that it refers to (1) a specific object already known to the reader, (2) one about to be made known to the reader, or (3) a unique object.

2. **a, an:** The **indefinite articles** *a* and *an* refer to an object whose specific identity is not known to the reader. The only difference between *a* and *an* is that *a* is used before a consonant sound (*a man, a friend, a yellow toy*), while *an* is used before a vowel sound (*an orange, an old shoe*).

Look at these sentences, which are identical except for their articles, and imagine that each is taken from a different newspaper story.

Rescue workers lifted **the** man to safety.

Rescue workers lifted **a** man to safety.

By using the definite article *the*, the first sentence indicates that the reader already knows something about the identity of this man. The news story has already referred to him.

The indefinite article *a* in the second sentence indicates that the reader does not know anything about this man. Either this is the first time the news story has referred to him, or there are other men in need of rescue.

RULES FOR USING ARTICLES

1. *A* or *an* is not used with non-count nouns.

   INCORRECT The crowd hummed with **an** excitement.
   CORRECT The crowd hummed with excitement.

2. *A* or *an* is used with singular count nouns whose identity is unknown to the reader or writer.

   INCORRECT Detective Johnson was reading book.
   CORRECT Detective Johnson was reading **a** book.

3. *The* is used with most count and non-count nouns whose particular identity is known to readers.

   CORRECT I bought a book yesterday. **The** book is about kayaking.

4. *The* is used when the noun is accompanied by a superlative form of a modifier: for example, *best, worst, highest, lowest, most expensive, least interesting.*

   CORRECT **The** most interesting book about climbing Mount Everest is Jon Krakauer's *Into Thin Air.*

Understand Verbs and Modifiers in English

Verbs, verb phrases, and helping verbs

EL5

Verbs in English can be divided between one-word verbs like *run*, *speak*, and *look*, and verb phrases like *may have run*, *have spoken*, and *will be looking*. The words that appear before the main verbs—*may*, *have*, *will*, *do*, and *be*—are called **helping verbs**. Helping verbs help express something about the action of main verbs: for example, when the action occurs, whether the subject acted or was acted upon, or whether or not an action *has* occurred.

Indicating tense with *be* verbs

EL6

Like the helping verbs *have* and *do*, *be* changes form to signal tense. In addition to *be* itself, the **be verbs** are *is*, *am*, *are*, *was*, *were*, and *been*.

To show ongoing action, *be* verbs are followed by the present participle, which is a verb ending in *-ing*.	INCORRECT	I **am think** of all the things I'd rather **be do**.
	CORRECT	I **am thinking** of all the things I'd rather **be doing**.
To show that an action is being done to the subject rather than by the subject, follow *be* verbs with the past participle (a verb usually ending in *-ed*, *-en*, or *-t*).	INCORRECT	The movie **was direct** by John Woo.
	CORRECT	The movie **was directed** by John Woo.

Placement of Modifiers

EL7

Modifiers will be unclear if your reader can't connect them to the words to which they refer. How close a modifier is to the noun or verb it modifies provides an important clue to their relationship.

Clarity should be your first goal when using a modifier.	UNCLEAR	Many pedestrians are killed each year by motorists **not using sidewalks**.
	CLEAR	Many pedestrians **not using sidewalks** are killed each year by motorists.
An **adverb**—a word or group of words that modifies a verb, adjective, or another adverb—should not come between a verb and its direct object.	AWKWARD	The hurricane destroyed **completely** the city's tallest building.
	BETTER	The hurricane **completely** destroyed the city's tallest building.
Try to avoid placing an adverb between *to* and its verb. This construction is called a **split infinitive**.	AWKWARD	The water level was predicted **to not rise**.
	BETTER	The water level was predicted **not to rise**.

Understand English Sentence Structure

Words derive much of their meaning from how they function in a sentence.

With the exception of **imperatives** (commands such as *Watch out!*), sentences in English usually contain a *subject* and a *predicate*. A subject names who or what the sentence is about; the predicate tells what the subject is or does.

The **lion** **is asleep.**
subject   predicate

A predicate consists of at least one main verb. If the verb is **intransitive,** like *exist*, it does not take a direct object. Some verbs are **transitive,** which means they require a **direct object** to complete their meaning.

INCORRECT   The bird saw.
CORRECT   The bird saw a cat.

Some verbs (*write, learn, read,* and others) can be both transitive and intransitive, depending on how they are used.

INTRANSITIVE Pilots fly.
TRANSITIVE   Pilots fly airplanes.

Formal written English requires that each sentence includes a subject and a verb, even when the meaning of the sentence would be clear without it. In some cases you must supply an expletive, such as *it* and *there.*

INCORRECT   Is snowing in Alaska.
CORRECT   It is snowing in Alaska.

INDEX

Note: **Boldfaced** page numbers refer to pages on which terms are defined; *italicized* page numbers refer to practices and applications.

A

Abbreviations
- capitalization, 301, *302*
- ending sentence, 231
- punctuation, 230

Abstract nouns, 2, *4*
Acronyms, 231, 301, *302*
Action regarding issue or problem, 325
Action verbs, 20
- direct objects and, 82
- indirect objects and, 87
- types, **21,** *22,* 24, *25*

Active voice
- choosing, in writing, 335
- identifying, **174**
- using, 176, *177*

Addresses, 247, *248,* 301
Adjectival clauses, 112
- combining sentence with, *113, 114*
- set off, with comma, 241

Adjectival phrases, 95, *97–98*
Adjectives, 29, 30–31, *32*
- adverbial clauses modifying, 115
- versus adverbs, **45,** *46*
- adverbs that modify, 42
- articles as, **33**
- fractions as, versus nouns, 265
- indefinite pronouns as, 15–16
- infinitive phrase as, 106, *108*
- nouns as, **36,** *37,* **38,** *40*
- order/rank/series of, 236
- pronouns as, **38,** *40*
- troublesome, **224–225,** *226*
- types, **35, 36,** *37,* **39,** 40
- using commas between, 236, *238*
- verb forms as, 101
- *See also* Compound adjective; Demonstrative adjective; Indefinite adjective; Interrogative adjective; Modifiers; Possessive adjective; Predicate adjective; Proper adjective

Adverbial clauses, 115–116, *117*
- *See also* Elliptical adverbial clause

Adverbial phrases, 96, *98*
Adverbs, 29, 41, 335
- adjectives versus, **45,** *46*
- adverbial clauses modifying, 115
- and words they modify, **41–42,** *43, 46*
- beginning sentence with, 134
- conjunctive, **44,** 58, *60*
- direct objects versus, **84,** *86*

- ending in -*ly,* **216**
- finding, in sentences, 44
- infinitive phrase as, 106, *108*
- prepositions versus, 52, *54*
- *there* and *here* as, 78
- troublesome, **224–225,** *226*
- *See also* Conjunctive adverbs; Modifiers

Advertisements, 306
Advertising, ellipses in, 279
Aircraft names, 263, 293
Anecdotes in writing, 323, *324*
Antecedents
- of pronouns, **9,** *10*
- pronouns in agreement with, **209–211,** *212*
- third-person singular, 211

Apostrophes, 271, *275*
- in contraction, 190, 273, *275*
- to create plural form of word, 273
- with possessive noun, 271–272, *274*
- with pronoun, 272, *274*

Appositival phrases, 99, *100,* 241
Appositives, 99, *100*
- comma to set off, 241, *244*
- dash to set off nonessential, 281

Art, titles of. *See* Titles of works
Articles, 3, 33, *34,* **333**
Audience, purpose and, 319
Autobiographical writing, 305
Awards, names of, 293

B

Bilingual dictionary, 332
Body of composition, 312
Brackets, 258, *259,* **277,** *278*
Brand names, 293, 295

C

Capitalization, 283, 284
- abbreviations/acronyms, 301, *302*
- concluding expressions, 254
- in good writing, 315, 330
- in parenthetical sentences, 276–277
- pronoun *I* (word), 284, *286*
- proper adjectives, 35, 295, *298*
- proper nouns, 6, 287–289, *290, 291–293, 294*
- sentences/quotations, 255, 284–285, *286*
- titles of people/works, 296–297, *298, 299, 300*

Cases
- nouns. *See* Possessive nouns
- pronouns, 185, **186,** *187*
  - nominative, **188,** *191*
  - objective, **189,** *191*

- possessive, **190,** *192*
- tips for choosing correct, 188, 189, 193
- *who, whom,* **193,** *194*

Cause-and-effect essay, 307
Celestial bodies, names of, 293
Chronological order, 321
Clause fragments, correcting, 137–138, *140*
Clauses, 93, 109
- commas and, 239, 240–241, *242*
- joining, 57, **129–130**
- types, 109–110
- *See also* Adjectival clauses; Adverbial clauses; Main clauses

Collective nouns, 3, *5*
- in pronoun-antecedent agreement, **210**
- subject-verb agreement and, **200,** *201*

Colons, 251, *252,* 254
Comma splices, 141, 234–235
Commands, 75, *77,* 178
Commas
- in addresses/letters, 247, *248*
- in compound sentences, 129, 143, **234,** *237*
- in dates/geographical names, 244, *246*
- in numbers, 245, *246*
- to separate
  - adjectives, 236, *238*
  - items in series, 235, *237*
  - main/dependent ideas, 58
- to set off
  - direct quotations, 247, *248*
  - expressions, 240–241, *243,* 250
  - interjections, 61
  - introductory words, 239, *242*
  - quotations with expressions (and other marks), 253–255, *256, 257, 259*
  - transitions (conjunctive adverbs), 58

Comments, final, 325
Common nouns, 6, *7,* **333**
Comparative forms, 214
- of irregular modifiers, **218,** *220*
- of regular modifiers, **215–216,** *217*
- rules for using, **218–219,** *220*

Comparison-and-contrast essay, 307
Comparisons, forms of, 214
- logical/balanced, **221–222,** *223*
- rules for using, **218–219,** *220*
- troublesome modifiers using, **224–225,** *226*
- using irregular modifiers, **218,** *220*
- using *other, else,* **222,** *223*
- using regular modifiers, **215–216,** *217*

Index   337

Time (hours of day), 251
Time periods, 289
Time line, personal experience, 317
Titles
    of people, capitalization of, 296–297, 298
    of works
        capitalization of, 299
        quotation marks in, 262, *264*
        underlining/italics in, 262–263, *264*
Topics, choosing/narrowing, 317–319
Topic sentences, writing, 309–311
Topical paragraphs, 313
Transitions, 58, 313
Transitional expressions, 250
Transitive verbs, 20, *22*, 336
TRI (Topic, Restatement, Illustration), 311

U

Underlining, 262–263, *264*
Usage, 149–151, *152–153*
    the, 333
    a, an, 33, 333
    accept, except, **149**
    advice, advise, **149**
    affect, effect, **149**
    ain't, isn't, **180**, *183*
    and, **202**, *234*
    at, **149**
    bad, badly, **224**, *226*
    be, forms of
        conjugating, 168, *169*
        in good writing, 335
        helping verbs and, **26**, 333
        linking verbs and, **23**, *25*
        singular, 197
    because, **149**
    beside, besides, **150**
    but, 234
    did, done, **180**, *183*
    different from, different than, **150**
    dragged, drug, **180**, *183*
    -ed, -d, or not, 159, *160*, **161–163**, *164–165*
    -er, -est, **215**, 219
    farther, further, **150**
    fewer, less, **224**
    for, 234
    gone, went, **180**, *183*
    good, well, **224**, *226*
    in good writing, 315, 330
    have, of, **181**, *183*
    in, into, **150**
    its, it's, **190**
    just, **225**

kind of, sort of, **150**
lay, lie, **181**, *183*
less, least, **216**
like, **150**
-ly, **216**, 266
more, most, **215–216**, 219
only, **225**
or, nor, **203**, 234
other, else, **222**, *223*
raise, rise, **182**, *183*
saw, seen, **182**, *183*
says, said, **182**, *183*
set, sit, **182**, *183*
so, 234
that, which, who, **151**
their, there, they're, **151**
there or *here*, **78**, *80*, 204
to, too, two, **151**
when, where, why, **151**
who, whom, **193**, *194*
yet, 234
you, unstated, **75**

V

Verb phrases, **26**, *27, 28*, 335
    participles and, 102, *103*, 158
    passive verb and, 175
Verbals, **101**
Verbal phrases, **101**
    gerunds/gerund phrases, 105, *107*
    infinitives/infinitive phrases, 106, *108*
    participles/participial phrases, 101–102, *103–104*
Verbs, **19**, 335
    active/passive voice, **174**, 175–176, *177*
    adverbial clauses modifying, 115
    adverbs that modify, **41**, *43*, 335
    agreeing with subjects. *See* Subject-verb agreement
    choosing active, colorful, 325
    compound, **72**, *73–74*
    conjunctions connecting, 56–57
    irregular, **161–163**, *164–165*
    moods, **178**, *179*
    no colon after, 251
    as nouns, 105, *107*
    objects of, **20–21**
    parts, 157, **158**, *160*
        irregular, **161–163**, *164–165*
        regular, 159, *160*
    regular, 159, *160*
    in sentences, **67**, *68*
    singular/plural, **197**
    subjects after
        agreement in, **203–204**, *205*
        for emphasis, **79**, *80*

in questions, **76**, *77*
for variety, **134**, *135*
tenses, 157
    conjugating, 167–168, *170, 172,* 173
    identifying, **166**, *169*, 171, *173*, **333**
troublesome, **180–182**, *183–184*
unstated, in elliptical adverbial clause, 116
See also Action verbs; Helping verbs; Linking verbs
Voice in good writing, 315, 335.
    See also Active voice; Passive voice
Vowel sound, 33

W

Word choice in good writing, 315
Word order
    agreement in inverted, 203–204, *205*
    normal/inverted, 75–76, *77*
    reversing, for variety, 134, *135*
    rewording inverted
        to identify pronoun case, 193, *194*
        to identify subject, 76–79, *77, 80*
Workplace writing, 308
Writing
    for assessment, **308**
    effective paragraphs, 309–311
    modes of, 305–308
    qualities of good, 315
    reflecting on, 331
    in second language, 332
Writing process (stages), 316
    drafting, 321–325
    editing/publishing, 330–331
    prewriting, 317–320
    revising, 326–329